wish you
happy forever

wish you
happy forever

❖

What China's Orphans Taught Me
About Moving Mountains

Jenny Bowen

HarperOne
An Imprint of HarperCollinsPublishers

HarperOne

HarperCollins books may be purchased for educational, business, or sales promotional use. For information please e-mail the Special Markets Department at SPsales@harpercollins.com.

HarperCollins website: http://www.harpercollins.com

HarperCollins®, ♨®, and HarperOne™
are trademarks of HarperCollins Publishers.

FIRST EDITION

Designed by Level C

*The credits on page 319 constitute a continuation
of this copyright page.*

Library of Congress Cataloging-in-Publication Data

Bowen, Jenny.
Wish you happy forever : what China's orphans taught me about
moving mountains / Jenny Bowen. — First edition.
pages cm
ISBN 978–0–06–233697–2 (Intl)
1. Intercountry adoption—China. 2. Orphans—China. I. Title.
HV1317.B677   2014
362.7340951—dc23   2013027751

14 15 16 17 18 RRD(H) 10 9 8 7 6 5 4 3 2 1

For Maya, who opened the door,
For Anya, who turned on the light,
And for all the little girls who showed me the way

Contents

Author's Note

This is the truth as I remember it—which doesn't mean it's precisely as it happened. I have consolidated a few events to better tell the story. For various reasons, I have changed some names of people and places.

I spend a lot of time in airport bookstores. They are full of books about how to do business wherever you're going. Bookstores at the Hong Kong airport are especially packed with tips for success in China. Most of them are written by Westerners who have succeeded in some small or large way or who have interviewed others who have. Most include cautionary tales and warnings that China will not be easy.

Although I am a Westerner writing about China, and although I have achieved a certain amount of success there (beyond my wildest dreams, actually), this is not one of those books. As you will quickly surmise, I am not an expert on much of anything.

But I still believe my story should be told, for it is not really *my* story.

CHINA
中国
Zhongguo

Urumqi●

Xinjiang

PAKISTAN

Gansu

Qinghai

Tibet

Sichu

INDIA

Kunmi
Yunna

Legend

◆ ~ First Half the Sky Children's Centers, 2000
● ~ Select Sites on Half the Sky's Journey
☆ ~ Beijing - National Capital
◎ ~ Sichuan Earthquake Epicenter, 2008

0   500 km
|___|___|___|___|___|___|
                              Estimated Scale
0   500 mi

RUSSIA

Heilongjiang

• Harbin

Inner Mongolia

Jilin

Liaoning

NORTH KOREA

Beijing

Hebei Tianjin
• Shijiazhuang

Ningxia Shanxi Shandong

YELLOW SEA

Luoyang Zhengzhou Jiangsu
•   •
Shaanxi   Gaoyou
Henan   Nanjing
• Xinyang   Changzhou

Hongbai Town
◎ • Mianyang Wanzhou Hubei ◆   Shanghai
• Chengdu   Hefei
Wuhan Anhui
•

Chongqing
•   Zhejiang

Hunan Nanchang   EAST CHINA
• Changsha   •   SEA

Guizhou Shaoyang Jiangxi
•
• Chenzhou   Fujian

TAIWAN

Guangxi Guangdong

• Nanning • Guangzhou
• Shenzhen
• Beihai Hong Kong

SOUTH CHINA
SEA

HENDRIKA
馬航凱

Hainan
• Sanya

Redthreadmaps

Prologue

One joy may scatter a thousand sorrows
一笑解千愁

Guangzhou, China
July 7, 1997

The others had come and gone. The little girls had been carried or marched into the room by smiling caretakers. One by one, they'd met nervous clutches of new mommies and daddies, aunties and grannies. Bright, tinkly toys had been passed into little hands, sometimes inspected, sometimes ignored. And then, gingerly, their eyes full of trepidation and knowing, the new mommies reached for their little girls. A few babies screamed bloody murder. Most went easily—another day, another pair of arms.

We still waited. I could hear the fading cries of the screamers. An official returned. *Please wait a moment. Please have a seat. Please have some water.* Then she left. We waited.

My heart had been in my mouth for so long I was afraid to swallow. Somebody, maybe Dick, my husband, told me to relax . . . take a deep breath. I didn't know where to start.

I blinked, tried to focus. I glanced out the window, at the building across the way. I thought I could see the desperate eyes of children peering through barred and blinded windows. Was it forbidden to see that? I shut it out, turned back to the reception room, and for the thousandth time scanned my surroundings.

The hot water they'd given us to drink had turned lukewarm. The fan blew warm, sticky air. Even the plastic flowers were limp. There was a yellowed calligraphy scroll on the wall.

"What does it say?" Dick asked, though both of us were beyond caring.

"It says, 'When the horse is on the brink of a precipice, it is too late to pull in the reins,'" our guide volunteered cheerfully. "Ha. Just kidding."

FORTY-EIGHT HOURS EARLIER I'd been on a film set, squeezing the last few moments of daylight on the last of the grand old California ranchos in the Carmel Valley. It was the finale of what would turn out to be the last independent feature film Dick and I would make together, the last I would direct: an earnest little potboiler called *In Quiet Night*.

So it was us and the crew, out there in rolling-hill oak-studded glory, trying to capture the climactic moment when a mountain lion springs from out of nowhere and does away with the villain. The lion, in real life, seemed friendly enough; he had been declawed and defanged and probably neutered. Still, he commanded your basic lion respect, and the crew was on its toes. Except me. I was already thinking *China* and *Let's get this killing in the can so Dick and I can board that plane and bring home our little girl.*

Poor baby (although she likely hadn't a clue) had been waiting for us for the twenty or so months she'd been alive. Enough, already! The endless pregnancy had done something to me, for sure. I was starting to believe in destiny—that we were meant for each other. I was ready and impatient to meet my fate. And we hadn't even seen her picture yet.

It was a different little face that led us to China.

●   ●   ●

EARLY ONE SATURDAY morning, eighteen months before we shot the lion pouncing on the bad guy and left for China, we were at home in Pacific Palisades, California. Dick, a cinematographer, was shooting a Chevy truck commercial and had a late call. A rare moment to kick back with coffee and the *New York Times*.

I was sitting at the kitchen table in my bathrobe, sorting seeds we'd ordered from catalogs at the start of the new year. Vegetables for Dick; herbs and flowers for me. This was sanity in our ever-precarious Hollywood existence. Today I was going to plant the first of my seeds in the potting shed. It was probably too early. Just as well, because I never did make it outside.

"Jenny, you've got to see this."

In the newspaper, a photo of a tiny girl—really just the shadow of a child—eyes crusted over, cheeks sunken and dark. Her body, all bones.

"*U.S. rights group asserts China lets thousands of orphans die.*" The story was about the just-released 1996 Human Rights Watch report, *Death by Default: The Policy of Fatal Neglect in China's State-Run Orphanages.*

Based on records smuggled out of a Shanghai orphanage along with a limited set of statistics relating to nationwide orphan mortality, the group claimed that thousands of healthy abandoned infants were dying of severe malnutrition only weeks or months after being admitted to orphanages across China.

And it said that the two thousand or so adoptions by foreigners couldn't begin to solve the problem. And it said that virtually all of the abandoned babies were girls.

Unwanted little girls.

I guess that somewhere I may have heard that children were given up in places like China and India because they were girls. I may have *heard* it, but somehow, reading it now, seeing the photo of a child nobody wanted, a dying baby girl . . .

Now we both knew what we had to do. Sort of.

"What can we do?" Dick said.

"I don't know. Send money?"

Isn't that what we usually did? But who would we send it to? How could our money make the slightest difference? We sat looking at each other, eyes red and throats lumpy.

"We could bring one home."

He said it. It wasn't even my idea. But I guess, to my credit, I knew he was right. That's what we would do.

So we set out on our adoption journey not to build a family—we had raised two lovely children, the nest was empty—but to save one life. That was how we saw it then.

Nanoseconds later, I was at the computer, logging on to the Internet, trying to figure out how the thing worked. It was 1996, and I'd only begun really exploring the web a few days before. I'd been having a rotten writing day—my screenplay wouldn't shape up—so I'd lost a few hours poking around cyberspace as a distraction. Or that's what I thought at the time.

Now I spent the entire day learning to "surf." There was no Google back then, but somehow I found the State Department guidelines for international adoption, the INS guidelines for orphan immigration, lists of adoption agencies, and information about an organization called Families with Children from China. I read personal stories. I called a friend who always seemed to know everybody and, sure enough, she had a friend who'd met somebody at a dinner party who had just returned with a baby from China. I got the name of a Chinese adoption facilitator to check out first thing Monday morning. I called San Francisco to give my grown daughter, Cristin, the news.

"I'm sorry I have to do this by phone," I said. "I'd so love to see your face right now."

"It'd make no difference, Mom. My face has no expression. I don't know what to feel."

Fair enough. Who knew?

I didn't get dressed until 5:00 P.M. When Dick called to say he was heading home from his shoot, I asked him to meet me at JR Seafood, our favorite Chinese place. I arrived with a giant red binder, crammed full and organized into categories—adoption agencies and immigration info and first-person adoption stories and lists of what to pack and what sorts of shots you need for China. Dick wasn't surprised to see the red binder. His wife was, if nothing else, a consummate researcher.

That night and all the next morning we talked. We tried to weigh the pros and cons. Were we doing the right thing? Would we be saving a life or taking a child away from her country? Away from what? What future could she have in China? We could find no wrong.

And then altruism began to morph into the endless pregnancy. We were like any other expectant parents, focused on one little life, eagerly waiting for the moment we would hold our daughter in our arms.

Somewhere in China, that one little life had already begun. Born but not yet abandoned. Fate was in motion.

EIGHTEEN LONG MONTHS passed. After the pre-adoption fingerprints, paperwork, home studies, FBI checks, and scrutiny of our now-fat dossier, and after China had taken a hiatus to completely reorganize its international adoption process—and while I was finishing my movie script, storyboarding each shot with Dick, scouting locations, casting actors, interviewing animal trainers and composers and editors, and then finally, finally rolling the camera—the telephone rang in the production office of the old California rancho in Carmel Valley. The wheels of Chinese bureaucracy turn slowly. No more so than making movies.

The phone call was for me, but I was off somewhere in paradise—a paradise of my own design.

EXT. IDYLLIC WILDERNESS VALLEY—DAY

Beside a meadow pond stands a tumbledown shack. Joey, a brash young lawyer, has escaped to the California hills to protect Dinah, her seven-year-old client, from further harm. This is their refuge. Joey, not exactly a natural mother, is giving it her best.

DINAH

I don't like it when there's brown
stuff on the side of the eggs.

JOEY

It's iron. It's a kind of vitamin.

DINAH

I'm not eating it.

JOEY

Fine.
(She drops the pan. It clatters to the ground.)
I'm not cooking.

"Cut."

That's me. I'm staring at a slip of paper someone has put in my hand. I'm hyperventilating. "Sorry, everyone: Dick and I are going to need a moment. Let's take a break."

We're already racing to the waiting truck. It flies over the bumpy roads, splashes through a muddy ditch, skirts a meadow, pulls around behind the hacienda-turned-production-office—

And just like in the movies, suddenly we're standing there, looking at the telephone with pounding hearts. I dial Los Angeles, call Norman Niu, our adoption facilitator.

"Congratulations. You have a healthy, beautiful daughter. Yue Meiying. Meiying means 'Beautiful Hero.' She's seventy-six centimeters. Nine kilos. Almost two years old. Playful. Smart. Guangzhou—best orphanage in China. You can come to China next week."

Oh my God. This is it.

I look at Dick. But we *can't* go to China. We have a cast and crew and investors depending on us here, and we can't go to the other side of the world to get our little girl who, even if she doesn't know it, has been waiting for us since the day she was born. Already we've failed her.

Somehow, we will make our way through twenty-two more shooting days, our hearts in limbo.

Guangzhou, China

By now we'd lost all sense of time. The plastic flowers had wilted. The hot water was tepid. We'd kept her waiting untold months and twenty-two extra days. Payback time? Was she old enough to decide she'd changed her mind?

And then Meiying was in the doorway.

Her hair was slicked down like a guy on prom night. Her big eyes looked tired and confused—and deep, old-lady sad. Her face was splotched with itchy-looking sores. A smiling woman in a rumpled white uniform lifted her up to me.

I felt my heart beating in every part of me. Ears. Knees. Toes. Eyelids. I reached out and took Meiying, my little girl, in my arms.

She barely glanced at me. Even my foreign face wasn't enough to rouse her curiosity. She'd been handed around to strangers before. Everybody was a stranger.

Meiying

The first time I held her is as immediate today as if I were transported back in time. The heat, the sticky air, the people all fall away. It is just us.

She smells of pomade and pee. She weighs nothing. She is all bits and bones. She doesn't nestle into my arms in that instinctive baby way, but rigidly arches her back. Her belly, too hard and round for this tiny body, pokes out of the thin white shirt. Her yellow pajama bottoms say *Novèlli Crayon* down one skinny leg. Her socks say *Baseball*. She is wearing clear jellies with pink rosebuds printed on the soles. They are too small. The bottoms have not been walked on. Her impossibly long, thin fingers tightly clutch a dried lychee nut in each hand, put there to keep her from scratching her face full of sores. She is beautiful.

What does it feel like to hold her? It feels both intensely foreign and awkward, and absolutely right. It feels like I am holding someone else's child, and yet there is no doubt that she is mine. That she has always been mine.

IT DIDN'T TAKE long to figure out that "healthy," "smart," "playful," and "best orphanage in China" were soothing gifts the Chinese bestowed upon all anxious parents-to-be. Within hours of returning to our hotel room, we'd seen the bloody diarrhea that turned out to be amoebic dysentery, we'd called doctors, arranged for urgent hospital visits, learned that our little almost two-year-old could barely walk and had no language at all. No Cantonese. No Mandarin. *Meiyou.* Nothing. Zip.

The one thing she could do like a champ was eat. Massive bowls of noodles disappeared into that swollen, malnourished belly. No wonder: she was feeding millions. A parasite zoo full of six kinds of creepy crawlies lived off our tiny girl. *Helicobacter pylori, Giardia intestinalis, Entamoeba histolytica, Clostridium difficile, Sarcoptes scabiei,* and *Ascaris lumbricoides,* better known as giant roundworms.

Healthy?—hardly. Playful?—under the circumstances, who would be?

As for smart, it was impossible to know. She didn't speak. She wouldn't even look at us. She didn't respond to anything except food. She was a little shell being eaten alive from the inside.

I'll confess we were a bit scared. We were exhausted from eight weeks of film production. It was our first trip to China. Our new daughter was sick and shut down and not doing any of the usual toddler things. Between useless (though undeniably cinematic) hospital visits, the three of us sat on the king-size bed at the China Hotel, two of us watching for hopeful signs.

Meiying wouldn't go near Dick (and barely tolerated me), but he soon learned that she would let him feed her Cheerios one by one. He went through dozens of flying cereal maneuvers, one at a time, each *O* finally making a perfect landing between sweet little rose-bud lips. Did I mention that she was beautiful as advertised? Even with running sores marring her pale cheeks, that part of Norman's promise could not be denied. Our new daughter was a stunner.

Day two on the big hotel bed, the first small miracle occurred. Bone-weary, I was propped against the headboard, watching on television as Hong Kong was officially returned to the motherland, ending 156 years of British rule. Despite the pomp and fireworks, my eyes drifted shut.

While awaiting her ration of incoming Cheerio flights, Meiying gradually began scooching backward on the bed, back toward my leg. I opened my eyes. Slowly . . . scooch . . . scooch. I held my breath. She wouldn't look at me, but I could feel the warmth of her little back coming closer . . . and then lightly touching—contact!— and then (bliss!) pressing against my leg.

Now we were ready to take on the world.

AFTER TWO WEEKS of appointments—visa photos, consulate clearance, inoculations, and a physical exam (which she mysteriously aced)—our new family flew home to California. Meiying was sick the entire flight, necessitating several wardrobe changes. She crossed the finish line at U.S. Immigration wrapped only in Dick's T-shirt.

The jet-lagged days back home were a blur of doctor appointments and preparations to start editing the movie.

The former Meiying became Maya, a name I'd heard months before in a dream. That it was so similar to her orphanage name seemed like another whim of fate. We were getting used to those.

Maya's new pediatrician told us that our daughter wouldn't have lived another year untreated. A life saved for sure. The facial sores began to heal. Dead worms appeared in the diapers (that is a *good* thing!). Weight was gained. But even as we dutifully stashed Flagyl in ice cream and force-fed our little darling the foul-tasting stuff, we quietly worried.

We celebrated the first steps, the first faint smiles, the first gluttonous pumpkin-suited Halloween—all milestones were accompanied by food—but Maya never seemed truly present. Even as she began to let me hold her and occasionally (briefly) rested easy in my arms, it was like she didn't get that cuddling was a worthwhile activity. The only sign that something was going on in that lovely little head was the furrowed brow that had appeared the moment we met her and refused to fade. In fact, the worry lines seemed to deepen when I held her. We had snatched her away from her everything. All was lost.

It seemed like our baby had never known love. She didn't know what to do with it. But could she be taught? Could she learn what should come naturally? Could these strange new people teach her to experience and accept love?

"Give it time," I whispered to her. "We'll find our way together."

I dearly hoped that was true. Was I mother enough to bring this hurt little being out of her shell?

I hadn't been exactly nurtured as a child. I came late in the post–Depression era marriage of two hard-working first-generation Americans who were entirely focused on making ends meet and saving for the rainy day that would likely come at any moment. My two sisters were born several years before me. I was not planned, and although it wasn't said (well, only once in anger), I never felt particularly loved or even wanted. Of course, decent families would never think of abandoning their unwanted babies in the 1950s in California, USA. Certainly not. But I don't remember being held or played with or talked to much. I wasn't unhappy. It was just the way it was.

When she wasn't off at work, my mother was tired and impatient and, it seemed to me, impossible to please. She never spared the rod. My father came home from work and lost himself in sports scores and bowling and his weekly pinochle game with the boys. We never talked.

When I looked at Maya . . . the utter aloneness of her . . . maybe I saw something of myself.

TO KEEP MAYA with me every waking moment, I decided to edit my movie at home. A film editor and assistant, trim bins, and editing equipment soon consumed our living room and all other available space in the house. I plopped Maya on my lap and did my best to make up for all the cuddles and kisses she'd missed out on, while we reviewed shots over and over, assembled and reassembled scenes.

Throughout that first winter, I tried to focus on both my babies—Maya and the movie. It was the best I could manage under the circumstances. Maya won hands down. While the editor cut, I sang silly songs and show tunes and lullabies and rocked and blew bubbles and fell in love. It probably wasn't an ideal introduction to family life, but at least our little girl knew somebody was paying attention.

Sometime around our first rough cut, as we replayed the opening courtroom scene for the thousandth time, Maya began to softly babble.

"What's she saying?" asked the editor.

I leaned down.

"*Tewwa twoo* . . . omigosh, she's talking! *Tewwa twoo* . . . Tell the truth! She said, 'Tell the truth'!"

Okay, so it was dialogue from the movie, but my little girl was talking! I covered her little babbly face with kisses.

July 1998

Whenever we can, we like to do something special on the Fourth of July to celebrate Dick's birthday (which falls on the fifth) without making too big a deal about it. Dick's the kind of guy who slips out the back door if you offer him a singing-waiter birthday cake in public. But a year earlier on the fourth we'd flown to China to adopt Maya, so his entire birthday had been wiped out by the International Date Line. Time to make amends and have a party.

Our house was full to bursting with a happy combination of film types and China adoption types. Conversations of every sort in every room. The mood felt upbeat, and why not? Our movie was done and in the hands of its distributor. That same distributor had offered to finance and distribute another independent film that I would write and direct. It was such a rare offer, I didn't let myself even think about whether I wanted to be consumed like that again so soon, or whether, in my heart of hearts, I really believed that the world needed another little movie by Jenny Bowen that would likely come and go, not adding up to much. I should be grateful for the opportunity. I started a new script.

We knew how lucky we were. We'd worked hard for the life we had. And, although we were yet again dreaming of and scheming about moving away from Los Angeles and back to our San Francisco roots (Chinese daughter, San Francisco—no-brainer), we were reasonably content. We were not thinking of turning our lives upside down again.

We were in the kitchen, refilling food platters. I could hear children laughing and playing a noisy game in the garden. I looked out at them through the kitchen window.

Somehow, through that kitchen glass, the world was a movie frame. Whatever was going on in the rooms of my house, beyond the edges of the frame, faded away. I could hear only the laughter of children.

And as I watched a gaggle of three- and four-year-old girls skipping up a path, trying to go fast, faster, yet keeping the line, giddy with the effort . . . I saw Maya.

She was positively radiant. Her cheeks red, her eyes bright. She was giggling so hard she could barely keep her balance. She called out and grabbed a friend's hand. A friend! The girls collapsed on the grass in laughter.

In that frame of light, I saw a child—*my* child—and she was okay.

Better than okay. She looked like someone who had known life only as it should be—a child who had been treasured from the moment she was born.

"Honey, come see."

We watched her through the glass.

"Look at our little girl," Dick said.

"Well, that was easy, wasn't it?" I said.

"Nothing to it." He smiled.

It was a miracle, this suddenly blossoming child. But a miracle that made perfect sense. Our girl knew, without doubt, that she was adored. It was that simple.

"Why can't we do that for the ones we can't bring home?" I asked—and meant it.

"Uh-oh," he said. We'd been together a long time.

When we talk about that day, he tells me I said something else after that. I don't remember saying it—

I know what I'm going to do with the rest of my life.

Part One

Laowai
(Foreigner)
老外

A way is made by walking it. A thing is so by calling it.
ZHUANG ZI (369–286 BC)

Chapter 1

Clumsy Birds Have Need of Early Flight

笨鸟先飞

Summer 1998

From the moment I saw Maya at the heart of that happy tangle of little girls outside my kitchen window, I felt absolutely compelled to act. I saw a solution, plain and simple. I couldn't ignore it. I would find a way to bring a family's love to children who had lost theirs. I'd bring Maya's miracle to China.

It's true that I didn't know anything about early childhood development. Or about China. Or about starting and running a nonprofit organization. On the other side of the world. Without any knowledge of the Chinese language. What I did know something about was dreaming stories. I'd been doing it all my life.

When I was tiny, I made up stories with buttons from my mother's sewing box, whole worlds of little button people. Then it was snail kingdoms in coffee cans in our foggy San Francisco backyard. At seven, I became a latchkey kid and quickly found my comfort and my dreams in library books. I checked out the eight allowed every Saturday; when finished with the pile, I read them again. The best hours of my childhood were spent in their embrace. And in time, the books inspired me to write my stories down.

I learned to look forward to a blank piece of paper. I could dream life just the way I wanted it. I was in control.

That was the best part of making movies—the part that kept me going despite the hurdles and uncertainties of Hollywood—dreaming a story and somehow making it real. Even if the films I made never mattered that much to me in the end, even if they didn't particularly give my life meaning, there was plenty to love about the process. I loved being challenged to use every skill I could muster from my meager bag of tricks.

And filmmaking had given me a few new skills. Perseverance for sure. But also how to pitch my story to anyone who'd listen in hopes of raising funds and followers. How to imagine characters, then cast them. How to imagine places, then scout them. How to visualize the way a scene should play, then guide my actors through the world I'd concocted.

I'd learned how to make something from nothing. Those babies in China had nothing. It seemed like a perfect fit.

THE NAME CAME to me in an instant. I would call my organization Half the Sky—named for the old Chinese saying, "Women hold up half the sky." Just what I dreamed for Maya's little orphaned sisters: I would help them hold up the sky.

I began to imagine the story, how it would play. I saw loving homes right inside orphanage walls—*real* homes designed to help young children heal and learn and trust. Places where, like our Maya, each child could know that her life matters to someone. We would find and train local women to look after foundlings as if they were their very own.

I imagined an infant program where babies could form bonds from the start. A preschool program for little girls who had no parents to go home to at the end of the day. The programs themselves would need to feel safe like family, full of love and comfort.

While I had no doubt that a world without orphanages would be a better world, I understood that China's orphans were wards of the state. Somehow we'd have to do all this inside existing institutions. That meant we would have to find a way to become partners with the Chinese government.

So I needed a pitch, a way to sell the story to China. Maya's sudden awakening made sense—I knew it did—but I'd need the science to convince others, especially government officials.

I found my science on the Internet; the words, stark and cold, came down to this:

The months immediately after birth are critical for orderly brain maturation. During this "sensitive period," the number of synapses—the connections that allow learning to happen—increase twenty-fold. An astounding 75 percent of human cognitive and emotional growth potential—the development of intelligence, personality, and emotional and social behavior—is finalized by age seven. Holding and touching a young child stimulates that child's brain to release essential growth hormones. Without stimulation from or experience with the world, normal development cannot occur. Conversely, "noxious" experiences can cause harm to the developing brain.

There it was. Our little miracle writ plain. Science says that our daughter's transformation wasn't a fluke but rather the result of stimulation of critical hormones and elimination of noxious experiences. And there was urgency, a time window during which children must be reached. So what more did I need to know?

Well. About creating a nonprofit organization. About how to pay for one. About early childhood education. About China.

Okay, I scored a perfect zero. I got down to work.

CASTING WITH A wide net, I returned to the Internet, where I found adoptive parents who were preschool teachers and doctors and child psychologists. I questioned everyone. I queried adoption agencies and Chinese language professors and people who ran Chinese restaurants—my Sinosphere was admittedly limited in those days. There had to be *somebody* out there who could help me make the China connection I needed. Honestly, it never occurred to me that it might be foolhardy to dive into building a program in a distant country where I didn't have a single acquaintance.

I found something online based in Beijing called the Data User Service of China Population Information and Research Center. They had posted an enticing note (in English!):

> DUS is ready to serve you with raw data of population censuses and surveys in China, publications both in Chinese and in English, and all kinds of machine-readable data on floppy diskettes, tapes, and compact disks. Any time, any data, please contact DUS!

What a find! I sent my urgent questions immediately:
1. *Approximately how many girls are currently in Chinese orphanages (welfare institutions)?*
2. *How many are adopted by foreign families each year?*
3. *How many orphanages are there in China?*
4. *Approximately how many abandoned children are brought to the orphanages each year?*
5. *Approximately how much money is spent per child for nutrition and care?*
6. *Approximately how many orphanages provide any sort of structured program that includes stimulation and education?*
7. *If there are any such programs, can you give us any data regarding teacher training, methodology, teaching materials, and class size?*
   Thank you in advance for your kind assistance.

I never heard a word in reply. And that was my first message from China on the subject.

No matter. I was on a vision quest. I completely ignored the fact that just about everybody I shared my brainstorm with listened politely and then said some version of "Impossible." "Can't happen." "The Chinese government will never let you do it." "Why would you want to help China anyway? They throw their kids away." "There are plenty of kids right here in the United States who need help. Do something in your own backyard." There was no shortage of advice. I pressed on.

I found, and followed to the letter, a do-it-yourself guide for setting up a California nonprofit corporation. I discovered that I needed a board of directors. Okay. Well then, I should start with an expert. I knew just the man.

Every adoptive parent online knew Dr. Dana Johnson—a professor of pediatrics, director of the International Adoption Clinic at the University of Minnesota, adoptive father, and maybe the top internationally renowned authority on the unhappy effects of child institutionalization.

I wrote. He called and talked to my answering machine. I called back and talked to his answering machine. He called again. (That's how it was in those days.) When at last we talked, incredibly, Dr. Johnson agreed to join Half the Sky's board of directors, even though it was still a figment of my imagination. I'm still not 100 percent sure why.

With a bona fide expert in tow, I wooed some fellow adoptive parents who'd become good friends while awaiting our daughters. Four kindhearted couples—including Terri and Daniel, dear friends who'd adopted their daughter from Maya's orphanage—agreed to join Dick, Dana, and me on the founding board. They joined us as friends and as caring new parents; I was the only one obsessed. None of us had any idea what we were getting into.

Considering that we were entirely focused on China, our new board looked awfully Anglo. Some prominent Chinese were definitely in order to round out the cast, so I tried to contact every name I recognized listed on the Chinese American Committee of 100, including Yo-Yo Ma, I. M. Pei, Jerry Yang (the Yahoo guy), and Vera Wang. Only Stanley Ho, the brother of AIDS researcher and *Time* magazine's 1996 Man of the Year David Ho, was kind enough to respond:

> *Dear Jenny:*
>
> *On behalf of Dr. David Ho, thank you very much for your important letter and the opportunity to serve on the Board of Directors of Half the Sky. Your efforts are truly noble and we salute you and your new foundation for your courage and determination.*
>
> *Dr. Ho would like to consider joining the board, but is unable to make a commitment now. His schedule is quite overwhelming. How much time do you envision being required? Would you be happy with the lending of his name only? . . .*

Would I be happy? "Absolutely, that would be terrific!" I replied. But Mr. Ho never wrote back again.

MOST IMPORTANT, I had to figure out how I was going to provide nurture, individual attention, and stimulation to large groups of abandoned, traumatized small children. Maya was one child and I was but one adoring mama operating on instincts that, thankfully, seemed to be working. Now I was envisioning rooms—maybe even multiple orphanages—full of thriving, cherished children. How could I take our little miracle to scale?

I scoured the Internet again, hunting down all the child development theories of the moment and corresponding with perhaps a dozen proponents of different methodologies. Then I learned about the town of Reggio Emilia, Italy, and how it helped its community and its children recover from the devastation of war. In a book called *The Hundred Languages of Children,* I found Loris Malaguzzi:

> Six days after the end of the Second World War. It is the spring of 1945. . . . I hear that in a small village called Villa Cella, a few miles from the town of Reggio Emilia, people decided to build and run a school for young children. That idea seems incredible to me! I rush there on my bike and I discover that it is all quite true. I find women intent upon salvaging and washing pieces of brick. . . .
>
> "We will build the school on our own," they say, "working at night and on Sundays. The land has been donated by a farmer; the bricks and beams will be salvaged from bombed houses, the sand will come from the river; the work will be volunteered by all of us."
>
> "The rest will come," they say to me.
>
> "I am a teacher," I say.
>
> "Good," they say. "If that is true, come work with us."

So Loris Malaguzzi, a young teacher from nearby Correggio, quit his job and became the father of the Reggio Emilia approach to early education. He understood from the start that to reach great numbers of children traumatized by war, he must find a way to be there for them one by one and all together. It was the opposite of what was believed in his day about the education of young children. "A simple, liberating thought came to our aid, namely that things about children and for children are only learned from children. We knew how this was true and at the same time not true. But we needed that assertion and guiding principle; it gave us strength and turned out to be an essential part of our collective wisdom."

Maya taught me that I could reach one hurt child by simply being there for her, responding to the need I saw in her. It seemed that Reggio might offer a way to reach any number of children like our little girl—to help build a new life for maybe thousands out of the rubbled landscape of loss.

An orphanage is not a town. Our children had no loving families to help them rebuild their lives brick by brick. Half the Sky's programs to nurture orphaned children must be placed in the hands of extraordinary caregivers who would be not simply substitute parents or nannies or even mere teachers. They must also become learning partners, able through careful observation to respond to children's needs and offer gentle guidance.

But how could an abandoned child, a child no adult spoke to except in group commands, a child whose eyes no one ever looked into—how could she possibly develop enough sense of who she was or what she needed to then tell us? If she *could* tell us—if she had a voice—what would she say?

I couldn't know the answers, but I could find the right people to help. People who knew how to turn ideas into practice. Over time, I told myself, the children would show us the way. We would have to watch carefully, listen to the hundred languages, the hundred ways that children communicate, and ask that question again and again.

"Learning and teaching should not stand on opposite banks and just watch the river flow by," said Loris Malaguzzi. "Instead, they should embark together on a journey down the water."

We wouldn't be afraid to take the journey together. We would learn from the children, and then they from us.

•   •   •

THE VERY DAY after discovering Reggio, I joined an online community dedicated to its teachings. There I found Carolyn Edwards, a psychology professor at the University of Nebraska, who, it turned out, had coedited *The Hundred Languages of Children*. I asked her if she thought such an approach, one that enables children to become partners in their own learning, could be a key to helping institutionalized children awaken.

"Absolutely!" she said, "Reggio, and its focus on learning through relationships, may well offer at least part of the answer you're looking for."

She told me about a young Chinese graduate student who might help me connect the dots.

Wen Zhao and her husband, Hong, had been among the thousands of Chinese students studying in the United States when Tiananmen Square erupted in 1989. Like so many others, they never went home. Hong was now a geology professor; Wen was a graduate student of early childhood education. Somehow exile had taken them to Lincoln, Nebraska, home, at that time, of the worst Chinese food I have ever tasted. Just before Thanksgiving, I bundled Maya up, we flew to the chilly plains of America's heartland, and I made my case.

Wen was a slender porcelain beauty straight out of the Qing Dynasty but tossed with a fluff of curly permed hair that was pure middle America. She listened carefully while I shared my vision of happy, healing preschools and infant nurture programs inside government orphanages. I explained why I believed that institutionalized children might thrive with a Chinese version of the Reggio approach.

Wen shook her head. "I just don't understand. Why do you want to do this for our Chinese children?"

I'd heard plenty of "Impossible," but Wen was the first to ask me *why*.

I wasn't entirely sure. I stumbled over my words.

"Well. Because I think I know how to help? Because no one else is doing anything for those kids? Because . . . look at this little girl on my lap—how happy, how alive she is. She taught me why. If you could have seen her on the day we met, Wen, you would just know."

"I can see she is in your heart," she said.

What I loved most about Wen was that she never did say, "Impossible." She just showed us around the university laboratory child development center, the walls bright with children's art and photographs of projects in the works, and told me she dreamed of one day returning to China to open schools like this. Good schools, inspired by Reggio.

"We'll do it together," I said. "Help me and you'll have your schools."

Maybe that's what convinced her. Or maybe she, too, was swept along by whatever wind was at my back. She got right to work developing a curriculum for an orphanage preschool. And when I thanked Carolyn Edwards for the great introduction, I asked if she'd also consider joining our board. Yes!

Early Spring 1999

I got my first truly practical Chinese lesson from Norman Niu, the sweetheart of an adoption facilitator who had helped us adopt Maya. "Uncle Norman" was the only Chinese person I knew at the time who had genuine dealings with the Chinese government. He was a natural for Half the Sky. Plus, while we were waiting to adopt, I'd given him and his cousin a bit part in my movie, so I liked to think we had a special place in his heart.

Dick and I invited Norman to lunch with our radiant little daughter and shared our plan. I told him about Dr. Johnson and Dr. Edwards and about Wen Zhao.

"Norman, we'd be thrilled if you'd consider joining our board and help to make Half the Sky a reality. It's really because of you and your work that all this is happening. So what do you think?"

Norman smiled. "It's a good plan. But difficult. China is not an easy place. Your daughter is very lovely. She must bring you much happiness."

He didn't seem dying to jump in. I went on to explain that all I really needed him to do was present the plan to the CCAA—the China Center for Adoption Affairs—in Beijing. Once the government agreed to talk to me, I would take care of the rest.

"You should go to the provincial authorities first. CCAA very difficult."

"I see. Well, would you do that for us, Norman? After facilitating all those adoptions, I'll bet you must have great relations in Guangdong Province."

"It is difficult. Did you try the shrimp?"

Okay. Well, he didn't say no.

And here was my first real China lesson: China is like Hollywood. *Nobody* likes to say no. In fact, it's almost impossible to make someone actually say the word *no*. In Hollywood, it's because nobody wants to be the one to pass on a future mega-hit. In China, it's because nobody wants to be the nail that sticks out and gets hammered. This I could live with. I just had to figure out the Chinese equivalent of not taking your phone calls. That's how they say no in Hollywood.

So lunch ended and Norman went to China and I eagerly waited for news.

BY NOW, I'D given up any thought of Half the Sky as a little project I'd do on the side while continuing to toil in the Hollywood trenches. I failed to turn in the screenplay for my next film; in fact, I barely wrote a word after seeing Maya through that kitchen window. Half the Sky was the story I wanted to write.

My dear husband, my soul mate, said he was with me all the way. We sold our house and moved back to the Bay Area, to an old farmhouse in the Berkeley hills. The new dining room became our Half the Sky production office.

The timing was great. Dick was helping out on a film project with Public Media Center, a nonprofit advertising agency in San Francisco. The company was run by Herb Chao Gunther, loquacious, sometimes brilliant, and definitely the cockiest, most opinionated Chinese German radical lefty ad guy around. We met.

"What makes you think you can make a difference?" Herb said.

"I don't know," I said.

"But that doesn't stop you?"

"No."

"Good."

Then the helpful hints came faster than I could write them down. Best of all, Herb was actually working in China. He had wangled some hefty grant funds from the Ford Foundation to train family planning officials in midlevel Chinese cities how to present sex education. He worked with a Chinese organization that might be willing to partner with Half the Sky. He had my China connection!

Herb promised to introduce me to Madame Miao Xia, secretary general of the China Population Welfare Foundation (CPWF), a Chinese NGO, or nongovernmental organization. "Well, actually, it's a GONGO," he said, "a government-organized nongovernmental organization."

"China's nonprofits are really run by the government?"

"Exactly," he said. "All truly functioning NGOs in China are, in fact, organized by the government and run by retired government officials. So you have to find a *nainai* GONGO."

"*Nainai* GONGO? Okay . . . I'm not following exactly."

"*Nainai* is 'grandmother.' You need a GONGO to look after you, like a *nainai*."

"*Nainai* GONGO. Got it."

"Anyhow, not to worry."

Herb said that Madame Miao was tough and political, but she was honest. A perfect *nainai*. We should be okay. And even though he had no authority whatsoever, I will be forever grateful to Herb for giving me my first yes. It felt like permission.

Herb was a man of his word. I soon received a letter from Beijing.

Dear Jenny Bowen:

It is our great pleasure to know your Foundation through our dear friends at Public Media Center. CPWF is a nonprofit NGO, to assist people, especially women, in their economical life, health, and social activities. Improving the conditions of the orphanages has been our concern in the past. Besides, we are in direct link with the government ministry—the State Family Planning Commission. In a word, as a Chinese NGO, we are greatly interested in a joint effort with your foundation to reach our common goal.

Truly yours,
Miao Xia, Secretary General
China Population
Welfare Foundation

Yes! We had a Chinese partner—a *nainai*!—nothing could stop us now! I faxed back at once with a copy of our proposal. I asked when we could meet in Beijing.

A week passed with no word. Hmm. I refaxed the letter and proposal. Bingo!

Dear Jenny Bowen,

We are happy that you have received our letter. At the time when we are looking forward to your reply we noticed unfortunately on our side the fax paper had been running out. We hope you will try it again and by that time the paper should be in position. Thank you for your attention and we are waiting to read your fax.

With good wishes,
Mrs. Zhang Zhirong,
Assistant to Mme. Miao

Three's a charm. My message was received and the assistant, Mrs. Zhang—who I now realized was the English voice of Madame Miao—sent a lovely note confirming that we were to be partners, and that there would be certain financial requirements on our side, and throwing in a little pitch for herself:

So far at this stage, I would be happy to appoint Mrs. Zhang Zhirong to be the contact person for this project. Mrs. Zhang graduated from University of Michigan, an MA in sociology, she has long years' experience in conducting and managing international aid programs. I am sure she will be a good helping hand in implementation of your program in China.

She'd written her own letter of recommendation! And I would soon learn that she had not oversold herself one bit. For now, I wrote back that it sounded like a great idea and I'd be in touch as soon as we heard from my friend Norman Niu.

Then NATO bombed the Chinese Embassy in Yugoslavia. The U.S. government said it had been a mistake.

•   •   •

BEIJING (*NEW YORK TIMES*), SETH FAISON—A powerful surge of anti-American sentiment was unleashed after last week's bombing of China's Embassy in Belgrade, sending rocks, bottles and slogans at the American Embassy here. The protests grew to become the largest anti-foreign demonstrations since the Cultural Revolution in the 1960s. . . .

"We are a very old and traditional nation," said Wang Yizheng, a government employee. "If you do not show us respect, we will hate you."

I wrote to my new friends at CPWF:

I'm writing to convey my sincere condolences and my outrage at the recent bombing of the Chinese Embassy in Belgrade. I am deeply sad and angry that the NATO countries have made such a terrible, tragic, and unspeakable mistake.

I am worried and frightened about how this will be played out. I feel that now, more than ever, it is important to keep our lines of communication open. I wanted to share these feelings with my friends in China.

Sincerely,
Jenny Bowen

I received an immediate reply:

Dear Jenny,

Your fax of condolences has been received. It's been circulated to all our staff and the translation copy has been sent to our newspaper, Population. We regard your attitude representing the sincere concern of the American people toward the Chinese people. We are here to express our heartfelt thanks and absolute agreement with you.

For almost two months, headed by the U.S., NATO countries
have launched an indiscriminate bombing of the innocent
people, especially killing and injuring innocent Chinese
journalists and diplomats, which is totally unacceptable by all
peace-loving people in the world. Justice would bound to defeat
all evils.

They went on to assure me that my country's wanton behavior
would not affect our future cooperation. It did strike me that I was
way out of my league here. I was a mere mom with a mission, and
here I was blithely exchanging diplomatic cables.

I had crossed a line, and I think I knew it. But there I was, on
the other side. And I was growing mighty fond of our new partners. I couldn't wait to meet them.

Do Not Hope to Reach the Destination Without Leaving the Shore

不下大海　难得明珠

There was one other bump on the road to China, and it wasn't getting any smoother with time. I'd lost count of the number of people who'd told me that what I planned was now absolutely impossible. Out of the question. The situation was worse than ever. Foreigners were no longer welcome to even *visit* government orphanages, let alone set up programs inside them. "Forget China. Your daughter's an American now."

And if it were up to the Chinese government, *everybody* would forget China, at least as it had to do with orphans. During the time that the Human Rights Watch report, the story that had opened our eyes, was being compiled, a British film crew, posing as an American orphan charity organization seeking to make a donation, had captured what they said was undercover documentary evidence of terrible and widespread neglect in Chinese orphanages. *The Dying Rooms* had been regularly airing ever since, even featured on *60 Minutes* in the United States. Rather than fading, the international uproar it had provoked continued to grow.

China responded to the loss of face by denying abuse, publishing a white paper refuting the allegations, thanking the world for its comments, and then . . . firmly closing the doors to all foreigners, well intentioned or otherwise. By now, even parents in the process of adopting had a hard time getting inside orphanages. If they did manage it, they rarely saw more than reception rooms.

FOUR MONTHS HAD passed since our lunch with Norman, and still no word. For all I knew, he hadn't done a single thing to secure permission for us to launch a program in Guangdong Province or anyplace else. Probably somebody who wasn't busy imagining a movie in her head would have predicted this back at the lunch table.

I couldn't let a few bumps slow me down. The children were waiting. Anyway, I had a real partner now—a partner with connections, the *guanxi* (special personal relationships) that could make things happen. I wrote CPWF again and explained that, actually, if they would be so kind, I needed some help with government introductions.

Ready or not, I was going to China.

THE CHINESE CONSULATE in San Francisco was full of would-be summer travelers waiting in obedient, ragged queues. When I finally made it to the first window, the clerk hesitated over my application. He put down his red rubber stamp. He gave my paper to the fellow on his left. He reached for the application of the person behind, dismissing me.

"Next window," he said.

"Is there something wrong?"

The clerk pointed to the window at his left and focused full attention on the document before him. I no longer existed.

There was no line at the next window. My new clerk did not look up when I arrived. He was sorting passports, rubber-banding them into tidy stacks.

"*Nihao,*" I said brightly. I nodded at my visa application, now on his counter. "That's me."

Not until all seventeen stacks of passports were filed into cardboard boxes did the worker bee pick up my application. Now he studied every line. After forever, he squinted up at me.

"Your occupation is writer."

"Yes."

"What kind?"

Ah, stupid me. "Oh! No—I'm just a screenwriter."

"For movies?"

"Yes."

"Let me understand, the writing you do is dramas?"

"Yes."

"You are not writing for the press?"

"No, no."

"You are not a journalist?"

"Oh no, definitely not."

He thrust a new form at me. "Write that down. What you just told me."

I did.

"Do you swear you will never write anything for the press?"

"Okay . . . yes . . . sure."

He took my papers and stamped them with three different red chops. Then he looked up at me and squinted through his glasses.

"This is for me: You go to China, you should write good movie about it. Not like *Red Square*. And why you not go to Shanghai? It best city. Write movie about *it*."

"MAYA, DO YOU remember the babies at the orphanage? All your little sisters? Some of them were so sad because they didn't have mommies to love them. Your mommy knows how to help those little girls not be so sad. I need to go to China to make that

happen. I'll be gone for just a little bit, and Daddy will be with you
every minute while I'm away. I'll always come back to you."

It was that fleeting and lovely after-bath ritual. Toweled dry
and sweet smelling, Maya was tugging on her pajamas.

"You know that, right? I'll always come back. . . . Maya . . . ?
Sweetie, your jammies are backwards. Let me help."

"I do it *all my byself.*"

Arrow straight to the heart. Parental guilt strikes. Big-time.
And, I admit, never quite leaves.

July 1999

Dear Friends:

*I am composing this while sitting in the lounge at the Tokyo
airport waiting for my flight to Beijing. I am going this time,
not to adopt a child, but to launch a very special project. It's
a project that grew from watching my precious daughter Maya
blossom from a sickly, scared waif into a happy, confident little
dynamo in two short years.*

*Last year, on the first anniversary of Maya's adoption, I was
feeling particularly grateful for the gift of my daughter's life in
mine. I decided I had to give something in return and, having
listened to your stories, I thought that many adoptive parents
like you might feel the same. My thoughts always come back to
the children who wait and to those who will spend their entire
childhoods without families.*

*When I was waiting for my referral, someone told me that
a girl who grows up in a Chinese orphanage has only three
choices in her adult life: to become an orphanage worker, to join
the military, or to become a prostitute. I never was able to check
out the truth of that statement, but I do believe that education
and self-esteem can give every kid at least a fighting chance to
do better.*

With a small group of adoptive families, I started
Half the Sky Foundation. Our plan is to establish early
childhood development centers in China's government-run
orphanages. We've joined forces with Beijing-based China
Population Welfare Foundation and, with their assistance, we
have received approval from the Ministry of Civil Affairs to set
up a pilot program in two orphanages. My trip to Beijing is
to visit orphanages in three provinces and to choose those two
sites!

We want to make Half the Sky a collaborative effort of all
adoptive families who share our desire to give something back to
the country that was their child's first home, and particularly to
its institutionalized children. Will you join us?

Well, there may have been a bit of wishful thinking in my message, but this was no time to be timid. I took a deep breath and sent the e-mail. A year and a week after I saw Maya through that kitchen window, here I was, off to Beijing to meet with officials of China's central government. To be allowed to tour I didn't know how many orphanages. To select sites for a pilot program. Nothing I understood of China (which was still close to nothing) told me that this would be happening. I couldn't wait to get on that plane.

As we lifted off from Tokyo for the last leg of the journey, I took it as a great sign that the entire Chinese women's soccer team was on my flight. Just the day before, they'd been barely defeated by the U.S. team at the Women's World Cup final game at the Rose Bowl. More than ninety thousand fans were silent in the stadium and forty million viewed on TV as the game was decided in penalty kicks. Even though they weren't victorious, the Chinese team could share credit for helping bring women's sports to a whole new audience. Let's hear it for the girls!

And when our plane touched down in Beijing, we did. The girls were welcomed like rock stars. Flowers and cameras flashing and tears and applause. What a welcome to China for Half the Sky! I smiled as I wove through the adoring crowd.

BEIJING WAS ONE big construction zone. Streets were being re-paved and buildings were being put up or taken down. The muggy skies were thick with dust. My eyes stung and my throat was sore by the time I reached our hotel.

"All of China is being rebuilt for October 1, National Day—our fiftieth anniversary celebration," the desk clerk at the Jianguo Hotel told me. "Just outside they're going to put in a new subway line."

"I don't see any construction out there," I said.

"It will begin tomorrow."

"But it's already July."

He smiled.

Sure enough, when I woke the next morning, I heard lots of pounding and crunching. I looked out the window at what ap-peared to be the entire People's Liberation Army (PLA) attacking the sidewalk with sledgehammers, pickaxes, and shovels. Not a sign of heavy equipment. When I asked later that year, I was told that the subway line had been more or less finished (or at least had *appeared* to be more or less finished) in time for National Day.

I spent my first full day recovering from jet lag. Wen Zhao, my Reggio expert from Nebraska, had arrived in Beijing sometime in the night and was bubbling with excitement about the adventure about to begin. She'd caught the fever.

We escaped the hotel and its PLA pounding and strolled through a tree-lined Beijing that was still, in 1999, full of bicycles and *hutong*s. We weaved among hawkers and their fake Pradas and Calvins in Silk Alley. We wandered past the elegant American Embassy, looking embarrassed behind smashed windows. (The bombing was not mentioned to me once during this entire trip.)

Little troops of tall, gaunt young men in uniform marched through the diplomatic area, saluting one another with white-gloved hands. Such perfect precision, such rigidity on such a blistering summer day.

"Wen, do you ever think the Reggio approach might be fundamentally contrary to the Chinese way of doing things?"

"You're not getting nervous now, are you?" Wen laughed. "Don't worry. Most Chinese people want to try whatever is new. Our plan should work if we can find the right teachers. We won't make our final hiring decisions until after our training, after we've seen how open these young teachers are to new ideas, after they've developed some mini-projects and then shared their reflections, and most important, after we've watched them with the children. Trust me, they will love Reggio."

"Oh, I do trust you," I said. "Completely. Hey, maybe we'll be famous. Maybe rich families will be begging to send their kids to our orphanage schools. We'll be turning them away at the door."

"Ha! You're right!" Wen said. "I suggest we'll have to name our schools Famous American Half the Sky Schools. China loves famous things and American things. Even private kindergartens are called Harvard and Princeton. With a name like that, we might even change the whole education system!"

"Let's go get our permission to do this thing!" I said.

"We don't have permission?"

WELL, WE SORT of did. No one had said no. In early June, I'd written to CPWF asking how the introductions and approvals were going. Two weeks had passed in silence. I then called Beijing and spoke with Zhang Zhirong, who was lovely on the phone. Yes, they'd received my letter and yes they were making plans for our visit. The next day I received a fax:

We welcome you visit China for a very significant project. For better preparation, first of all, we had meetings trying to figure out our future cooperation. Meanwhile we have also contacted the relevant government agencies such as the Ministry of Civil Affairs and the CCAA to make introduction of your foundation and to share with them your good intention and the program action plan. In general, we all recognize the goodwill of the program, but for better understanding, the following questions need to be explained further. After receiving your response, we would follow up with further coordination and writing report to the Ministry, and afterwards to respond to you as soon as possible since time is pressing for your coming visit.

The letter went on for two more pages. It sounded sort of positive, but endless. I immediately wrote back, announcing the firm date of my arrival. I answered questions as well as I could, laid out as much as I knew of our plans, then guessed at the rest, figuring it was all going to change anyway. I'd learned this from film production. You pitch a great story and lay out a careful and highly detailed plan and budget, and the moment the crew sets up for the first shot everything begins to unravel and plans are revised. Constantly. The trick is to keep the momentum. Keep moving in a more or less forward direction.

Just two days before I traveled, Mrs. Zhang finally replied, "After back and forth negotiations, we got approval from the Ministry to visit three institutions."

Well, I figured we'd have to visit at least six institutions if we were going to find the right place for the pilot. If we failed, we wouldn't get a second chance. And there was no word about approval to actually start programs. So it wasn't exactly a yes. But it certainly wasn't a no. That was good enough for me. I decided not to burden anybody else with the details.

• • •

THE LADIES OF CPWF were an hour late for our breakfast meeting. "So sorry," said Mrs. Zhang. "Terrible traffic jam. Construction everywhere nowadays. It is a great, great pleasure to meet you!"

If it weren't for the fact that Mrs. Zhang's boss carried herself like someone important, I might have hugged Madame Miao at first sight. Everything about her looked soft and cuddly. Chubby face, rosy cheeks, fuzzy halo of dyed hair. Yet there was no doubt who was in charge.

Mrs. Zhang, on the other hand, even though sixty-ish, was as playful and available as a puppy. She had a gigantic warm smile, dark eyes that shone behind big round glasses, almost perfect English. I felt like I'd always known her.

"Now please you will tell us how we can help you," she said.

I explained a little about Maya, about how she'd come alive after finding the love of a family. But I sensed that I shouldn't linger on the dark side of Maya's story. No dredging up ghosts of dying rooms from Half the Sky.

"I represent a group of parents just like me," I said. "We are so grateful to China for the gift of these beautiful little girls in our lives. Now we want to give something back to their sisters who still have no families."

I told them about my idea for infant nurture programs where retired women could be trained to help the babies form healthy attachments and to give them the kind of individual attention and stimulation that would allow them to thrive. And about preschools, in which children would be gently guided to develop self-confidence and a love of learning while being prepared to enter primary schools in their communities. I told them about Reggio and threw in a few of my statistics about brain development.

"You are a teacher?" asked Mrs. Zhang.

"Well . . . no. Um, I'm mostly a screenwriter. And I've directed a few little films. But that's not—"

"But *why*?" she asked. There it was again.

"Because . . . well, because, most of all, we want to give orphans the love they have lost. Every child needs to know that she is loved and valued."

"But you have come all the way to China. You want to do for Chinese children? *Why?*" said Mrs. Zhang, her eyes now glistening.

"Well, because we have Chinese daughters. The children we had to leave behind are our girls' little sisters. We can't just go on with our happy lives and forget about them. They're family, just like our daughters."

Mrs. Zhang wiped her eyes and slapped the table.

"Understand. We must help you do this."

"Madame Miao, Mrs. Zhang, I think we may have found the perfect partner," I said.

Madame Miao nodded. "We think the same way."

"Well, okay! So what I think we need, to get things off to a really good start—well, we need to visit more places, more orphanages. Three's fine, but do you think you could get us into six? And we don't want to go only to model institutions, okay? Can you show us the not-so-good ones too? Because if they're perfect, there is nothing to improve."

Somehow I doubted that perfection was going to be an issue, but I wanted our new partners to have a mission, to feel driven. Heaven knows I needed them.

HERE'S WHAT IT'S like to travel China by car:

There are eight of us plus luggage in what is optimistically called a nine-passenger minibus. Madame Miao, Mrs. Zhang, Wen, the driver, yours truly—plus assorted others. There are always assorted others.

And the driver always smokes. He is willing to hold his cigarette outside the cracked-open window, but he just can't survive the drive smoke-free. As a result, I always feel bleary-eyed and hungover on road trips. Nobody else seems to mind.

Just about everyone is talking on a cell phone. Different conversations, all at maximum decibels. Chinese cell reception far outclasses that of its Western predecessors. On one of my rare sightseeing excursions in China, I once received a perfectly clear call from Los Angeles while at the bottom of an impossibly narrow mountain gorge. I'd walked 6,566 stone steps down to the bottom, and the line was crystal-clear.

In addition to the competing phone calls and the smoke, there is snacking. Bags of watermelon seeds and salty-sweet crackers and peanuts in their shell, along with dragon's eye fruit and mandarin oranges and lychees and bottles of water or sweet green tea, are produced from thin air.

You would think all this would make time fly. Au contraire.

It was a five-hour minibus ride south of Beijing in interminable traffic to our first destination, a place with the unpronounceable name Shijiazhuang. It would have been three hours without the traffic, but then it wouldn't have been China. Whenever the traffic opened up a bit, the driver went into high gear, pushing the minibus until the windows rattled, passing everything he could. He accomplished this by driving on the wrong side of the road, playing chicken with oncoming truckloads of melons, rusty scrap metal, and pigs, ancient putt-putting tractors and sleek official vehicles with black-tinted windows.

The air was hot, thick, gray-brown. The landscape was flat, green-brown, and went on forever. There was not a single piece of modern farming equipment to be seen. I was dripping and my brain had gone to mush. China in July. Avoid in future.

At long last, we turned off the expressway.

After we'd passed through the tollbooth, the driver pulled the minibus over to the side of the road behind another car. A man and a woman got out of the parked car and squeezed into our already cozy minibus. (We were up to ten of our allotted nine passengers.) The man was Mr. Bai of the Shijiazhuang Family Planning Association. Nobody introduced the woman.

We zipped into town, mostly by driving on the wrong side of the road. Then we sat in another traffic jam. The downtime was not wasted, though. Mr. Bai took charge. He shared with us the entire history of Shijiazhuang going back to 206 BC. He told us the current population—almost ten million, and I'd never heard of the place before! It seemed like no town in China had fewer than a million residents. After a while the mind is so boggled by people numbers that none of it registers.

Mr. Bai also managed to share Shijiazhuang's agricultural output, important historical sites, and what the place is *most famous* for. In this case, it was smokestacks. More smokestacks than any other city in China. There was plenty of visual evidence to back him up.

When we finally reached our destination, it was not the orphanage, but a restaurant. It did absolutely no good to protest that we weren't hungry; we'd been snacking on the drive. In China, I soon learned, hunger is not the point. No meals will be missed. Ever. I am to this day, whenever I visit government friends anywhere in China, reminded of meals I foolishly begged off from a dozen or more years ago.

"Remember when you drove all the way from Gaoyou to Lianyungang and then *only* visited the orphanage? You left without lunch!"

THE RESTAURANT LOBBY was palatial. Crystal chandeliers, rococo gilded wing chairs, and massive potted plants. The pseudo-Aubusson carpet was grimy, as was every single carpet in China as far as I could tell. (In the new, improved China, the carpet grime situation is likewise improved. It seems to run about fifty-fifty.)

We were greeted by a beautiful, tall young woman in a pencil-thin red-satin *qipao*. She was wearing a white-fur shorty cape, even though it was close to one hundred degrees outside. I was the only one in our party who was soggy from the heat.

We followed our greeter into an elevator. The doors closed but the elevator failed to move. Our driver muscled the beautiful young woman aside and punched the buttons in a more manly fashion. Nothing happened. The beautiful young woman opened the elevator doors and we followed her up three flights of stairs.

She guided us down a hallway with dozens of open doorways. Cigarette smoke poured out of every one. Raucous laughter and shouts punctured the haze. Somebody was having way too much fun for twelve thirty on a Tuesday afternoon.

The woman who'd arrived with Mr. Bai pushed ahead and entered one of the smoky doorways. A lot of pushing and shoving goes on in China, but nobody minds.

By the time we arrived, our hosts were stubbing out their cigarettes and gulping the last of their tea. They stood to welcome us with wide smiles. I'm not sure who most of them were. There was a vice mayor and a party secretary, and apparently they were the only ones who merited an introduction. Everybody else came for lunch. Mr. Bai vanished and I never saw him again. I decided that maybe I didn't need to memorize everybody's name.

There was a great deal of bickering about who should sit where around the big round table. I got the message right off the bat that this table-arranging business is a highly complex matter that all foreigners should stay out of. Almost as complex as food-ordering (but here you are invited to participate if you dare).

Certainly the highest-ranking person must sit at the head of the table (which at a round table is the place with the pointy napkin) and/or facing the door. And the honored guests (that would be me in this situation) are invited to sit to the right and left of him according to somebody's idea of what each one's respective rank is. But then there are the seats remaining. Everybody vies for the *least* important. At a not hugely formal banquet like this one, there's always a fair bit of friendly shoving before everyone finally settles down to eat.

The meal featured local delicacies with a special focus on meat and seafood. The Chinese were poor for a very long time. Vegetables don't get much respect when people have guests. Cheap stuff like noodles or rice is an afterthought. Visitors are a great excuse for a proper carnivorous feast, even in the poorest places.

The vice mayor was hosting a couple of other banquets at the same time. After he told me about his town's historical highlights and the trip he made to Disneyland and Las Vegas and Miami and we toasted a few times, he excused himself to make the rounds. I never saw him again.

I picked at my meal and tried to make sense of the conversation. When the topic bored her, Mrs. Zhang translated only every fifth sentence or so.

The meal was punctuated with toasts of *baijiu*—seriously hard white liquor—required for men, optional for ladies. Then fruit. Then all the men lit up. Then it was time to leave. Everyone stood at once. Exited abruptly. Lunch over.

This would normally be naptime in China, but this particular foreigner was the restless type. Somebody would have to take her to the orphanage.

ESCORTED BY THE still unidentified woman who'd joined us with Mr. Bai, our minibus made its way through a poor part of town. Kids playing in muddy sewer water. Hawkers hawking whatever—

food, cigarettes, underwear, VCDs (ubiquitous first-run movies of suspect origin)—from plastic tarps spread on crumbling pavement. Horse-drawn carts, pedestrians, and tiny three-wheeled trucks transporting refrigerators and mattresses competed for space along the narrow road. Our driver leaned on the horn and bullied through. No one on the street even glanced at him as they edged aside just enough to not get killed.

At long last we arrived at the orphanage gate. A woman in a grungy nurse's uniform was swabbing the tile lobby with a dirty mop. She ducked out of the way when we entered.

THERE WERE NO signs of children living there. No cries, no laughter. I wanted to ask where they were, could we see them? But I obediently followed the group into the reception room. The unidentified woman brought up the rear, keeping an eye on me.

The room had a big oval conference table with an open space in the middle. Sort of an elongated doughnut. Dusty plastic flowers only partially filled the hole. Chairs and leatherette sofas lined the walls. It looked familiar. Another version of the place we'd met Maya. *Every* orphanage has this reception room.

But now there were plates of fruit and bottles of water and unopened packs of cigarettes and paper cups for tea poured by a pretty girl. A new trio of women came in and sat with us at the big table, smiling and peeling oranges for me. Then we waited.

At last Director Kong, the orphanage boss, entered the room. All the ladies stood until he sat. He was in his midforties, wore his pants pulled high over a premature paunch, and sported a rather extraordinary black rug atop his head, apparently held in place by a thicket of eyebrows.

One of the orange-peeling women passed out brochures and a three-page report densely packed with Chinese characters. Everyone took out a notebook and started writing. So I did too.

Director Kong introduced himself and the others on his team. Each stood and bowed slightly. The unidentified woman turned out to be Mrs. Li, in charge of the children's department. Another woman, a deputy director in charge of logistics, then read the report aloud. She was nervous. Mrs. Zhang translated every word.

I learned how many *mu* of land the institution occupied and how many square meters the building was. I learned about the history of the institution and about the various divisions of work and, finally, about the children. I learned how many were "brain-damaged" or "deformed" and how many were "normal" (which, in the deputy director's opinion, was almost none).

Madame Miao then introduced Half the Sky. In a tribute to the Chinese educational system of rote learning, she recited to Director Kong and his staff exactly what I'd told her the day before. Everybody wrote in their notebooks. Another orange was shoved my way. More tea was poured.

Then it was my turn. It was my very first time speaking to an orphanage director about my plan. I hadn't thought about what I would say. But I felt oddly calm. I'd now spent twenty-four hours in semiofficial China and I was starting to get the formality, the rhythm, and the tone of things.

Before I made movies, I was in theater. I directed a little bit, but in the beginning I was an actor. When I was a young acting student in San Francisco, I used to ride the bus to my classes and eavesdrop on conversations. I'd pick up on the rhythms of speech; I'd watch people's mannerisms and how they connected with one another. And then I'd get off the bus and *become* those people for a little while . . . simply let them inhabit me, and continue the conversation until I arrived at class. Despite the alarmed glances of passersby, that was how I learned to become an actor, I think—much more than in the classes. Just by absorbing the world around me.

When I sat before Director Kong to make my pitch, that's pretty much what happened again. I became him and Madame Miao and Mrs. Zhang and Mrs. Li and the orange-peeling women, in addition to being entirely myself. I don't mean to suggest that my audience thought of me as simply one of them. Far from it. But this slipping into their skin—this chameleon-ness of me—made me comfortable in an otherwise impossible situation. I don't think I'd ever done that before in my regular life. Maybe because this was all so irregular—so utterly foreign and impossible to prepare for—it awoke some old actor's survival instinct. I became of the moment.

"Director Kong, everyone—first I want to thank you for giving us such a warm welcome. Madame Miao explained that it is our love for China's children that brings us here to see you today. As the lucky parent of a Chinese daughter and the representative of many foreign adoptive parents, I thank you for the loving care you give to the children who need you so much. Now we want to join you and give a gift to the children who remain in China's orphanages."

Careful not to criticize, I noted that the institutions' staff helped the children as much as they could but that, with so many to care for, it wasn't possible for the caregivers to provide all children the kind of individual attention that each needed to thrive. I told them about research that tells us that infancy and early childhood are critical times for healthy development.

"Half of a child's intellectual development potential is established by age four," I said. "Seventy-five percent is finalized by age seven." Everyone wrote.

"If we want these children to succeed in school and in life and not become a burden to society, we can't afford to waste the early years. And think of this—if a baby hasn't bonded with a caring adult by the age of two, she may *never* learn to develop a healthy, trusting relationship with another human being. Not in her entire life."

Everyone looked appropriately worried. Except, perhaps, Director Kong, who was whispering behind his hand into his cell phone. I paused. He got up and left the room. Oh well, the ladies were with me.

"We know you are concerned about the children in your care. The good news is that we think we can help you give them everything they need to succeed in life. With the help of Zhao *Laoshi* [Teacher Wen] and other experts, Half the Sky has developed two programs just for this purpose."

I told them a little bit about the *very famous* and innovative and scientific Reggio Emilia approach, and about the plans we'd drafted for Reggio-inspired Little Sisters Preschools and Baby Sisters Infant Nurture Centers.

"When children feel safe and loved, it is easy and natural for them to learn. Reggio is all about opening doors for the children, giving them rich experiences, helping them to fall in love with learning. Then they can reach their true potential. The founder of Reggio said, 'Our job is to help children climb their own mountains, as high as possible. No one can do more.'"

By the time I wrapped it up, Director Kong was back in the room. The ladies waited for him to speak.

"It is a very good plan."

"Thank you, Director Kong. I really hope we can work together."

"Certainly. What we need is an elevator and a new washing machine."

I looked at the ladies. No one seemed to disagree.

"I see. Well. May I visit the children?"

Chapter 3

Do Not Upset Heaven
and Earth

不知天高地厚

I entered a room full of orphans. It was the first time.

There were maybe twenty, maybe thirty of them, all little girls—toddlers. But no one was toddling. They were all sitting on little paint-chipped wooden potty chairs in a small dormitory. The children were tied to the chairs at their ankles and chests with strips of rag.

There was a scratchy black-and-white television in one corner playing a soap opera. The sound was low. There was no other sound in the room. No cries. No little kid noises at all.

A young *ayi*—which means *auntie,* but in this context, *caretaker* or *maid*—in a wrinkled, once-white uniform arrived. She was carrying a metal bowl of rice mush with bits of something brown. She was maybe sixteen. *"Nihao,"* I said. She nodded with a shy smile, eyes averted, then grabbed a spoon and sat down on a small plastic stool before the little girls. She started scooping food into the first three little bird mouths. The other children watched her, mouths open, waiting for their turn.

"Why are they tied?" I asked Mrs. Li.

"We don't have enough workers to control them," she said.

"Well—do they have any toys to play with or anything?"

"Oh yes."

I murmured to Mrs. Zhang, "Where are they? The toys?"

Mrs. Zhang asked. "She says they're locked up."

"Why?"

"The children will break them," Mrs. Li said.

"But–"

And then I shut up.

I knelt beside a small girl who wore a red string tied tightly around her tiny wrist. It was digging into her skin.

"Ow," I whispered. I touched the string. She looked at me with pure terror.

"It's too tight . . . the string . . ."

"Her mama gave it to her. She won't let us take it off."

I stood up, shaky on my feet. I tried to touch each little rough cheek or hand before I left. Pathetic gesture.

THE NEXT ROOM was full of older girls–another twenty or so–maybe three to twelve years old. They were arranged around two large, bright-colored tables. The tables looked brand new–completely out of place in the otherwise dingy surroundings. A brand-new, seemingly never-touched toy had been placed before each child–plastic puzzle discs and stuffed animals and toy military vehicles, some still in packaging. No one played. I don't think the children had ever seen toys before that day.

They were a sad-looking lot. Unrepaired cleft lips and spastic limbs and bad haircuts on misshapen heads. Way too many bruises and scars for such a young crowd. Most of them were foggy-eyed, glazed. But a few watched us–especially me, the foreign freak, the first they'd ever seen. They were curious, and a couple were frightened when I came close. I took any emotion as a sign of life.

One sweet-faced little girl, maybe three or four years old, sat alone against the wall on a towel-covered stool. She watched me, and when I approached, I thought I saw a tiny fleeting smile.

"Hello," I said, crouching beside her. "*Nihao ma?*"

I took her hand. Her skin was coarse, dry. She looked down at our fingers touching. She reached up and touched my yellow-brown hair.

"Why is she sitting here alone?" I asked, trying to sound friendly and nonthreatening. "Can't she join the other children?"

"She had a tumor removed from her brain. It was benign, but she lost control of her bladder."

"But she's so young. Can't she be helped? Can't she have a diaper?"

Nobody had an answer for me. Something was growing tight inside me. My eyes were stinging.

"Would you like to see the babies?" Mrs. Li took me by the arm, her grip firm. I wanted to shake her off. I wanted to run away from this place. But I didn't.

THEN THERE WERE the baby girls. Rows of them in squat wooden cribs. And these tiny creatures—stuffed two to a bed—they were tied to the railings.

Where could they go?

I walked up and down the rows, gazing at each. I tried to count them. I couldn't focus. I thought of who might have left them. Each one a different story. Each a tragedy that could not be spoken.

I touched the pale forehead of a tiny child, maybe two months old, with spindly arms and doll-size fists. I stroked her cheek with the back of my fingers. Her mouth didn't turn toward them. She'd forgotten every newborn's instinct to suckle.

I picked her up and held her close. She weighed nothing. The makeshift diaper, a rag really, that was tied to her waist sagged, soaking wet. I must have reacted. An *ayi* rushed up and snatched her away, then quickly grabbed dry rags to change her.

To be honest, I can't remember the rest. I wasn't really there anymore. I remember in my throat. I remember the tightness inside me, the rush of anger, pushing at my chest. The wanting to scoop them all into my arms and get them out of that place.

But I can't remember the faces anymore. Or when I do, when I force myself to remember, those dear little sad faces are multiplied into thousands I've seen since, like an impossibly miserable hall of mirrors.

THAT NIGHT, AFTER the requisite evening banquet with a new set of officials, we finally arrived at a government hotel. The entire troop of hosts insisted on riding the elevator up to our rooms. It seemed as if the party would continue in the hallway, even after we got the bags sorted out and assured everyone that our rooms were just fine. The concept of private time was nonexistent. Finally, I apologized for my unfortunate jet lag, thanked everyone for the hundredth time, and closed myself inside the room.

I sat down on the rock-hard bed. I stared at the laminated chart on the dresser. It listed every item in the room and what it would cost if you were thinking of stealing it. Starting with the easy (ashtray–1 *yuan;* towel–2 *yuan;* tea cup–1 *yuan*) and finishing up with the ridiculous (armchair–230 *yuan;* television–1,100 *yuan;* mattress–750 *yuan*).

I carefully read the entire list. And then I fell apart.

I sobbed for those little babies who were in nobody's arms tonight and the children who'd never touched a toy and the toddlers who always had to wait their turn.

I thought of the lunch banquet and the dinner banquet, tables heaped with more food than could be eaten, and the reception room full of oranges, and the little bird-mouthed babies.

I despised Director Kong and his toupee and Mrs. Li and the lazy *ayi*s and even the nice ladies who did nothing more than pour tea and peel oranges. *How on earth would I get all those chil-dren out of that place?*

Still snuffling, I undressed for bed, brushed my teeth, and tried to cook up a rescue plan. I'd set up a private-care home. We'd move to China and use the money from selling our house and we'd build something like a residential school and nursery. Or maybe I'd go back to that orphanage tomorrow and somehow gather them all up and . . . what?

I splashed water on my face and looked in the bathroom mirror (85 *yuan*).

What if I did? How many could I save? What about their thou-sands upon thousands of sisters? Was it all truly impossible?

But maybe it's not Mrs. Li's fault. Not even the smarmy direc-tor's fault. Maybe it's the system that's rotten. There is no system. Broken. Broken. Broken. That's what has to change.

Don't fight the people. Join them. Fix it together. Write a new story.

Strangely relieved, I slept a solid three hours before popping up, wide-awake. It was 4:00 A.M. That's 1:00 P.M. in California; I called home. Dick was reassuring as always. "With you all the way, honey," he said. "But I'd rather not run an orphanage in China."

"No, me either. Put Maya on, okay?"

He tried. Came back.

"She doesn't want to talk to you. I asked her if she was angry with you for going to China. She said she wasn't."

"Really?"

"Hang on—"

"What's she saying?"

"She says she's not angry. But she might be tomorrow."

THE NEXT DAY, as our minibus plowed through Beijing traffic, Madame Miao snapped her cell phone shut.

"Good news!" she said. "We have received permission to visit institutions in three provinces! You will go to the south! Now, in the capable hands of Mrs. Zhang Zhirong, you will have a big trip!"

"That's fantastic! And after we've visited, will they allow us to select which of the places we want to work?"

Madame Miao smiled and completely ignored the question. Even a China dummy like me could see from that smile that there was no point in pushing for an answer. Nobody had ever said we could actually do what we proposed.

I first became aware of the China Smile at an ever-so-brief meeting with a government official the morning before we left for Shijiazhuang. Ministry of Civil Affairs Section Chief Ma, a small man with a perfectly round face and perfectly round eyeglasses, came to the hotel to join us for breakfast and see us off.

Before the meeting, Mrs. Zhang had told me he was an important connection from the very government ministry that would be essential to our work. As she explained it, the Ministry of Civil Affairs sounded like a cross between today's U.S. Departments of Health and Human Services and Homeland Security, among other things: "It is responsible for welfare—for old people, poor people, mentally sick, handicapped, veterans, and orphans. Also NGOs and funerals and disasters and riots. This is a good sign, that Section Chief Ma wishes to meet you."

It was only day two, and already anything that woman told me was golden. I did my best to charm the section chief. I told him my story and about my desire to help. I explained what I understood about the developmental stages of children and about how we might help at each stage. The whole time I talked, he smiled. The smile was fixed; his eyes, behind their round frames, were absolutely blank. I could read nothing. Suddenly paranoid, I wondered whether Mrs. Zhang was actually translating anything I was saying. She assured me she was. It was kind of like the old song lyrics, "Your lips tell me no-no, but there's yes-yes in your eyes." Only in reverse. The China Smile.

IT SEEMED PRETTY obvious that the ministry had selected Shijiazhuang for our first visit largely because it was in the north, close to Beijing, and easier to keep an eye on us there. In the end, I was grateful they had, for I'd been able to get a glimpse of orphanage life close to what it really was. The south was a different story.

For reasons I wasn't China scholar enough to understand, abandonment (and infanticide) of girl-children had been going on south of the Yangtze River long before institution of the one-child policy in 1979. Even when unofficial policy was relaxed in rural areas to permit a second child if the first was a girl (boys were needed to work the land, provide for the family, carry on the family name), orphanages in the south continued to fill with little girls, likely second daughters.

Before the bad publicity of *The Dying Rooms* and the Human Rights Watch report, those southern orphanages were fairly easygoing and accessible. "The mountains are high and the emperor is far away," as the saying goes. But, as the subject of both the film and the report, those orphanages had paid dearly. They were still feeling the sting when I showed up with my bright idea.

So despite the fact that they had been ordered by the ministry to allow our visit, orphanages in the south were not about to be stung again. The banquets were as lavish and frequent as in that first town, but caution was most definitely in the air.

Here was the routine: When we arrived at the gate, the "normal" children and staff were all outside, applauding. Everyone was dressed up and adorable. Cute little girls with lipsticked smiles brought us flowers.

First stop was the scale-model-of-our-future-orphanage ex-hibition. Usually that was in a giant glass box in the lobby. "Everything that we see today will be torn down soon," they said. Although they definitely did look the worse for wear, most of the buildings were no more than five years old. (Mrs. Zhang told me that China is the land of instant antiques.) We spent more time looking at the models than visiting the children.

Then there would be the standard reception room visit, with fruit and speeches.

Finally, we'd make a quick pass through the children's rooms. All was clean and orderly. The children were perfectly washed and combed. No less-than-perfectly-formed child specimens were on display. A brand-new toy had been placed in front of every child. It sat untouched, a foreign object. Most of the children had been given sweet treats to keep them in line. There were few caregivers present, though, and nothing could disguise the blank faces of the children.

A couple of the little ones escaped from their assigned chairs and clung to my legs, demanding to be picked up. The *ayi*s grabbed them away with a nervous, apologetic laugh. The babies were snug in their cribs, each with a bottle propped at her mouth. When I picked up a bottle that had rolled away from a newborn too small to grab for it, it was quickly snatched up by someone and popped back into the tiny mouth. All shipshape.

Sometimes there'd be a little performance in our honor. We sat in little chairs. Wee tots wearing paper bunny ears sang a song about pulling carrots. The slightly older kids offered a Vegas-esque fashion show to a disco beat. The staff might treat us to a song or two. We applauded with great enthusiasm.

It was a year or more before I was able to walk into an orphan-age in the south on a first visit without encountering some version of an orphan's Potemkin village.

The one exception to the carefully staged but warm southern welcome was in Guangzhou, the capital of Guangdong Province, and Maya's first home. The week before, while we were visiting two orphanages in southern Jiangsu Province, the Chinese government had begun a ferocious crackdown on the Falun Gong, a fast-growing sect of seemingly ordinary middle-aged citizens who engaged in qigong-like exercises and meditation and who had lately been staging public demonstrations, some drawing tens of thousands of followers. The government declared that the evil cult's founder was pursuing a hidden political agenda. Police in several cities detained the group's leaders. Thousands started gathering to protest the arrests—most visibly, in Beijing.

While we were in the air, flying south to Guangzhou, there'd been an emergency meeting, and by the time we landed, the government had announced a nationwide ban on Falun Gong on the grounds that it engaged in superstition and disrupted public order, thereby damaging social stability.

So instead of an escort to the orphanage, a phone call was waiting for us. All government workers, including those at the institutions, would be engaged in reeducation meetings. There would be no visits allowed that day.

WE WERE ORDERED instead to spend the sweltering day at the Bird Park on White Cloud Mountain. Wen went off to visit some Guangzhou cousins (she appeared to have cousins in every town in China), and I had an opportunity to begin to get to know Mrs. Zhang.

"I really feel very positive about your plan," she told me. "I can tell from the questions you ask that you are sincere. When you are talking, I am feeling there is a light in the darkness."

"What great good fortune that we found you!" I said.

"I should tell you," she said, "that I am an orphan myself. Both my parents died when I was young. My aunt raised me and my sister. People often said my aunt should send us to an orphanage, but she would not. So you see, I know how sad that is to not have a mother and father."

"Oh, Mrs. Zhang—"

"Foreign friends usually call me Joan. Zhang Zhirong is a difficult name. Not only that, do you know it's a name for a man? When I went to college, I found they'd assigned me to the boys' dormitory!"

The screenwriter in me knew she wasn't a Joan. I tried it for a while, but eventually I just called her ZZ. It stuck.

"Do you remember when Herb called and you first heard about Half the Sky?" I asked her. "What did you think? That I was just some crazy foreigner?"

"Not at all," she said. "The timing is good. China is just starting to open up. It may be possible. When later I speak to you on the telephone, I know for sure."

"Why?"

"I can feel you are sincere. This is something different than the others. Not just sending money. You know, I've been doing foreign affairs for years. I talk to you and I know you don't want to invade us or make trouble for China. You just want to make friends and help the children."

"So what did you do after that first call?"

"I discuss with Miao. I tell her I can feel the seriousness. And I know the situation about the conditions in the orphanages."

"You knew?"

"CPWF works with Family Planning Commission. A great number of babies are abandoned in these times. Besides, I work at UN International Women's Conference in 1995. Foreign Affairs Office prepares us. They tell us about *The Dying Rooms* movie.

They say women coming to Beijing from all over the world will criticize us. Be prepared, they tell us. Not everybody says China is good."

"But you weren't nervous about me?"

"No! I want to do this. I took a very active part. We are very close to Vice Minister Wan at Family Planning. He has friend, Madame Jiang, at Family Planning, formerly of Ministry of Civil Affairs. Madame Jiang has good *guanxi* with Civil Affairs Welfare Department Director General Yan. Short man, very nice. I personally bring letter to Director Yan explaining the purpose. He is expecting me. It's kind of a friendly talk."

"You made it happen."

"*The Dying Rooms* is a bad situation. We say bad things always have a good side. This is a turning point. China wants to turn the page, but gradually. At the same time, they need help from outside. Of course, you have to have a friend or you can do nothing. Still, it is sensitive. When I take you on tour of orphanages, I must not say anything wrong. Not say too much straightforward with officials. Not too much detail because I don't want to give them any chance to say no."

As long as they don't say no . . .

This I understood.

And I was smitten. What good fortune to find this woman, this ZZ! I adored and trusted her already. She would become my best friend, my big sister. My better half in China.

With ZZ beside me, I felt new confidence when we arrived at Maya's orphanage the next day.

THE RECEPTION WAS anything but warm.

I'd been surprised when ZZ told me that Guangzhou was on the approved list of sites. I hadn't even considered trying to launch

Half the Sky there. Sure, the children were in dire need of help; Maya was proof positive. But from the little I'd been able to learn, Guangzhou seemed too big, too secretive, and too troubled. Despite Norman's glowing report on that first telephone call—"best orphanage in China"—I'd learned from media reports and rumors that weak babies had a slim chance of surviving, let alone thriving, in that orphanage.

One thing was certain—this little dream of mine had to succeed and quickly. We had to begin with conditions where success was at least imaginable. That eliminated Guangzhou. But I was in no position to argue.

"I'm so pleased to meet you," I said to the closed face of Guangzhou Director Zheng, a compact fellow whose pocket protector held a single pen. Despite his controlled demeanor, a forelock of hair refused to stay in place and his shirt kept coming untucked. I concentrated on good thoughts: I was really trying to like him. "I was here two years ago to adopt my daughter."

He grunted and frowned even further if that was possible. "No pictures," he said.

He glanced down at the big bag of toy musical instruments we'd purchased the day before—"the Chinese way," according to ZZ.

"And you can't bring those toys inside," he added.

He led us into what appeared to be a spanking-new showroom. The walls were lined with photo blow-ups of the children with various celebrity officials and assorted highlights of orphanage life.

One display featured three medals that had been won by older children competing in the Paralympics. "It would be great if the kids could hang those medals in their rooms," I said. Then wished I hadn't. Director Zheng appeared to be considering whether he should have me arrested.

Instead, he whisked us through a lightning-quick tour of one floor of one building in the massive complex. It was spartan but clean, and the many dozens of children looked physically healthy. That was all the opinion there was time for. Then we were outside. He couldn't get rid of us fast enough.

"So Director Zheng," I said as he ushered us out, "might you be interested in hosting some programs that are designed to provide nurturing care for orphaned children?"

I think he may have physically shuddered, insulted that we thought perhaps his institution might be improved upon.

"There are procedures that must be followed," Director Zheng said.

And so we said our thanks and goodbyes.

SOUTH OF GUANGZHOU, near Hong Kong, Shenzhen was our final destination. It was, in those days, a long drive from Guangzhou through miles of lychee and banana groves dotted with new high-rise apartment buildings and construction cranes.

ZZ told me that this was the richest farmland in the nation. *Soon it will be gone,* I thought, just as the apricot orchards of my childhood had become Silicon Valley. Make way for New China.

We stopped at the border crossing to the Special Economic Zone (SEZ) and secured an entry permit for ZZ, required for Chinese nationals only. A dozen or so years earlier, before Deng Xiaoping's policy of "reform and opening" established it as China's first SEZ, Shenzhen had been a poor fishing village. Now the government feared that, without entry restrictions, all of China would move there.

No wonder. Shenzhen was another Hong Kong but, in that uniquely mainland way, flashier and tackier. Tucked between brand-new skyscrapers were budget hotels, job boards, streetside barbers, and vendors hawking junky bright clothes, cheap bus tickets, phone cards, and snacks. Factories of every kind encircled the city. And nobody was *from* Shenzhen. The place, at least in 1999, was overwhelmed by a steady stream of young migrant workers from every rural corner of China, making their way from farm to factory to take care of their families back home. They were China's "floating population." "You are a Shenzhener once you come here," the saying went.

THE ORPHANAGE HAD a swank mirrored front. The Shenzhen director, a tiny spark plug in spike heels, was savvy enough to take advantage of the place's relatively upscale location and open a public kindergarten for the community. The tuition she collected helped support the institution, with the added benefit of potentially (in my mind anyway) allowing orphaned children to mix with those from town. There was nothing special about the care in Shenzhen, but this setup, along with an unusually large population of about six hundred children—maybe something to do with all those young migrant workers—made it look promising for a pilot program. Furthermore, the Shenzhen director seemed open to new ideas and promised she could blast through any potential government obstacles. She guaranteed absolute, 100 percent cooperation.

Perfect! We had our first pilot site. I was elated. We wouldn't exactly be saving the world on our first outing, but if the goal was to have a successful first year so that we'd be free to expand to more challenging areas, Shenzhen was definitely the place.

We still needed a second pilot site—someplace a little smaller, but with a large enough group of children to demonstrate positive impact. I asked Wen to return to Jiangsu Province, on China's more sophisticated (and hopefully more open-minded) east coast, while I returned to California to tackle the practical side of developing the dream.

C h a p t e r   4

To Move a Mountain, Begin with Small Stones

移大山始于运小石

No one had said no, but they hadn't really said yes, either.

No matter; I returned home without the slightest doubt that Half the Sky was on its way. I reported back to the board, and they were maybe a little surprised, but definitely pleased and excited, when I told them that we were actually going to do this thing!

A week later, Wen called to report that she'd found the ideal spot in Jiangsu Province for our second pilot site—Changzhou, a small city not far from Shanghai. There were about 120 children, which would make it a midsize orphanage. As in the majority of places we'd visited, the children's basic needs were taken care of, but that was it. Wen sent photos. When I saw the barren rooms and blank faces of the children, I agreed: Changzhou would be pilot site number two.

Now we began to make detailed plans. Wen started reaching out to her connections in China to identify a pool of young teachers for the preschools, and I set to work on a plan for the babies. Beyond adopting Malaguzzi's inspiration about children and caregivers learning together, I hadn't made much progress in thinking through how the infant nurture program would work. When I suggested to the orphanage directors during our recent visits that the residents of the adjacent senior housing could come over daily and cuddle the babies, out came the old China Smile.

Fixed grin, eyes glazed over—no way was *that* idea going to fly.

So now I created an early childhood advisory group online. I invited adoptive parents who were child development professionals to help us plan our approach. Our first two volunteer nanny trainers were selected from that very committed pool. Even better, I met Janice Cotton, an early childhood professor, researcher, and practitioner who, although not available for this first outing, would not only design our infant nurture program, but one day oversee the development of an elegant and comprehensive child development curriculum for Half the Sky.

I informed the board that there would be a few other things to figure out quickly, before we returned to China. I explained that, on my trip, when I'd begun to see a few too many of those China Smiles, I may have made a few impromptu and rather bold promises:

"We will not only transform the children. We will turn orphanage rooms into playrooms of the highest international standards! We'll fill them with colorful and sturdy developmentally appropriate toys!"

It hadn't taken long to get the message that many of our potential Chinese partners (especially the men) were really into enhancing their real estate holdings. They wanted the shiny toys and plaques and other assorted symbols of success. So, of course, I obliged. Now we had to figure out how to deliver.

Lucky for us, we had talent in the house. Our good pals on the board, Daniel and Terri, were experienced designers. Daniel had been a cabinetmaker before becoming a screenwriter and professor; he'd even designed and built play equipment for the children's ward of a hospital. Terri was a painter with a gorgeous sense of color. They designed the play equipment, furniture, and color scheme that we still use in our children's centers today. And, best of all, they volunteered to lead our builds.

Paying for this grand plan would be tricky. We'd already tapped out friends and family. Not a single one of the very promising foundations I'd researched was willing to even look at a proposal. We had big ideas but had accomplished nothing yet, and Chinese orphans were not high on any funder's priority list—actually not on the list at all. Ours was not considered a pressing global issue.

Still, we launched our first public fundraising effort with great optimism. We collected names and addresses of anyone we thought might want to help the children. I wrote an appeal letter. Rob Reiner, a colleague of one of our board members and an advocate for early childhood education, helped us with an insert stating his support. By New Year's Day 2000, we were ready. We sent our first direct appeal off in the mail and held our collective breath:

On the July Fourth holiday last year, the first anniversary of our daughter Maya's adoption, I watched her playing in the backyard, exuberant with friends and family. I marveled at this little being who had taken over my life and so fiercely captured my heart. And I was overwhelmed with gratitude for the gift of her life in mine.

I know you'll understand when I tell you that my happiness that day was tinged with sorrow. I couldn't get the image out of my mind—the image that haunts me still: the babies lying alone on their backs, the toddlers strapped to walkers . . . all those abandoned little girls in orphanages in China who will never know families. Who will never know Maya's joy. . . .

Like many developing countries, China has extremely limited resources for its orphaned children. The main priority in welfare institutions is, and must be, food and health care. Everything else is an unaffordable luxury. Caretakers want to give the little ones more, but they are simply overwhelmed. So the children languish.

*The lucky ones find families. For those who don't, the future
looks bleak. Chinese society is rooted in the family. Life for
a girl-child in China is not easy. Life for a girl-child with no
family is unspeakably tough. Education is their best hope . . .
for most, their only hope. But many of these little girls will get
no education.*

*Although mandatory to ninth grade, school in China is not
free. But even when the orphanage can raise the funds to send
its children to local schools, they face obstacles. Deprived of
the nurturing and stimulation they need to develop normally,
the orphans learn to speak late, walk late. They suffer so many
developmental delays that, by the time they reach school age,
many local schools refuse to admit them.*

*There is a clear and simple way we can change all this. A
way people like us, on the other side of the world, can give
China's orphaned babies and small children a shot at a better
future.*

*We can set up and support high-quality, caring enrichment
programs right in China's orphanages. We can prepare those
children to enter the world. . . .*

And just as I dreamed it, the money rolled in. We raised almost
100,000 dollars! Checks and faxes and phone calls flooded our
dining room. The three thousand names of potential supporters
I'd collected in the first year had multiplied as those people shared
our story with family and friends. By the year 2000, there were
perhaps thirty thousand families around the world who'd adopted
children from China, and few did not ache at the memory of the
children they'd left behind. I knew now, for sure, that we were not
alone.

Then, days after the mailing went out, and six months after
my visit, we received semiofficial approval (nothing in writing

yet) from the Ministry of Civil Affairs. Half the Sky would (probably) be allowed to create its two pilot programs. We would have one year in which to prove ourselves. I don't know if other nonprofit organizations typically begin on such a high note, but I was pinching myself every day.

I announced that we would launch our programs in the summer and invited volunteers to come to China to help us do the job. It began to sink in that I wasn't just telling a story anymore. It wasn't just another adventure; I wasn't just making a movie. The story I was writing was about to affect real lives—real little girls tied to chairs and cribs on the other side of the world. Nothing would stop us.

As plans took shape and it all became more real, some on our board grew nervous. I, on the other hand, felt strangely calm. It was time for a return trip to photograph and measure the rooms we'd be renovating, to recruit teachers and nannies, and most important, to meet the children whose lives we were about to change.

I couldn't leave Maya behind again. Dick managed to rearrange his life, and in March 2000, eight months after my first official visit, the three of us headed back to China.

ZZ MET US in Shanghai. Dick and Maya loved her instantly, and it was clearly mutual.

"There is some news," ZZ said over breakfast the first morning. "The Ministry of Civil Affairs informed me that the coordination of the Half the Sky programs is being shifted to the China Social Workers Association, which is a new NGO under the ministry."

"There are social workers in China?"

"I don't think so."

"Right. Okay. Well, will we still work with CPWF?"

"Yes. Should be. Maybe."

"Okay." Not that I had a choice.

"On the telephone they sound nice. The new vice president, Mr. Shi, is a good friend of our friend at the ministry. Next week we will visit Mr. Shi and bring some nice gift according to our Chinese custom."

"Definitely."

What would I do without her?

We took a train from Shanghai to Changzhou. As we settled in our seats, ZZ got a call from Shenzhen. A high-energy, high-volume Chinese debate ensued. I wished I'd paid more attention to my teach-yourself-Mandarin CDs.

"The Shenzhen director apologizes that she can't prepare name list of children for us," ZZ said, snapping her phone shut.

Swell. To help fund the programs, we'd decided to offer donors the opportunity to sponsor individual children. We would provide each sponsor with basic information on the assigned child, along with a photo that Dick would take. We knew that, as in all Reggio-inspired programs, documentation of the child's progress would be an important component of our work, and every child would have her own "memory book," her own history. It would be an easy matter, we thought, to share regular progress reports with sponsors so that they could feel connected to the children they were helping. Without even the children's names, this would be tough.

"Did she tell you why?"

"She says that she needs more formal written instruction from Beijing. I'll call our new friend, Mr. Shi."

Mr. Shi promised to fax something to Shenzhen immediately. Even before meeting him, I already liked Mr. Shi! But now I wondered if I should be just a little bit nervous about that promised 100 percent cooperation from the Shenzhen director.

•   •   •

DEPUTY DIRECTOR ZHANG Yunyun, or "Small Cloud" Zhang (*yun* means "cloud"), met us at the Changzhou train station and whisked us off to the orphanage. Small Cloud Zhang was a super-competent pint-size dynamo with painted-on eyebrows and close-cropped hair. Her boss, the actual director, whose name I don't remember, couldn't be bothered to spend time with us. He was one of those I came to call the *ganbei* guys (*ganbei* means "dry glass/bottoms up")—the minor officials who, when they're not drinking tea and reading the newspaper or napping, spend all of their time toasting each other at banquets.

But the person who actually ran the place was Small Cloud Zhang, and although a bit nervous about what we had in mind, she seemed agreeable. Even better, she actually knew the kids—knew their names and a little bit about each one.

We photographed and measured the rooms and made lists of supplies we'd need to buy. Small Cloud Zhang followed us around on her spindly high heels.

"Do you think we could use *these* rooms instead of the ones you've chosen, Deputy Director Small Cloud Zhang?" I asked as we walked through a space that seemed inviting. I wasn't quite sure she understood my request, but it seemed to me that she nodded her head. Wen and I conferred.

"And do you think we could knock a hole in this wall to open up the space into one big room?" Small Cloud Zhang hesitated a moment. Then nodded, perhaps with less enthusiasm.

"Those cartoons will have to come off the walls," I said.

Every orphanage had primitive Donald Ducks and Mickey Mouses on the walls. What was later called piracy was then just the way it was.

The cartoons? Small Cloud Zhang blanched. But she didn't say no.

"Of course, our crew of volunteers is going to be painting everything. The walls will be beautiful." Better get the worst over with.

"Volunteers? *Foreign* volunteers?"

"Just a small group for the build. Most will be adoptive parents. And their children!"

The China Smile twitched. Just barely.

WE SET UP in the reception room to take photos and a brief history of each child. More important than giving us something to offer our child sponsors, this information, in combination with some baseline developmental assessments that Dana Johnson's International Adoption Clinic would perform, would help us track each child's progress.

The children were brought in one by one. Dick took photos of each, and I wrote down what little information the orphanage had. Approximate date of birth, date of abandonment, medical condition . . . anything else? There was never anything else. Even the medical condition seemed like a best guess.

I watched as each tiny girl was marched in and plunked on the sofa. Each one carrying her own sad mystery. Not one of them cried as they were stuck in front of the foreign man's camera. There was not a single boy. I tried to focus on my notebook, swallowing tears for these brave little girls.

"Be still, my heart," Dick whispered.

"What?"

I looked up at him and then at the little girl he was photographing. She was perched on the doily-draped blue sofa. She did not look pleased to be there.

"She looks like Maya!" I said.

"Like Maya's sister," he said.

Xinmei

She was twenty-eight months old when we first saw her dark, quiet eyes and solemn face. Abandoned at birth, Xinmei had been taken to a welfare institution that cared solely for old folks. They had no adoption program, foreign or domestic, so Xinmei had spent her infancy as the institution's first child resident.

She had a large hemangioma—a tangle of misplaced blood vessels that caused a swollen mass to bulge from her neck. "As big as her head when she was brought to us," a caregiver told us later. I imagined some poor country couple seeing their new baby, *this* baby, for the first time—their one and only child.

The very day we arrived in Changzhou, Small Cloud Zhang returned from a visit to Xinmei's welfare institution. She'd seen Xinmei there and felt she might have a chance at international adoption—it was the rare *domestic* Chinese family that would adopt a child considered less than perfect—and so she brought the little girl back with her. Xinmei had not been in the Changzhou orphanage twenty-four hours when we met her.

She looks like Maya's sister, Dick said. And if fate would have it, that's who she would become.

We still have the photograph Dick took of Xinmei that day— almost Victorian in its posed formality. But now, strangely, the child in that picture looks nothing at all like Maya.

OUR RETURN TO Shenzhen was far less promising.

The Shenzhen director greeted us warmly again but noted that she needed something even more official than a fax from Beijing before we could photograph the children or do any baseline testing. And, despite the fact that there were about a hundred infants in residence, our infant program would be allowed to work with only fifteen babies in one small room.

We did our best to make a plan for the rooms allotted to us, but with trepidation. That 100 percent cooperation was starting to feel like 50 percent at best.

• • •

WE FLEW BACK north to Beijing, and in the morning ZZ and I visited CCAA (China Center for Adoption Affairs). The vice director had summoned us. He wanted to know more about Half the Sky. Exactly what were our intentions?

I told him about the gratitude we felt to China, how we wanted to give back. In my new chameleon habit, I slipped into his skin and figured he might be worried that Half the Sky would lure foreign adoptive parents' donations to places unknown, beyond CCAA's control. I assured him that we hoped for and needed CCAA to help us. We knew that there was no one more familiar with the institutions than he was. I asked for his help in selecting the sites that could most benefit from the programs.

The vice director warmed up a bit and shared his carefully phrased view of conditions in the orphanages. Then he passed along a few pointed warnings.

1. Don't grow too fast.

I wasn't sure what he meant but readily agreed. "We won't," I promised.

2. Don't put children's pictures on the Internet in a way that they can be identified.

Made perfect sense. "Certainly not," I said.

3. Stay away from adoption.

In other words, adoption is government business. No trespassing.

"I understand," I said. "Our purpose is only to help the children who are living in the institutions. We will not touch adoption. Not ever."

Fingers crossed behind my back, I wondered if our hopes for little Xinmei could possibly count as adoption meddling. Was I breaking the rules before I even got started?

•　　•　　•

BEFORE WE LEFT Beijing for home, I made a last attempt to seal the deal. I booked a room at the elegant Fang Shan, a Qing-era restaurant (supposedly the imperial dining hall of Empress Dowager Cixi) in the middle of Beihai Park and invited all of our new government friends. Mr. Shi of the Social Workers Association, a shy man with a sweet high-pitched voice and a perpetual smile, arrived at the stately retreat an hour late, red-faced and puffing. He'd ridden his bicycle from the other end of town.

The food, all thirteen elegant courses, was tasteless. Maya, indifferent to the cuisine, adored the pretty young waitresses in their bright silks and seriously high platform clogs. The next time we entertained our Beijing colleagues, they asked to go to TGI Friday's.

C h a p t e r 5

Pick the Roses, Live with the Thorns

爱花 爱它的刺

I've been a mother since I was nineteen years old. When I was a girl, it was what girls were supposed to aspire to. Marriage and motherhood. I wasn't too keen on the marriage part, but went along with the requirement. I wanted the baby. I'm not sure what drove the desire; maybe I wanted to know what unconditional love felt like. At the time, all I knew was that I wanted to leave my childhood behind and start living a life like I imagined in stories.

When I was ten, I won a writing contest sponsored by the *San Francisco Chronicle* and received a big book as a prize. It was a picture encyclopedia. I thought it was babyish, for little kids, so I gave it away to a friend. My mother gave me the worst beating ever for that. She was furious; she kicked me and pulled my hair. I got a tirade of *ungrateful* and *spoiled* and *That book was worth a lot of money* and *Who do you think you are, Miss Priss?* and *I wish you'd never been born*—words I pretended not to hear.

I didn't understand why she was so angry. But somehow, maybe from reading all those library books, I understood, at least intellectually, that she didn't know any better. She was probably giving what *she* got. Anyhow, when I grew up and had a child, I would be different.

I might have stopped writing that day, for all the grief it brought me. Instead, I opted for the theater. I wrote plays and studied acting. No one in my family ever came to see me in anything, but I told myself I didn't care. It didn't matter. I didn't need anybody. I'd found out I wasn't the only misfit in town. Theater was full of them.

So I married too young, and when my young husband (who was about as mature as I was) wasn't around much because he was busy trying to make it as a folksinger, I quietly left my marriage and threw myself full-time into theater and motherhood. I pretty much grew up alongside my daughter Cristin and my son, Aaron. I didn't have a clue what children needed, but I knew that my own upbringing was not the model to follow. I went in the opposite direction. My children played backstage and traveled where the work was, and somehow we all survived and, in many ways, flourished.

From time to time, I'd hear my mother's words starting to come out of my mouth—*I'll give you something to cry about*—and I'd swallow the words and hold my children tight instead. It wasn't easy and I didn't always succeed. Sometimes my babies and I would cry together. My love for them came naturally, even though its expression did not. Like Maya, I suppose, I had to *learn* loving and being loved—as basic as those things are.

BY THE TIME Maya came into our lives, my first children were grown. Dick (then a longtime loving stepdad and my spouse for twenty years) and I loved having a child in our lives again. I guess it was natural that, as Maya settled in, we began to talk of a little sister—someone who shared her background and who could grow up with her. They'd be there for each other, even if something should befall their not-so-young parents.

The dossier for our second adoption was already in Beijing when I called Norman one jet-lagged morning right after our return home and told him about Xinmei.

"It's not so easy," he said. "Pre-identified adoption is not allowed."

"I know, Norman, but will you ask? Richard and I . . . we just have this feeling that she's meant to be Maya's little sister. She looks exactly like her!" I was still delusional on that front.

"It is difficult."

"Please, Norman. Just try? Oh . . . and when you call, please explain that this has absolutely nothing to do with Half the Sky. We didn't know this would happen. We had no idea. Will you tell them that, Norman?"

Dear Jenny,

The e-mail is quite like magic! I am thrilled to see such quickest ways of communication like we were talking face to face!

I am returned to Beijing. The baseline testing of children in Changzhou is complete and went very well. We are not so fortunate in Shenzhen. Approval documents still have not arrived from Guangdong Provincial Bureau. I will contact Mr. Shi to find out the result of his further negotiation and report to you afterwards. If negative, you have to consider the change of pilot institution.

Zhang Zhirong (ZZ)

Ugh. We'd come so far—things *couldn't* unravel now. Almost two weeks passed before I heard again from ZZ.

Dear Jenny,

I finally found Mr. Shi who is right now in Shenzhen for a meeting organized by the ministry! Mr. Shi agreed to do the negotiations there to find out the attitude of all parties and reasons. For the last two days, I almost called him every few hours. The answer from him yesterday afternoon was that we have to change the site from Shenzhen, for the reason now, even the ministry does not agree to set the pilot there.

Also, from our conversation yesterday I know that we do not yet have official permission to begin the project. Why it takes so long, the problem is because of the shifting of our project to the Social Workers Association. Now we are asked to report to a new department which does not know much about the project. Usually they would like to know the whole story from the very beginning.

I understand the heavy responsibility as a representative of Half the Sky. I should do my best to make your load lighter if I can. However, certainly if you will come to China it is quicker to resolve.

Zhang Zhirong (ZZ)

THE PEACE HOTEL in Shanghai had seen better days. Once the Cathay—a glittering symbol of British occupation and opium booty—in its heyday the hotel hosted Charlie Chaplin, George Bernard Shaw, and Noël Coward (who wrote *Private Lives* there).

The night I arrived, I couldn't have cared less. My flight out of San Francisco had been delayed seven hours. I had missed my connection in Taipei. I was exhausted and grumpy when I checked in.

Knowing the Chinese penchant for making phone calls without apology up until 11:00 P.M. (ZZ being no exception), I unplugged the hotel telephone and collapsed on the bed.

Within five minutes, somebody was outside my door, pounding and shouting and ringing the doorbell. I crawled out of bed and opened the door.

A security guard was screaming at me.

I did my best to respond. "*Wo bu hui*—ah . . . look, I don't speak Chinese. *Meiguo* . . . American—"

"The telephone! The telephone—!" he sputtered.

"I unplugged it so I could sleep," I said, pointing impatiently to the DO NOT DISTURB sign on my door.

"Not allowed!" He tried to shove past me. "May I come in?"

I shoved back. "No! I'll plug it in. I'll plug it in."

I shut the door as forcefully as I dared—and plugged in the darn phone.

The ringing woke me at 11:00 P.M. It was ZZ.

"I figured out how they bug the rooms," I said.

BEFORE HEADING TO Changzhou, we planned to visit some potential toy and materials suppliers around Shanghai. We hailed a cab and headed toward a paint factory that manufactured "environmental" paint. One of our supporters had kindly equipped me with lead-detection swabs and I intended to swab every surface, toy, or product before allowing it into our new children's centers. ZZ called the factory manager to tell him we were on our way.

"My boss is coming with me," she told them.

"Is she Chinese or a foreigner?"

"Foreigner."

"No foreigners can come."

"She's Chinese, sort of. She does good work to help China."

"Tell her not to speak any foreign language."

We arrived at the factory. It was situated in what had to be the most polluted pocket of metropolitan Shanghai. The air was opaque.

The cab pulled up to the gate. It didn't open. The cab driver honked. The guard stood inside his little guardhouse talking on the telephone—I assumed to our friend, the factory manager. The cab continued to honk.

ZZ called the manager again on her cell phone.

"He says you must remain in the cab," she reported.

I decided that now would not be the right time to pass ZZ my lead-detection swabs.

ON THE WAY to Changzhou, our next stop, ZZ told me that Xinmei was looking forward to seeing me.

"Really?" I said, feigning indifference. "I'm not sure we should tell her about the adoption. What if they turn us down?"

"We Chinese know we must accept life as it is."

At two years old?

When we arrived, Deputy Director Small Cloud Zhang greeted us in front of the Changzhou orphanage with Xinmei bundled in her arms. Xinmei looked adorable, all gussied up for the occasion. She didn't have much hair, but what was available had been fashioned into a pert little topknot, secured by pink butterfly clips.

Small Cloud Zhang passed the baby to me, cooing, "Mama! Mama!"

I took her, of course. I couldn't turn away my little daughter-to-be. "Xinmei," I whispered. "Please forgive me if this doesn't work out."

Xinmei tolerated me for the ten minutes I got to hold her. Just another *ayi* to her. I tried to pretend she was just another kid. I was almost relieved when we arrived at the children's activity room and an actual *ayi* came to take her away. If she was to be my child, this didn't feel like the right way to get acquainted. The minute she was out of my arms, I felt sick that I'd been so hard-hearted. I watched her toddle alone across the barren room lined with sad little chairs and too-quiet little children. I turned away, trying to imagine a preschool in that dreary space.

•　　　•　　　•

SMALL CLOUD ZHANG led us into the orphanage reception room. Madame Miao and Mr. Shi were waiting for us there.

"We have good news!" Madame Miao said.

"We agree to change the pilot institution from Shenzhen of Guangdong Province to Hefei of Anhui Province," Mr. Shi said. "The needs are more great there."

"The Association has good relations with the institution," Madame Miao said. "And the director of the Provincial Civil Affairs Bureau is my relative! Tomorrow we will go there and meet him for dinner."

"This is wonderful!" I said. "Dear Madame Miao and Mr. Shi, you have saved the day. Wait . . . can you translate that?" I asked ZZ.

"*One sings—all follow.* We are happy to have agreement," ZZ said.

Not to be outdone by the Civil Affairs director of Anhui Province, the Civil Affairs director of Changzhou's Jiangsu Province invited us to a very special banquet at a *famous* scenic spot.

"We will drive some distance," ZZ said. "We must finish our work quickly."

A meal always takes precedence in China. Per instructions, we were ready to climb into the minivan by 11:00 A.M.

"How far is this place?" I asked ZZ.

"Oh look, Xinmei will join us!" she replied.

Small Cloud Zhang scuttered toward the minibus in her spiky heels, Xinmei bobbing in her arms.

"Oh . . . but—" I murmured. And then that little baby was on my lap and there was nothing to do but hold on. She looked up at me curiously. *You again?*

I touched her soft hair and whispered, "Hello, sweet baby."

•   •   •

THE ANSWER TO my question was that the place was far. It was easily a two-hour drive. We drove through a hilly, denuded landscape. Every now and then, giant billboards would appear, promoting something that looked a lot like Yosemite and nothing like the current view. Then we arrived.

Our destination was a reservoir ringed by neatly clipped and stunted trees and shrubs. The minivan stopped beside a small dock. Some men were waiting there. Cigarettes hanging from their mouths, they were holding aloft bright orange life vests. There was even one for Xinmei.

Obediently, we tugged and tied on our vests. When everyone was suited up, we all climbed into a skiff with an outboard motor. There were eight of us in that little boat. The two smoking guys took us for a spin around the "lake." Everybody but Xinmei and me was talking on a cell phone. We raced from one shore to the other. Xinmei was petrified.

After multiple circumnavigations and high-speed sprints, the boat pulled up at the opposite shore.

We were escorted to a small building and into a dining room with a smudged plate-glass view of the "lake" and the boat. Thankfully, our minivan was parked in front; we wouldn't have to get in that boat again. The air inside was thick with cigarette smoke. I worried about Xinmei's little lungs but figured she'd probably breathed worse.

The moment she was seated in a baby chair next to me, Xinmei started crying. I tried holding her; I bounced her; I slipped her bits of food. She was inconsolable. Small Cloud Zhang took over and Xinmei was instantly silent. She sat on the deputy director's lap and ate every bite proffered. The Jiangsu Provincial Civil Affairs director was charming, I'm sure. I can't remember. I had descended into kind of a dazed, smoky stupor.

•   •   •

AFTER THE MEAL, I squeezed into the back of the minibus for the long ride home. Xinmei was plopped on my lap. She looked like she was about to cry again. "Shh . . . shh, Xinmei. It's okay," I whispered.

I smoothed the mussed little hairdo. Snuggled her into my arms. Hummed a little.

Then she pinched me.

It was definitely a pinch. I pulled back, looked at her. She wouldn't look at me. She inched to the very edge of my lap, where she sat for the rest of the trip. Seat belts are not a Chinese thing.

When we finally arrived at the funky-but-with-a-certain-charm Changzhou Binguan (guest house), Small Cloud Zhang sprang her next surprise. She grabbed my arm and presented me with a knotted plastic bag.

"What's this? What did she say?" I asked ZZ.

"She said that Xinmei will spend the night with her new mama! She wants to know if you're happy to do so?"

Well, exhausted is what I was (day three of jet lag is my worst), and my throat was sore from all the cigarette smoke, and Xinmei and I weren't exactly hitting it off. But Small Cloud Zhang was now beaming.

"Oh . . . yes. Sure!"

I PULLED MISMATCHED flannel pajamas and a disposable diaper from the plastic bag. Xinmei watched me warily from the bed. I tried to make conversation as I peeled off her jumper, T-shirt, and other assorted layers.

"So this must feel really, really strange, huh, Xinmei? Here's this funny-looking person you don't even know, and now you find yourself in a hotel room with her—whatever a hotel room is."

I took off her soggy diaper.

"Oh God—"

Two years of neglected wet diapers tied tight with rope rags had caused bone-deep scars on her hips.

"Oh . . . poor baby . . . oh, let me—"

I tried to gently clean the still-raw wounds. She rolled away from me.

"No? Okay . . . it's okay . . . it's gonna be okay . . . C'mere, little one." I pulled her close, quickly slipped on the disposable diaper. "There now . . . that's better, isn't it, Xinmei?"

And she slapped me in the face.

I'm ashamed to say my instinct was to slap her back. Instead, I sat there, staring at this strange little creature, my hand in midair. My daughter? She spat at me. That stopped me cold.

My hand fell against my mouth and the tears came. Mine, not hers. She watched me from across the bed. A safe distance. And from there, I could see her little bare feet. They were scarred as well—burned to the ankles, evenly on both sides, like bobby socks.

When a child is naughty, holding her in scalding water teaches her not to misbehave again, someone told me later.

"Who did this to you?"

I took a deep, shuddery breath. "Okay. All right. Don't worry, Xinmei, we'll work it out."

I sure hoped that was true. We spent the night on opposite sides of the bed. She cried out in her sleep. I longed to hold her, to try to soothe away the sadness that filled the room. But I didn't dare pull her to me. I reached across and stroked her back as she slept.

China was breaking my heart.

Chapter 6

A Good Beginning Is Half the Journey

良好的开端　成功的一半

Berkeley, California
June 2000

The next month flew by in a frenzy of preparation for Half the Sky's first build and training. My garage was piled high with newly purchased toys and art supplies and princess dresses and tiny high heels and tutus. Along with their birthday money and lemonade stand proceeds, children adopted from China sent us dress-up clothes to fuel the dreams of their little sisters.

I sorted the treasures into boxes lined up in the driveway to send along with our first volunteer building crew. I picked up a cheap plastic diamond tiara and imagined it perched above Xinmei's sad little face.

When I was a child there was a delivery van always parked in a driveway down the street. A boy named Andrew lived in the house belonging to that driveway. He would let us look inside the truck sometimes. Its walls were lined with little toys in cellophane bags. Andrew's father drove the truck to deliver the toys to the wire racks that tantalized small children in grocery stores and five-and-dimes. And sometimes, if we helped him, Andrew's father would let us choose a toy.

One day, when I was seven years old, I was heading home from school with my house key on a chain around my neck. I'd been a latchkey kid for only a few weeks.

Andrew's father was in his driveway, working in the van. He called out to me and said I could choose a toy. I climbed into the van. Before I could select a toy, he told me to close my eyes for a surprise. I did. He put his hand on me and he said, "It makes me sad that I don't have a little girl like you to love." I kept my eyes closed, listened to a song in my head about camels and bears and ponies prancing on the merry-go-round, and thought about how I should feel sad for Andrew's father.

Do you love me? he said.

Yes, I said.

Did I? Is this what love is?

Then he was angry. He pushed me out the door of the van and told me never to tell. I never did. I didn't know who I could tell. After that day, I went straight to the library from school. I read books there until my parents got home.

What Andrew's father did to me was unforgivable, but far from the worst thing a grown-up has ever done to a child. Perhaps the greater hurt was that I didn't know who I could tell.

Three years later, a girl on my street reported that Andrew's father was gone. She'd told her parents what he did to her, she said, and he'd been sent away. It had taken three years for a child to speak out.

Now I stood in my driveway full of toys and dreams for the future and thought of the children waiting in China. The secrets. Xinmei, her scars. No one to speak for her. Not for any of them.

I knew I couldn't speak loudly in China. The doors would be closed again if I did. But we would find a way to be a quiet voice for those children. There is a Chinese saying, "Whispers on earth are thunder in heaven's ears."

We would quietly make thunder.

•   •   •

To our first-ever Half the Sky volunteer crew—

We can't wait to welcome you to China! It's hard for me to believe, but it's been two long years since the idea of Half the Sky began. And, as you can imagine, it's been an extremely delicate operation to get access to the children in China's orphanages in order to help them. We don't want anything to happen now to shake the trust that has been placed in us.

So here comes a necessary little speech:

I hope that when you are in the orphanage, you will think of yourselves as ambassadors of Half the Sky and of all foreign adoptive families. You are there to work—to give your loving energy to help the children. You are not there as sightseers. Please save your cameras for excursions outside the institution. Orphanage administrators are very protective of the children and their surroundings. Dying Rooms–type coverage has made them justifiably worried about the image of the care they give the children and how it is portrayed. They really are doing the best they can. The fact that they are allowing a bunch of foreigners in to revamp and reorganize the children's lives is proof of their concern. So, rule number one—no cameras!

Now, there is some nervousness afoot about the possibility that someone traveling with Half the Sky will be smitten with a particular little one in the institutions and will feel compelled to move heaven and earth to try to adopt her. Or that someone will see the perfect child for a best friend or sister back home and suggest she call her agency to petition CCAA. It can't happen. It would jeopardize Half the Sky's programs and, indeed, the entire China foreign adoption program, if Half the Sky volunteers ever, intentionally or not, use our programs to pre-identify children.

This is only the beginning of a very long journey. We have a year to make this program work and to prove its worth. And

then we have many miles and many orphanages before us. We
are honored and privileged to have the doors opened to us. And
we are grateful to you for helping us keep those doors open.
*   End of sermon. See you in China!*

About now, I wasn't exactly sure how clean my own hands
were on the topic of pre-identified adoption—officially forbidden
in China at the time—but I could only imagine what would happen
if our very first volunteer build disintegrated into an adoption
shopping tour. Whether or not I had practiced what I preached, the
warning had to be sent.

Changzhou, China
July 2000

"Do you think we've just ruined our lives?" I asked Dick.

"Do you?"

"She really hates us. Me anyway. Where does a two-year-old
learn to spit like that?"

"I don't want to think about it," Dick said.

"And she bit Maya in the bath."

Dick groaned. I stuffed my face into the hotel pillow, shutting out what was left of the sweltering day. Our future daughter,
Xinmei, soon to be Anya, was by the door, screaming to be let out
of our room, where we were clearly torturing her. Maya looked
shell-shocked. Dick too.

I reached out, rested my hand on his chest.

"She seems to like you, though."

He went to the door, gathered the miserable little bundle up in
his arms, and carried her to the bed. She stopped screaming but
kept a wary eye on me. She snuffled pitifully.

Maya climbed up beside me, keeping a careful distance from
her new sister. We were a pathetic-looking family.

When we had arrived from California that morning to prepare for our first crew of American volunteers, Small Cloud Zhang surprised us with our little daughter-to-be. Even though we didn't quite have approval to travel to adopt her yet, we were now officially "matched." There was no reason she couldn't stay with us while we were in Changzhou.

"Great," I said, just a bit on edge at the prospect.

In less than two months, Anya had gained two kilos. She was almost unrecognizable. Small Cloud Zhang beamed. "We've been taking her to KFC every day to get her used to eating Western food!"

I didn't think food was going to be our problem. Now I touched our baby's small scarred foot. She pulled it away.

Well. One day at a time, I guess.

"I'm sorry, sweetheart," Dick said. I didn't know if he was talking to me or to Anya. He really was smitten with that child.

"WHY ARE WE here in July?" Terri moaned. "Could there be a more unpleasant month in China?"

Our friends and volunteer crew leaders, Terri and Daniel, clustered with ZZ, Dick, and me in a tiny patch of shade in front of the orphanage. We were waiting for the volunteers to arrive from Shanghai. Our children were off somewhere with Feng *Ayi* (Auntie Feng), the nice lady who would be our official crew nanny. Despite the soggy heat, I was loving the quiet.

Ten Americans, most of them parents of Chinese children, climbed down from the bus. Small Cloud Zhang came outside to greet them. She was nervous. Everyone was nervous. It was the first day of school for us all. Our first official Half the Sky build.

"Welcome to China," she said. "Welcome to the Changzhou Children's Welfare Institution!"

Small Cloud Zhang led us inside. We sat in the reception room, drank tea, and learned how many *mu* of land the institution covered. I thanked Small Cloud Zhang for the zillionth time. Then I asked if we could visit the children.

I WALKED INTO the children's ward behind my little crew of eager parent volunteers, took a very deep breath, and watched. I knew what they would see. I'd prepared them as well as I could. *Just remember, we're here to make it better. Keep your cool.*

Okay, I could exhale. Every one of those folks handled themselves better than I had back in Shijiazhuang. They were just happy to be there with those kids. They didn't seem angry. They didn't seem to take the conditions personally.

I wasn't sure why they weren't haunted and furious. I couldn't fathom how they'd be able to go back home and back to their lives—or why I never could. But I watched those good hearts blowing kisses and wiping runny noses and pouring love all over those babies, and I knew I was not alone in this. I would never be alone, for I was among family, doing exactly what I was meant to do. And one day, if the stars aligned and I didn't screw it up, all of China would be with us too.

Then, *whoosh* . . . someplace deep inside, I completely, absolutely knew for certain that that day would come. "We can do this," I said to nobody in particular. I could already hear distant thunder.

I found a way to touch every child in every room that morning. I smoothed scratchy, wrinkly dry skin, tiny bird-boned fingers, and oddly coarse malnourished-orange hair. I whispered to the littlest who struggled, "Hang on. We can fix this. You're going to be okay."

Calm now, anger safely stowed, I asked the *ayi*s to lift the babies and toddlers out of their cribs, then started doing it myself. The volunteers joined me at once. And nervously, the *ayi*s began to help, if only just until we were gone. But now, as I watched the volunteers, with tears in their eyes, lifting tots free, tickling and dancing and crooning, I saw how it would work.

Every day, we would come back. We would come back with reinforcements—nannies and teachers and foster mamas and babas, and before long this would be a place where babies were cuddled instead of trapped and tied, and every single vacant-eyed toddler and scrawny six-year-old would know what it feels like to be the apple of somebody's eye.

TERRI AND DANIEL set about organizing the troops as Small Cloud Zhang watched their every move. There was something about seeing this group of large Americans scrubbing down orphanage walls that just about stopped her cold. When they began to wash away the giant fake Disney cartoon figures, I thought she'd pass out. *What in the name of Mao had she let happen?*

Oblivious, the volunteers merrily cleaned and then painted the walls white, adding what would become our signature pastel stripes, leaving plenty of room for children's art and photo documentation of their projects.

Meanwhile, ZZ and I went shopping—not just once, but for the next three days.

We bought books and baskets and bikes and feathers and beads. Despite the dripping summer heat, we came to know every corner of Changzhou, a funky little town (little by China standards) laced with canals and bridges—and *most famous* for hand-painted wooden combs carved in whimsical shapes. We prowled every narrow street, every market, every dusty shop.

Here's how shopping went:

"How about a cozy reading nook for the preschool?" I suggested.

"Sure," said ZZ. "What's that?"

"You know, a place to enjoy books together. Warm and homey—
the opposite of institutional. We need a sofa to start with."

So we set out to find a sofa. Most Chinese homes, especially in
the steamy south, had wooden benches rather than plush uphol-
stery. Finally, we came upon Furniture City, a multistory block
of showrooms and warehouses all linked together. Everyone we
asked pointed us in a different direction for sofas.

Soggy and exhausted, at last we made our way to the top floor
of a metal-roofed building. The showroom was an oven. But we'd
found the sofas!

"Wait." ZZ clutched my arm. She didn't look so good.

"ZZ, are you okay?"

She dug into the backpack, which she wore backward because it
was stuffed with our shopping money. She pulled out a little vial and
deposited some tiny brown pellets into my hand and then her own.

"Chinese medicine," she said as she gulped hers down. "Save-
your-heart pills. Eat them."

I obeyed. Thus fortified, we cruised the sofa department—rows
of red, chartreuse, and hot-pink velveteen with swirly patterns
and black-leather cushions and fish gargoyle feet, and then quite
a few swan-shaped, phoenix-embellished fainting couches that
looked like they came from New Orleans bordellos in 1895.

As we wandered, a small sales team began to form behind us.
Just a couple at first, then—as word got out that a foreigner had
reached this godforsaken outpost—more and more. I don't know
where they came from; the place had looked empty when we got
there.

At last we came upon a lone little blue-and-green, not-too-
gaudy love seat. I could live with the tassels dangling here and
there. "This one," I whispered to ZZ, then kept on walking, as
she'd taught me to do, pretending I hadn't even seen the thing. ZZ
then began to bargain.

The first price, no matter what it was, was an outrage. ZZ bargained as if Chinese pride depended on it. The crowd grew. Everybody got involved. It was unclear who were the merchants and who were the bystanders. I stood a few rows away, my foreign face forgotten, and observed total mayhem. Everyone shouted at and argued with one another. Then a moment of quiet as ZZ held the room. She spoke from her heart. The crowd looked over at me. I smiled, waved a little.

Inevitably, ZZ cried. Then the merchants, crying a little themselves, threw their hands in the air. The matter was settled. And the price they gave us for the little love seat was very, very good.

"I just tell them about the orphans and about the love that you and the foreign friends are bringing into their lives," ZZ explained.

SOMEHOW, WHILE WE were away, the volunteers had managed to cajole Small Cloud Zhang into letting the children help. When we returned, little ones were wandering around underfoot as the crew happily sanded and painted. Even Small Cloud Zhang, in her spiky heels and minidress, was painting stripes. We set up our newly purchased boom box. Tina Turner was soon rattling the walls.

Changzhou was not yet accustomed to foreign faces. By the end of day one, the local media were on high alert. We were on TV and on the front page of the daily news. Curious neighbors came by to check out the situation. Some women from a nearby apartment block told me they'd had no idea there was an orphanage in their town. I saw the concern on their faces. If I'd had doubts before, our first build taught me that the problem is not that people in China don't care about children. Ignorance was our only enemy.

•   •   •

BY THE END of our two-week stay in Changzhou, four new babies, in the arms of police officers, had arrived at the orphanage gate. Not one child had left for adoption. It didn't seem that the orphan problem would get better anytime soon. Still, there was reason to feel hope for the children. Surrounded by caring volunteers, nannies, and young teachers-in-training, they showed the first signs that they were beginning to wake from their orphanage slumber.

"What are the babies eating?" Wen asked two little girls who were feeding their new baby dolls with plastic spoons.

"Egg," said one child.

"Do you know where the egg comes from?" Wen asked.

The girl didn't miss a beat.

"From *Ayi*."

"But where does *Ayi* get the egg?"

No answers.

"This is your opportunity," said Wen to her future preschool teachers. "When you see them begin to wonder, think about where you want to take it. The kitchen? The market? The farm? Learn about animals? How life begins? These are the moments you look for."

THE YOUNG TEACHERS were gathered listening to one another read from their training journals. They were beginning to feel at home on the mini-chairs at the mini-tables in the spanking-new, pastel-hued Half the Sky Little Sisters Preschool. Behind them stood an array of multicolored shelves stocked with art supplies, books, and developmental toys. Around the room were balance beams, a puppet theater, a mirrored triangle, tunnels and trikes, and baskets full of well-loved dress-up clothes from America. It could have been a high-priced private school on Manhattan's West Side.

"When I came to bring Tianyu to the classroom on the first day, she was so emotionless that I could not get any response from her," read Liwei, one of the teachers. "When other kids grabbed toys from her, she just allowed it and never showed any anger or upset. Every day I spent time with her, I took her to explore the leaves and flowers. I constantly talked to her and asked her questions even though she made little response. But today, when I told her my training was finished here and I would go to train and then work at the new preschool in Hefei, she turned her head away from me with tears in her eyes. Then she ran and hid."

"Why do you imagine she did that?" Wen asked. Liwei was silent. She looked at the floor. The room was quiet.

Liwei slowly raised her head. Her own eyes welled as she spoke, her small voice breaking. "I think . . . I think we were beginning to have a special bond. She was coming to trust me. I worked hard to be at her level, to understand what she needed. I was there for her. Now I see she's mad at me for leaving her. She's been abandoned before."

Wen took Liwei's hands and looked around at the rest of her teary-eyed young converts.

"Now you see," Wen told them, "we can be much, much more than we were taught at teachers' college . . . more than stern ladies at the front of the room who teach children to recite by rote. We can be, we *must* be, learning partners, champions, observers, explorers, friends—and, for these special, hurt children, we need to be family."

ON THE LAST day of our build, the new teachers and nannies proudly escorted the children into beautiful spaces that promised happy days ahead. The volunteers gave out sweet treats and dress-up clothes. We served a bunch of watermelons that we'd bought from a local farmer. We turned on the music. We all signed our names on the new preschool wall. Above the names, across the top, ZZ and I wrote in English and Chinese: BUILT WITH LOVE AND HOPE.

And then we had a party. A massive, everybody's-invited extravaganza of a party.

"THAT PARTY!" ZZ said to me years later. "You bring everyone—blind children, children who'd been lying on their back for years, the disabled children, *everyone*. That so touch the heart of the people like Small Cloud Zhang. At the beginning she say, 'Difficult. No, it's difficult. They never been out. We don't have the equipment to take those children out.'

"But when the volunteers pick those children up and carry them to the party, then they understand. And for me," ZZ said, "*I* understand. It's really moving, how much you wanted those children at the party. And we all think, 'Thanks for Half the Sky to bring those people to help the orphans.' The fear begins to fall away.

"You know, I am not a typical Chinese," ZZ said. "I've been working with foreigners a long time. I understand them. I have no fear of them. But what is difficult for Small Cloud Zhang is that it is one thing to allow you, a foreigner, to come inside her institution. But then you, as the leader of Half the Sky, can bring a whole group of volunteers inside and she has no control. Who knows if they are 100 percent friendly? So she feels fear. The dark influence from *The Dying Rooms* is still there.

"The fear from my side is that Half the Sky doesn't make any mistake. But what taught me very early that I don't need to worry is what you did to one of the volunteers in our second build right after Changzhou. Hefei! Remember the volunteer in Hefei?"

"The one that I asked Dick to put in a taxicab?"

"You treat her even worse than the Chinese!" ZZ said, laughing.

"She broke all our rules," I said. "She smuggled in a camera. She roamed around the orphanage by herself. She took photos of the kids."

"If I were you, I would give her another chance. I give her some criticism—a warning."

"I was terrified they'd make us all leave and that would be the end of Half the Sky," I said.

"But you say, 'Go back to the hotel, pack, go away!'—so that really tell me I don't have to worry about you," ZZ said. "After that, every time I go to the institutions, when the directors or the officials—they worry that this is a whole group of foreigners come. We have rules, regulations, this and that. I always use this example and tell them, 'You don't have to worry about Jenny Bowen. She is one of us.'"

ANYA STOOD ON the white carpet of the Businessman's Suite at the White Swan Hotel in Guangzhou, the city where all Americans must go to finalize adoptions. Except for the Pull-Up she wore on her head, she was stark naked.

"You and Maya go ahead down to dinner," I said to Dick. "Anya and I will just stay here and glare at each other."

"You sure?" he said. "Not much of an adoption celebration."

"Mmm-hmm."

"We'll bring you something."

"Mmm-hmm."

They left. I ran cold water over my fresh-bitten finger.

If this child had come to us first, before Maya, it's hard to imagine anything like Half the Sky emerging. But who said it should be easy? Anyway, I reminded myself, we weren't alone. Thirty-two new teachers and nannies and one hundred sixty-five children were starting this journey alongside my family. We'd all have to find our way.

Pull-Up jauntily perched over one eye, Anya was struggling into her adoption-celebration going-out-to-dinner dress—*all my byself.*

"So now you think you'll deign to join the party?" I asked.

She ignored me. Put her shoes on the wrong feet.

"We're in it now, kiddo," I said. "You and me. We're going to learn to love each other. Like it or not."

Enough Shovels of Earth, a Mountain; Enough Pails of Water, a River

积土成山　积水成渊

Just a few months after the builds in Changzhou and Hefei, the first Half the Sky success stories began to arrive. Our pilot programs would eventually spark 165 little miracles. Just as Maya did, and I prayed that Anya would, the children of Changzhou and Hefei began to heal and even to blossom.

Feifei

The police had taken Feifei to an orphanage when she was about a year old. She'd passed through a few sets of hands by the time she was turned over to their custody, so no one was clear about where she'd been abandoned or how she'd been found. In those days, record-keeping wasn't a priority at the orphanage. If and when her file was submitted for foreign adoption, someone would fill in the blanks, make it up.

She didn't seem in crisis on arrival, so after a brief quarantine she was bathed, diapered with clean rags, clothed in several layers, and deposited in a small blue wooden crib, in a room full of small blue wooden cribs full of girl babies of similarly uncertain origin. There she remained for the next ten months.

She was fed on schedule, a bottle propped on a folded towel.

Her diaper was changed on schedule, three times a day. She was bathed in a plastic tub every morning. That was her only human contact. She was never cuddled or rocked or kissed. Not once.

When Half the Sky programs began, our caregivers also began keeping "memory books"—individual albums for each child—full of reflections, artwork, photos, conversations, and milestones. The books serve as a sort of history for children who have lost theirs. From Feifei's memory book:

> Today is Feifei's first day in the Little Sisters Program. She is two years old and very pale and weak and shy. She doesn't interact with other children. She can't walk or even sit by herself. The teacher is propping her against the wall to help. But Feifei doesn't want to sit and she cries to lie down, for that is how she normally spends her days. For a whole day she struggles with the teacher, refusing or unable to use her legs and hips. She seems to have no language at all. The teacher is having difficulties communicating with her. No one knows what is wrong with Feifei. The orphanage says it is brain disease.

Two weeks later:

> After much patient help from the teacher, Feifei now is sitting up straight all by herself. She is beginning to play independently and shows a growing curiosity.

After another month:

> Feifei walks by herself for the first time! She opens her arms to reach her teacher.

And just four months from that first day, Feifei began to care for her baby doll:

> TEACHER: What are you doing, Feifei?
> FEIFEI: It's cold.
> TEACHER: Oh, Baby is cold, so you help her by covering her with a blanket?
> Feifei nods. She is very serious, but we can see a little smile.

Two years later, Feifei was adopted by a family in the Netherlands. Feifei's mother wrote to us once Feifei had settled in:

The idea that anyone thought that our daughter had serious brain disease made us feel very sad. There is nothing wrong with her! She rides her bicycle, plays computer games, needs an agenda to keep track of her play dates, and practices all day long for her career as a singer. She is fond of (pink) clothes and can't wait for the time when shoes with high heels and makeup are allowed. She fights over toys with her brother and argues over who has to feed the rabbits and cats. If you could see her, you wouldn't believe our girl was once little Feifei!

Feifei got a second chance. She learned to walk and eventually to talk and sing (and argue) because she came to know that somebody cared whether she did or not. She *mattered*.

Loris Malaguzzi got it right. The children, including Feifei, would become Half the Sky's teachers. As we observed them and responded to their needs, they proved to anyone who cared to look that what had happened for our Maya could happen for every child. Half the Sky's programs were developed from observations made within China's welfare institutions about what children need, along with a dose of early childhood theory. Yet they continue to prove over and over again the same simple, universal truths. Every child needs to know that she matters to someone. And every child has potential. One little girl's miracle would become an everyday story.

Within six months, the new preschool teachers and nannies were reporting back to ZZ and Wen steadily, giddy with small triumphs. We shared the coming-out stories with our supporters in newsletters and e-mails. The children's victories might seem slight against the soap opera of our own behind-the-scenes adult machinations, but there was no doubt in our minds who the true victors were.

As word got out, government study groups were sent from Beijing to examine the situation. Small Cloud Zhang was invited to give a few lectures at local teachers' colleges. She told ZZ that we'd changed her life. Suddenly she was *the* authority on child development, and in steady demand. "But I'm not a teacher!" she protested happily.

ONCE HOME IN California, Anya and I had begun an uneasy and cautious rapprochement. After a couple of weeks, she let me dress her now and then. I was sometimes allowed to give her food. Occasionally she even joined us on the big bed for a family snuggle, though she carefully kept her distance from me. She eased up on the spitting and biting business (that slap, thankfully, was a one-time thing), and she began doggedly tailing five-year-old Maya, who must have ascended a pedestal while the rest of us were sleeping. Suddenly, Anya was handmaiden to her big sister, responding to her every whim and parroting her every move.

Our new daughter seemed to have decided that this family stuff wasn't a complete disaster after all, and neither, possibly (time would tell), was her mother.

•   •   •

MOST CHINESE WOMEN were required to retire when they reached the doddering age of fifty or fifty-five (and just try to get a new job if you're a woman laid off post-forty), but because she had useful language skills, ZZ managed to hang on at CPWF until she turned sixty. The moment she retired, Half the Sky hired its first employee, and ZZ began what she now calls her "real career."

While still in graduate school, Wen became our second, part-time employee. Half the Sky now had two staff plus me. I then hired Ivy Yu, a recent Berkeley grad and our most loyal volunteer, to help me run the Berkeley office (our dining room table). Still not imagining the day would come when we'd need seventeen hundred staff to keep our operations going, our team of four marched boldly into the next phase of Half the Sky's development.

I'd been gathering names of potential program sites from the beginning—orphanages whose kids came home to their new adoptive families with attachment difficulties, hints of abuse, or signs of neglect. Whenever I read a sad story on the adoption lists, I took notes. With increasing frequency, parents were writing directly to me, sharing their stories of troubled adoptions and traumatized children.

Letters of thanks from adoptive parents came to us too. After a period of adjustment (and some healthy grieving for their nannies), children from our Half the Sky programs seemed to be thriving in their post-adoption lives. Infants and toddlers who attached early were able to transfer those attachments to their new parents easily. With plenty of evidence of success in hand, it was time to expand our efforts.

Using my trusty World-Cart map of China and assorted plane, train, and bus schedules, I figured out how we could visit twenty trouble spots in six provinces in just nineteen days. ZZ and Wen didn't even wince at the itinerary. As far as I know, nobody in China ever winced when I announced an all-new plan, a whole new deal. This is one of the many things about the Chinese that I love.

Then bad news. Kindly Mr. Shi, our handler at the Social Workers Association, had been transferred from orphan issues to veteran affairs. I was crushed. The new guy was Mr. Yang. ZZ called him Lao Yang (Old Yang), so I did too. Thin, drawn, and humorless, Old Yang was a cipher. Even when we eventually met in person, I couldn't glean anything about him except that he was embarrassed by his bad teeth. (I knew this only because he covered his mouth when he spoke, and so nobody ever understood what he was saying.)

ZZ submitted my orphanage request list. Old Yang came back to us with approval to visit ten cities—none of them on my list of trouble spots. That news reached me two days before my departure for the big trip.

Hi ZZ,

Can you help me figure out how we might convince Old Yang and the ministry that it is not sufficient to send us to ten of the nicest institutions in China? If we accept only institutions on the approved list, we won't be going to a single place where the children are most in need.

Hi Jenny,

I am a Chinese, and have been working and dealing with the leaders for long years. Thank you for your trust of my hard work to let them understand your heart. I have spoken to them on your good intentions for the children, but still they have to discuss and think about and negotiate with each other. It has been driving me crazy in the past years! But I believe also, like you, as long as we try, nothing is impossible!

Yet again proving herself our secret weapon, ZZ negotiated further and won. Our Half the Sky Study Tour of 2001 was set.

Over eighteen days, ZZ, Wen, Old Yang, and I visited fourteen cities spanning the country from Shanghai to Chengdu and points south; most of them had been on our trouble list. We breezed through the provinces of Anhui, Jiangsu, Yunnan, Sichuan, and Guangdong and the municipality of Chongqing. We dined at banquets and shook the hands of smiling strangers. Tailed by endless entourages of anonymous officials, we wandered through bleak orphanages—hallway upon hallway, room upon room.

To our hosts' dismay, we always asked to skip the *famous* tourist attractions and headed straight for the places that made nobody proud. This became our modus operandi at Half the Sky. Another four years would pass before I finally visited the Great Wall.

I knew that this failure to tour was frustrating for ZZ; she'd cut her teeth as a government tour guide. I finally relented and took a break in sunny southern Yunnan Province, *famous* home to fifty-two minority groups. The Kunming orphanage director escorted us to that capital city's *famous* botanical gardens. My eyes glazed over at *mu* upon *mu* of floral displays.

In fact, all I could see or think about were the young girls in tattered ethnic dress, some of them no more than eight or nine years old, begging out front, cute hungry babies strapped to their backs. When we exited the gardens, I stopped to give them a little money. I took their pictures. A policeman stuck his hand over my camera lens. "Forbidden! No pictures!"

Now the Kunming orphanage director—who I think had liked me when I smiled nicely after she proudly told me that she'd been a factory manager and that she ran her orphanage the same way she'd run the factory—didn't trust me anymore. She snarled at ZZ that I didn't understand and made things worse for the children by giving them money. I was chastened and apologized for my bad behavior.

"I guess she won't welcome Half the Sky to Kunming any time soon," I said to ZZ with regret.

"One day they will all welcome us," she said.

IN EACH CITY, we were met at the airport or train station by the orphanage director or a local Civil Affairs official or the vice mayor or a department head from the institution. How high the rank of the welcoming delegation told us plenty about the degree of enthusiasm for our programs. In any event, first stop was food, always.

Over lunch and the mandatory reception room pit stop, I'd try to take a quick read on the director and staff. *Did they get what we were talking about? Did they care? Would they try?*

Finally, when we saw the children, all the lost little girls, we had a brief golden moment to draw our conclusions. They were, again, our teachers and true tour guides. Their faces, the texture of their skin, the language of their bodies, and especially their eyes told us all we needed to know about the level of care and caring. So I studied the beautiful faces, hundreds upon hundreds, acres of innocence betrayed.

In central China, they were bundled against the winter chill—puffy little mummy-babies, two to a crib, immobilized by layers of clothing. In the steamy south, less clothing but no more action. Tied or bundled or unfettered, it didn't seem to matter—the children had forgotten what children do. Almost everywhere we went, they lay flat on their backs or were propped in walkers or lined up in little chairs. Almost everywhere, they barely moved; their eyes were vacant, noting their visitors with indifference, if at all. I longed to hear them cry or laugh or have two-year-old tantrums. Almost everywhere, it was quiet.

We had only a short time with the children in each place, but when I looked into the faces of those in charge, I just *knew* where our programs could thrive—I could see it in their eyes. In fifteen years, in more than fifty orphanages, we've had to close only one program because the administrators were too corrupt and too indifferent to do what they knew was right for their children. In that place, the nannies we paid and trained didn't do their jobs because, although we sent it faithfully, they didn't receive their pay. The children spent their days alone. Nothing felt more horrible than shutting down that program. Even if the children never saw the benefits (and in that place they never did, except on our visiting days), while we were still in their lives at least they had a chance.

Despite the gloom of the places we saw on that Study Tour of 2001, I was filled with hope—for now I felt sure we could change things in a big way. Again and again I whispered my pep talks and promises—this time with full confidence that I knew what I was whispering about.

Better than my promises, ZZ and Wen seemed to derive new energy and authority now that they were full-fledged Half the Sky staff. Wen waved orphanage directors over to bedsides. "See here, how this child won't make eye contact? See how her arms and legs are so limp? Her brain is being damaged from lying here day after day like this."

ZZ chimed in, "You should let the children run free. That is how they grow normally. You are stunting their growth."

The locals looked worried. They clucked and murmured among themselves. I stood by and silently cheered Wen and ZZ on. Despite a dedication to preserving face for themselves and those they respect (or think they should), the Chinese seem to be capable of criticizing one another with a bluntness that no Westerner would ever dare. ZZ, who was of a certain age (the worst offenders, for sure) and knew all too well what a good humiliating tongue-lashing felt like, thought nothing of pushing to the front of queues and telling young guards and ticket-takers and shop girls how poorly they were doing their jobs.

And in one town, our aging minibus driver plowed into a young woman on a bicycle. Even as she tumbled, he started yelling at her. She sat up, dazed, in the middle of the road, cars whipping by, and our driver screamed at her about the rules of the road. Thankfully, she was only bruised.

The woman limped away. Dumbfounded, I looked at ZZ. "He lost face in front of a foreign friend," she explained without a wince.

DESPITE MY FOREIGN ignorance of Chinese ways (ZZ kindly explained I was "the other kind" so couldn't possibly understand), things were definitely looking up for Half the Sky—even in the apparently unreceptive-to-change Guangdong Province. Old Yang, who had reluctantly arranged our trip and now never let us out of his sight, told us that the Civil Affairs people in that intensely competitive provincial office quarreled over who among them would get to be our escort and enjoy all those tasty banquets.

While driving through Guangdong, provincial Civil Affairs Bureau Division Chief "Call me Jane" Wu, the victor, was in a grand frame of mind. She told us she didn't think her main competitor, Ms. Yeh, should be doing PR because Ms. Yeh was unattractive and brash. Old Yang said there was some truth in that.

"In what way is she brash?" I asked.

"For example, she demands your name card instead of asking sweetly," Jane said. "It's obvious this shows she thinks she's the boss."

Obvious. Everyone agreed.

"Let's sing!" said Jane. And so they did.

ZZ's rich contralto soared along with Jane's hearty soprano in a medley of favorites from the Cultural Revolution ("The East Is Red"; "Sailing the Seas Depends on the Helmsman"; "I Am a Little Member of the Commune").

The more I work, the more I love it. Aye-hey-hey! Aye-hey-hey!
Always thinking of the good character of poor and lower-middle
  peasants,
Loving the collective and loving labor,
I am a little member of the commune!

Through the minibus window, I could see old tower houses scattered here and there in the lush southern landscape. They were elegant fortresses that had been erected by the families of men who'd traveled to North America, their "Gold Mountain," at the turn of the previous century to build railroads and pan for gold—the young men who helped to build my hometown, San Francisco. While they toiled in that hostile distant country and judiciously sent their earnings home, their women built towers and ramparts to protect the new family wealth from bandits.

I leaned against the glass, my ears humming with songs of revolution, and thought about how far I was from San Francisco—how much my life had changed and yet how much I felt at home in this faraway place. I wondered how many young men ever returned from Gold Mountain.

The crumbling towers looked lonely and oddly feminine now among the squat, tile-faced blue- or green-windowed village homes favored by later generations. Near one village, we drove past a young woman working in the fields with a baby on her back. A shutter clicked in my brain. Time stopped. I saw a still image of the two in my mind's eye and for an instant I knew they were Maya's mama and little brother. We were only a few hours from the bus station in Guangzhou where our baby had been abandoned. It was possible. In fact, I was certain. I wanted to yell out, *Stop the car! Turn around!* But the ladies were in full voice and I did nothing.

BEFORE HEADING HOME, we flew to Beijing to meet with Madame He LuLi—vice chairman of the Standing Committee of the People's Congress, president of CPWF, and former vice mayor of Beijing. There weren't all that many powerhouse women in China in those days. I hoped she might give me some advice.

The Party Congress was in session, and central Beijing traffic was pretty much shut down. When we finally reached the China World Hotel, we were escorted into an elegant formal reception room. It would be my first meeting with a true dignitary. I scanned the room, trying to figure out how to have a conversation when all parties sat lined up around the perimeter of the room, facing center. No looking in the eyes for this bunch. Madame He arrived, and we all stood. She was seated (center chair, of course), and then we all sat. After introductions, I perched sideways on my gilded throne and did my best to make contact.

"Madame He, we saw many beautiful buildings on our tour of the welfare institutions, but we didn't see much activity inside. Unfortunately, it seems there is very little being offered to stimulate the children and give them the love that all children need," I ventured.

"When people have money to spend for the first time, they do with it what they understand," she said.

I shared a bit of our Half the Sky story and hopes for the future. When I asked her for advice about how to best proceed in the Chinese way, Madame He said we should actively seek media attention, especially at the local level. She said we should get the ordinary people involved.

"Tell the Chinese people, and they will want to help you!"
Could that be true? So simple?

I'D RECEIVED QUITE different official advice at a U.S. Consulate
residence a few days earlier when ZZ and I were in Guangzhou.
We watched the elaborate southern Chinese tea ceremony performed flawlessly, respectfully, by our American host, a U.S. visa
official. But the words . . .

"First thing to know is that you can't trust the Chinese," our
host said. "They look at you and just see money."

"Stay under the radar. If you don't, the government will throw
you out," said the commercial officer.

"You'll never get the Chinese to go along with your ideas," said
a man from public affairs.

"If I were you, I'd just go home," said our host.

I looked at ZZ's face. Impassive. A polite smile.

"Thank you for the advice and the delicious tea," I said.

"Be careful," they said.

WE MET BRIEFLY with Old Yang's boss—the president of the China
Social Workers Association, our new partners. President "Red
Sun" Liu's freshly dyed, greased-flat helmet-hair glistened in the
afternoon light as he made a direct play to push our trusted CPWF
right out of the picture.

"CPWF functioned as our matchmaker," President Liu explained. "Now that the match is made, we don't need them
anymore."

ZZ fumed as she diligently translated every word.

"We also suggest that the salaries and benefits Half the Sky
pays should come through our association," he oozed.

"But President Liu," I said, doing my best ooze back, "your association has signed an agreement with CPWF and Half the Sky that defines everyone's responsibilities. This has been settled. And just today Madame He LuLi took time away from the People's Congress meeting to reaffirm her support of our partnership."

His face folded into the China Smile. The meeting was adjourned.

PRESIDENT RED SUN Liu would not stand in our way. Nobody would; I was determined. And I came away from my meeting with He LuLi convinced that, at least at that time in China, no loyal Chinese would be congratulated for dismissing foreign funding for "good works" or anything else without a darn good reason.

So we seized the moment. In 2001, we expanded our programs in Changzhou and Hefei and added one new site from among those we had visited on the big trip. Then, working hard to nurture government relations, we offered to do our bit to help China "develop the west." Our plans for fall 2001 included new centers in Chengdu and Chongqing in western China.

But then came September 11.

Unless There Is Opposing Wind, a Kite Cannot Rise

逆境成才

September 13, 2001

Dear Chengdu and Chongqing volunteers,
    This is simply the worst of times. In the last couple of days we've heard from a couple of you expressing concern and anxiety over the idea of traveling away from home and to the other side of the world next month. This is completely understandable, and is certainly compounded by the prospect of either bringing or leaving behind your family. If you know that this is not the right time for you to make this trip and wish to withdraw, please know that you are not alone.
    Before we make a final determination, though, as to what should be the next step for Half the Sky, we would like to hear from the rest of you. Ours is a charitable mission and needn't operate on a stringent timeline. It is very possible that the wisest thing for us to do would be to postpone these builds until the world situation stabilizes. . . .

Big mistake. I had written to the volunteers on impulse—not the first time I'd charged ahead before consulting the board.

Maybe I was paranoid, but it seemed to me that there was a

growing tension among some on our board. We were all on edge. Everyone was. Except for Dana, none of us had been on a board before and didn't know exactly what boards of directors did. Some just knew they didn't want me blithely making all the decisions. I felt it, but no one said it, and so I just kept doing what I thought was best, as if I were directing a movie. The director calls the shots: that's the only way good movies get made. It didn't occur to me that running Half the Sky might require a different set of skills.

The day after my e-mail, my pal Terri, our volunteer crew leader, sent an e-mail to the group:

> *Dear Board,*
>
> *I have decided I will not be going to Chongqing. I find the timing of this project to be unmanageable and profoundly difficult. I don't feel comfortable trying to make arrangements involving other people's lives in a time that's filled with so much uncertainty.*

She then listed all the things that could go wrong. A lot. Two pages worth of things: stranded or detained volunteers, missing luggage, confiscated supplies, separated families in panic, a new attack, a retaliatory attack, airline shutdowns. The volunteers must not be allowed to participate in making decisions, she urged. In fact, she said, the build *must* be postponed and I had absolutely no business consulting with the volunteers directly.

I had rocked what was not a very stable boat. No surprise, most of the volunteers asked to postpone the trip, and so we did. But the unease among our founding families would never go away; Half the Sky was entering nonprofit adolescence.

THE FOLLOWING SPRING, we made good on our promise to "develop the west." None of the board members joined us.

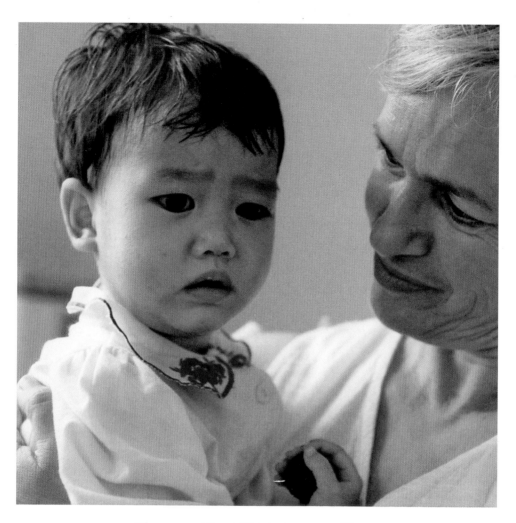

The moment I met Meiying, now our Maya.
Guangzhou, 1997.

On the set of my last movie, *In Quiet Night,* but dreaming of China.
Carmel Valley, 1997.

Maya and me, happy together. Berkeley, 1999.

Our first glimpse of Xinmei, now our Anya.
Unlike her father-to-be, Anya was not in love at first sight. Changzhou, 2000.

Maya, Dick, me, and Anya at the notary office. The red thumbs mean Anya's adoption is official. Nanjing, 2000.

Welcome to China!
Above: In the early days of Half the Sky, we'd be greeted with flowers, banners, and once, even a brass band. *Below:* A surprise outing on a reservoir. *Below:* Anya, me, and ZZ. *Below right:* Miao Xia, Mr. Shi, Small Cloud Zhang. Jiangsu Province, 2000.

Above: The good women of China Population Welfare Foundation. *(From left)* The amazing ZZ, CPWF President Wu, me, and CPWF Secretary General Miao Xia. Beijing, 1999.

Then: An all-too-common sight during my early orphanage visits and in some areas Half the Sky has yet to reach.

Now: A typical Half the Sky Infant Nurture Center where each nanny provides loving attention and bonding for orphaned babies.

Above: Wen *(standing center)* trains her first group of young teachers in a Half the Sky Little Sisters Preschool. Hefei, 2000. *Below:* Volunteer crews transform a bleak orphanage room into a colorful preschool. Chuzhou, 2001.

The difference we make: Half the Sky exists to bring a meaningful connection with a loving, responseive caregiver into the life of every child.

Above: In a child-centered Half the Sky preschool, teachers and children become learning partners. *Below:* The caring mentors of Half the Sky's Youth Services program help prepare school-age children and teens for independence.

Above: Half the Sky's Family Village program provides permanent loving families for children whose special needs make adoption unlikely. *Below:* In Half the Sky's China Care Home, orphaned children receive life-saving medical care while watched over by their own loving nannies.

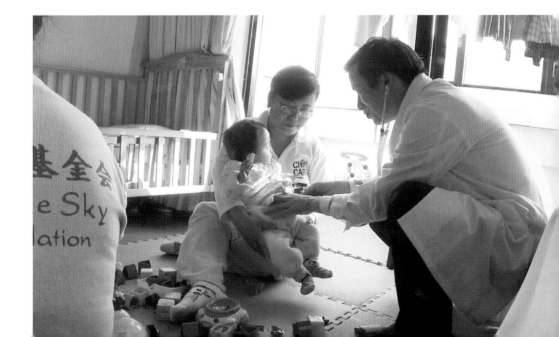

Above: Anya and Maya, first day of school, Beijing, 2004. *Below:* Christmas in California. Our son Aaron and his wife, Tamara, Maya, me; Dick, Anya, our daughter Cristin, her son Colin and husband Jim, and ZZ. Berkeley, 2002.

Jingli, Maya, and Anya in Tiananmen Square, Beijing, 2004.

Hard as we tried to stay on the government's good side, we didn't always succeed. *Above:* The AIDS-affected family we quietly supported. Henan, 2004.

Above: The forbidden photo of children begging I took in ignorance. Kunming, 2001.
Below: The government-supported Baby Bubbles experiment I failed to appreciate.
Chongqing, 2005.

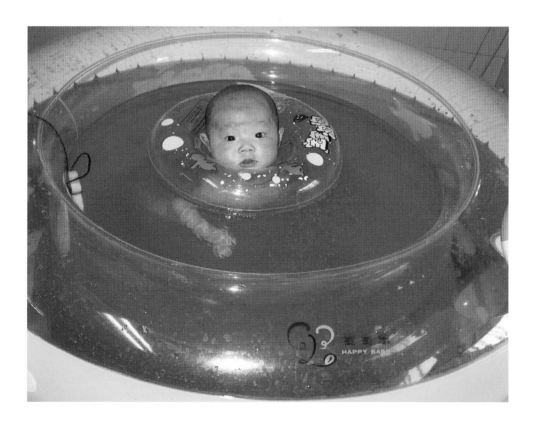

Above: Dick and friends load a relief truck bound for the Chenzhou orphanage. *Below:* The government roadblock turning back cars on the mountain road to Chenzhou, 2008.

Above and Below: Babies safe and sound during freak snowstorms in Chenzhou, 2008.

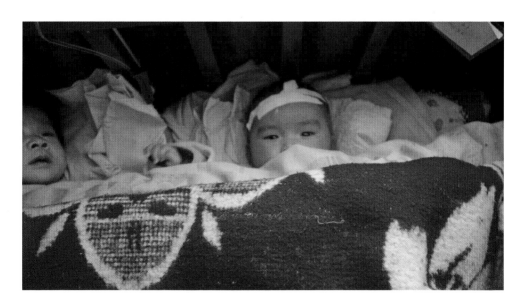

Above: Hongbai Town Primary School after the Sichuan earthquake. *Below:* In Half the Sky BigTops, children find a safe place to play and to heal. Sichuan, 2008.

Above and Below: On the makeshift playground outside a BigTop, children play at being Red Cross workers and survivors.

With Vice Minister Dou YuPei, the man formally responsible for child welfare.
Ministry of Civil Affairs. 2008.

Above: Joint conference with Ministry of Civil Affairs Director General Wang Zhenyao. *Below:* Professor Wang and Mrs. Gan discuss the future of child welfare and Half the Sky in China. Yangtze River, 2010.

Maya and Anya in Tiananmen Square, Beijing, 2013.

We began in Chongqing, China's largest city. Before it became the poster child for China's western development campaign, old Chongqing, with its winding lanes and steep, staircased hills reminded me of San Francisco. At the confluence of three rivers, the city was always enveloped in mist. It felt like the foggy hills of my childhood.

Staircase shopping was tricky, though—no bicycles, no pedicabs, no trucks or taxis—and, on every Half the Sky build, serious shopping must be done. Naturally, the citizens of Chongqing had solved the problem decades before we got there. *Bongbong*s, men bearing stubby wooden poles, trailed behind us as we shopped. Our purchases—paint cans, rocking chairs, rugs, art supplies, whatever—were tied to the ends of the poles and easily hoisted onto strong shoulders. When we ran out of shoulders, more *bongbong*s magically appeared. By the time we arrived at a street wide and flat enough to accommodate three or four taxis, we had a dozen heavily laden but laughing *bongbong*s in our wake. They thought we were hilarious.

One day, after shopping, our car crept through traffic, leading a parade of supply-laden taxis.

"Why do you think there are so many women outside that little red temple, ZZ?"

"Must be because today is International Women's Day. Good day for women of China. Most work only half day or even have the whole day to enjoy outings and shopping."

She quizzed the taxi driver.

"Ah yes, see," she said. "That is the Guanyin Temple. Guanyin is Goddess of Compassion. Taoists, Buddhists, even Christians—all Chinese love her."

"Can we have a look?" I asked.

"Yes, sure we can."

We hopped out of the cab and ZZ instructed the whole fleet to pull over.

Inside the lovely old sanctuary, it was dark and crowded with women—worshippers and the nuns who ran the place. We bought joss sticks from a nun stationed near the door. Her shaved head and faded red robes blended into the ancient walls. Everything about her was serene. Only the little rubber-banded stack of bills she carried brought her into this century. She was about my age. We might have been born at the very same instant. *There are a million different ways to live a life,* I thought. Look at us now—standing here together as if it were always our destiny.

A couple of young shop girls, arm in arm, nudged me aside to pay for their incense.

"Why do they come here on this special day?" I asked. "What do they pray to Guanyin for?"

"They say she hears the cries of the world. She takes care of poor and suffering. Maybe there is sickness in the family. Maybe someone in trouble. Guanyin is there for the ones who are forgotten. Usually most pray for her to bring them sons."

I watched the women, young and old, solemn in their prayers, and wondered which ones were praying for sons and grandsons. Which ones, because of government policy or sheer poverty, might give up their daughters if Guanyin failed to hear their prayers?

After a while, I lit my incense in the fire and, following ZZ's lead, bowed to the giant golden Guanyin. Then I knelt on threadbare silk cushions to pray.

I asked Guanyin to please remember the little girls. Please watch over them too.

"And, if you can, will you keep an eye on Half the Sky as well? Just in case we need some extra help?"

A COUPLE OF days later, ZZ and I were on a four-hour (or so we had been told) bus trip from Chongqing to Chengdu, the capital of Sichuan—trying to manage two concurrent builds without our crew leader. Training would start at Chengdu in the morning. Six hours had already elapsed. It was close to midnight. No Chengdu in sight. ZZ chattered to Old Yang on the phone and slapped my leg happily.

"Good news! Guangdong now welcomes Half the Sky programs! We can choose the sites! Old Yang says he just needs to reconfirm with Mrs. Wu. I am sure this is because President Red Sun Liu's boss, the former vice minister, said such nice things to you at dinner the other night in Beijing! What's that, Old Yang?" ZZ shouted into the phone. "Speak up!"

I could hear Old Yang straining to be heard over the bus noise. Poor fellow was even more impossible to understand on the telephone.

"It should be no problem . . . mmmrfughm . . ."

"Old Yang says please tell what cities you will choose. It seems to be with the support of the former vice minister, everything is moving faster than in the past!"

"Who's Mrs. Wu again? What's the name of the person in Guangdong Province who didn't want us to open programs in Shenzhen?" I asked warily.

"Mrs. Wu is the division chief of Civil Affairs Bureau in Guangdong Province who traveled with us last year when we sing songs together," ZZ said.

"Oh, *Jane?*—the one who knows all the verses of 'I Am a Little Member of the Commune'? That's wonderful! Please tell Old Yang thank you for the great news and for his hard work," I said. "We can choose the cities just as soon as we're absolutely sure we have permission to set up our programs in Guangdong from Mrs. Wu and her boss and Foreign Affairs and everybody else.

"And this is just for you, ZZ—if this is true, it's fantastic news. I think we should try for the fall. There are two families who say they'll support programs in Guangdong. They want to help only the place where their daughters are from. I want to talk to them, but I'm afraid to if permission might be withdrawn again—if this is another Shenzhen. Old Yang needs to confirm it's a definite yes."

"Understand," ZZ said.

ZZ shouted into the phone and Old Yang mumbled back for another half hour or so. Still no city lights ahead. I began to wonder if we were on the wrong road. Finally, ZZ hung up and yelled at the bus driver a bit. Then she just stared at the gloom.

"Well?" I said.

"Driver says less than one hour to Chengdu. Maybe."

"What did Old Yang say?"

"Yang asked again what your plan of Lanzhou. He hope Lanzhou is included in Half the Sky program in some way. I am sure Miao likes that too. Lanzhou is her hometown," ZZ said.

"Lanzhou? But isn't Lanzhou in Gansu Province? Not Guangdong?"

"Sure it is. We went there!"

"The desert place in the northwest, right? Sort of ugly?"

"Not ugly to Miao," said ZZ.

"But I thought we were talking about Guangdong. Where Maya is from."

"Of course, we are," ZZ said.

"Right. I'm confused."

Sometimes even though we were speaking the same language it was as if we weren't.

"Don't worry." ZZ shrugged. "It's not your fault; you're just 'the other kind.'"

"You've said that before."

"*Mei wenti*," ZZ said. "No problem."

I slumped deeper in my bus seat and pouted for a bit. Just for a bit, though. She had a point.

When I arrived home from that whirlwind tour of trouble spots, Anya, who had just turned three and was starting to like me a little, said, "Mom, you Chinese."

"You mean Mommy was in China." She'd been hearing English for only eight months now.

"No, Mom. You Chinese. I mean, Mommy Chinese," she insisted.

I knew better than to pick a fight with my most avid critic.

"Okay," I said.

But her pronouncement got me thinking. In four years we'd accomplished a lot, but it seemed I understood less about China now than I did back in 1998 when I devoted all those days to research. I was learning to love the country and adore the people and even decipher them a little, but I was in no way assimilating. Even though I liked to think there was no role too challenging for the actor in me to inhabit, in some elusive way it seemed that the more time I spent in China, the less "Chinese" I became.

Anya was wrong for once. I am *the other kind*. This may be for the best. The Chinese seemed to let foreigners get away with more.

Chengdu, Sichuan

The interminable bus ride finally came to an end. At 2:00 A.M.

Somehow, we managed to drag ourselves to Half the Sky's training at the orphanage first thing in the morning.

Wen's happy and productive Reggio-inspired preschools had already become legend; her exuberant training style was a must-see for anyone who happened to be on the orphanage campus while she was at work. She soon had a devoted band of young teachers who would follow her anywhere.

Meanwhile, Janice Cotton, the early childhood specialist from Alabama (also mom to a Chinese daughter) whom I'd met online, had taken my infant nurture idea and shaped it into a beautifully teachable program that spoke to women of even the humblest backgrounds. The locals we hired were, in the early days, mostly semiliterate factory workers, laid off from state-owned companies that had recently shut down. Janice had an intuitive connection with these undervalued women, who were just thrilled by the idea that someone would actually pay them to cuddle babies.

After the trainings, and after they'd been at their new jobs for a few months, the nannies often told us that they had been given another gift, one they hadn't understood before: purpose. Their babies needed them. The women began knitting sweaters for their little charges during their free time. They came in on Sundays just to make sure everything was okay. With such loving attention, the babies blossomed. They bonded with the nannies who loved them so. And then the thriving, happy babies were adopted. Soon we had to add another unit to our training: one on saying goodbye to the ones you love. That part still isn't easy. I don't know how they do it. The best nannies, the ones who manage to open their hearts again and again, only to have them broken—they suffer (and perhaps benefit) the most.

"Babies cannot take care of themselves," Janice told her new trainees. "They need you to care for them—not just in a physical way, but in an emotional way. Babies in institutions don't have parents to give them love. The babies in this orphanage are totally dependent on you nannies and *ayi*s to take care of them when they are hurt, to love them when they are lonely, and to challenge them to take risks and to learn new things. This is what we call 'responsive care.'

"We talk a lot about responsive care and how important it is to a baby's development. Babies who have responsive care grow up to be happy and able children and adults. Research studies show that babies who have *not* experienced responsive care often have difficulty in many different areas of development when they are older. The purpose of Half the Sky is to make sure that the babies in this institution have the responsive care that they need to grow up to be happy and healthy. Your job is very important. The kinds of care that you provide to babies here will have lifelong effects for them when they grow to be children and later adults."

Then Janice went on to demonstrate responsive care by inviting Dr. Huang, her training partner and interpreter, to dance. As music filled the training room and they waltzed around, Janice called out, "See how I'm letting Dr. Huang lead? I'm giving him responsive care. But see how he pays attention to me too? If I want to twirl, he is ready to help. Responsive care is a dance."

Before long everyone was dancing, caught up not only in the music, but in a whole new way of looking at their world.

ZZ and I wandered away to explore the orphanage to make sure no children had been forgotten in the excitement. Sometimes orphanage directors didn't understand or truly believe that we were trying to help *all* the children, including those with severe special needs. On occasion, we'd find them still waiting in dark rooms, months after our programs were under way and their sisters were beginning to flourish.

ZZ and I came upon a wide rooftop balcony where a young *ayi* was hanging piles of wet diapers to dry. The girl looked no more than twelve or thirteen. When I asked, she told me that her name was Baimei and she thought she was thirteen, but nobody knew for sure. She'd had no schooling. She spent her days cleaning up after the younger children at the institution. I asked her about her dreams for the future. She shrugged.

"But if you could do anything you wanted—go anyplace in the world—be anybody?"

"Maybe . . . I don't know . . . maybe a pop star?"

"A singer? Do you like to sing?"

She shrugged again.

"Do you think you have a pretty good singing voice?" I asked.

"No. I don't think so."

"But you wish you could learn?"

"I don't know."

"Well . . . do you know why you might like to be a pop star, Baimei?"

"Oh yes." She didn't hesitate. "They make people happy."

The absence of childhood dreams seemed unbearably sad. My dreams were what sustained me. But in the early days of Half the Sky, I never once met an institutionalized child who could share her dreams with me. They didn't seem to know that dreams were possible.

During an orphanage visit that first summer, I met a sixteen-year-old who'd spent her life in an institution. Unlike many of her sisters, she was articulate and unsettlingly straightforward. She said to me, "I have no plans for my future. None at all. Sure, I would love to find a family. But I'm too old to be adopted. And for girls like me there is nothing. My education will soon be over, and then that will be the end of it."

But your whole life is ahead of you! You're a smart girl—it's ridiculous to say that you have no hopes! I thought this, but I didn't say it. Part of me knew she simply spoke the truth. Even Half the Sky, so keen to remember forgotten children, put all of its resources into transforming the lives of the young ones. They were resilient. They needed so little in order to thrive. It was as if we held the key to their happy futures. But older children who'd never known love, or who'd had it taken from them—theirs was a different story.

As I watched the little ones begin to flourish in our new infant centers and preschools, I often thought about that girl and about all the other big girls whose fates were sealed when their lives had barely begun.

•   •   •

OVER HOTPOT, AT a posh restaurant with a live tree growing in the dining room, I asked Chengdu Director "Little Pretty" Chen about the older children in her orphanage and how they did in school. She was, as always, in full face paint and perfectly coiffed. Today she'd chosen knee-high lavender platform boots and a red leather miniskirt. Little Pretty Chen carried a cigarette at all times, even an unlit one in the baby rooms. "One must smoke because it is fashionable," she'd told me when we first met.

Now she took a drag on her cigarette and piled live shrimp on my plate. I watched their little tentacles wave in the air.

"Orphanage kids are not welcome in our community schools," Little Pretty said. "They are poor students. They have no motivation. We do everything for them. We feed them and clean up after them. They want for nothing. They're lazy and spoiled and don't care to work hard at school or at anything else."

Right then, while listening to Little Pretty Chen, I decided that we must design a program for older children, one that would try to meet their individual needs and interests. Besides the loving attention and guidance that the kids so obviously hungered for, we would provide opportunities to study music, art, computers, languages, dance, sports, or anything else they could dream up. We would offer vocational skills and school tutoring. We would find a way to pay for college tuitions. We would be doting parents and mentors for big kids who had no one at all.

The next morning, Baimei became our first Big Sister.

Baimei

Baimei was three or four years old when she was found wandering in the vast Chengdu train station. The police thought she told them that her uncle had taken her there and instructed her to wait for him. He never returned. That's what the police understood. But the child couldn't speak clearly and no one could be sure.

Baimei doesn't remember much about her early years at the orphanage. She remembers that no one liked her. The *ayi*s and the other children called her the Garbage Picker because they said she ate garbage. She doesn't remember eating garbage.

Baimei attended first grade at the local community school. She thinks she did well. But at the end of the year, there was an exam. Baimei didn't understand that the test had a time limit. She lent her only pencil to a classmate who'd forgotten to bring one, and waited for her turn. When the girl finished, Baimei wrote her name on her own exam paper—and then the time was up. Her test score was zero. Little Pretty Chen told Baimei that she was stupid and could no longer attend school.

For the next two years, Baimei begged to be allowed to return to school. Finally Little Pretty said, "All right. If you can learn to recite the multiplication tables before the next school year begins, you can go to school."

The new school year was only three days away. Baimei borrowed a book and, in just three days, somehow managed to memorize the tables. She tried to recite them for Little Pretty, but Little Pretty had no time to listen. Baimei was never allowed to return to school.

When the Big Sisters program began, Half the Sky hired basic education and music teachers for Baimei. Her quarterly progress reports were glowing:

Baimei's enthusiasm for learning grows more and more. She has changed from one who received knowledge passively to one who is actively exploring, seeking new information, and sharing it. She understands what she is taught in class and raises very good questions. She has even been able to correct me, her teacher, on more than one occasion!

She always prepares for class ahead of time, writing the *pinyin* and words for new characters with the help of a dictionary. Once when I wrote a new character incorrectly, she looked it up in the dictionary and showed me the correct way. I praised her, and she told me shyly that she had looked it up the day before. Her vocabulary is growing rapidly. I am so proud of her!

Our Big Sisters were also required to send us their own quarterly reports. Baimei's written Chinese was rough, but it was easy for our translators to find the heart of her story:

Dear Uncles and Aunts at Half the Sky,
    I have made a lot of progress. I feel that my Chinese and math are much better than before, and I even know some English! I want to tell you that it's your support that makes me full of self-confidence. I am no longer a girl that fears things. Now my life is going well for me. I love studying, especially English. I only know a little about that, but it is enough to me to fall in love with it. I can have a short conversation with my teacher. I am very happy and grateful for the opportunity you provide for me, and I won't forget your love.

An American family learned about Baimei and wanted to adopt her. Adoption of an older child was rare in those days, but these people were eager and well prepared to give Baimei a good home. She would have siblings also adopted from China, and a friend from her orphanage lived close by. Baimei was excited. A whole new life! But Little Pretty Chen said she was too old. Never able to turn chameleon with Little Pretty, I stammered in frustration, "But she's only thirteen! Chinese law allows children to be adopted until fourteen."

"The papers are wrong," Little Pretty said decisively. "She is fourteen."

A few months later, Little Pretty Chen was arrested for embezzling 750,000 *yuan* (about 90,000 dollars at the time) from foreign adoption donations. She received brief Public Enemy fame in hopes of deterring others who might be considering venturing over to the dark side. She was sentenced to fifteen years in prison; she was in for ten. "Her husband didn't even divorce her," ZZ said wistfully. "He must love her very much."

Baimei lost her chance to have a family, but she kept working. She decided she wanted to become a makeup artist because "beauty makes people happy." Half the Sky sent her to beauty school, where, in time, she became a cosmetician.

> *I remember the first time I served the customer I felt very nervous, but now I feel much better. Sisters in the beauty shop told me that I have made great progress, which makes me very happy. But don't worry, I won't be conceited on these praises. I will continue working hard and I won't let you down.*

If I ever had my doubts about the futility of trying to reach older, institution-damaged children, our first Big Sister wiped them out. She taught me never to walk away. Not from *any* child. Since I met Baimei in 2002, Half the Sky has helped more than 6,500 teens attend universities and vocational schools; study languages, computer science, music, art, sports, and dance; and begin to dream. It's never too late to start . . . and our dreams set us free.

> *My dream now is to study in Beijing with Mao Geping, China's famous makeup artist. If I can improve my skills, I will work for the TV crew. Sometimes I feel I am an unfortunate girl, but still, I always have my dreams.*

Chapter 9

A Burnt Tongue Becomes
Shy of Soup

烫了舌头怕喝汤

Summer 2002

Old Yang told us that Guangdong Province was a definite go. So that summer, while our volunteers and trainers established a new Half the Sky center in Shanghai, I made an exploratory trip to Guangdong with a young adoptive mother whose daughter was from Yangdong, a small Guangdong town (population only four hundred thousand!) and one of our now-confirmed orphanage build sites for the fall. Her family had committed to sponsor the new center. We were welcomed with enthusiasm.

Another family had agreed to sponsor a new center in Huazhou, the second Guangdong site. Both of these orphanages had elicited dozens of e-mails from concerned adoptive parents whose children had come to them with an array of typical post-institutionalization problems—emotional distance or shutdown, food hoarding, nightmares, developmental delays, and, as with our Anya, just plain anger.

Eager to launch their own Half the Sky programs, the Huazhou and Yangdong directors attended our training in Shanghai. After three years of trying, we were finally going to Guangdong!

Organizing each build and training is a lot like preparing to shoot a movie. We recruit a crew of volunteers. We order developmental toys and books and supplies from multiple sources. We organize hotels and transportation. We interview and hire local teachers and nannies and mentors and supervisors. We measure and photograph rooms and prebuild bookcases and climbing equipment and puppet theaters and plenty more. Our two-site Guangdong build was scheduled for October 2002. When I arrived back in Beijing in September to make final preparations and sign agreements, everything was lined up and ready to go. Fortunately, Terri had agreed to lead the builds. Things were looking up.

ZZ MET ME at the Beijing airport. Bleary-eyed from what was becoming my regular twelve-hour commute, I was ready for an uneventful evening. That wasn't to be.

"We must go to the Social Workers Association. They wait for us," ZZ said. Not good. We made our way to the association offices as fast as Beijing traffic would allow. When we walked into the reception room, the gentlemen of China Social Workers Association were already lined up in the formal configuration. Our only booster at the association, Old Yang, had been demoted to the end of the row. He studied a blank piece of paper with great interest.

President Red Sun Liu motioned us to sit. Even as my tea glass was being filled, Red Sun Liu started in on ZZ. Spittle flew. ZZ calmly wrote until the boss finished his harangue. She looked up at me—her face impassive.

"He says this: 'When we brought the American mother to Yangdong for the visit, it was not the right way,'" she began.

"In June?"

"In June. 'The proper procedure is to advise the association, who then advise the ministry, who then issue written documentation for approval.' But I don't do it right," ZZ said. "So he think this is why Guangdong Province now reject Half the Sky to start programs."

"No programs in Guangdong?"

"Proper procedures have not been followed."

Not again.

"President Red Sun Liu suggests he may help," ZZ continued. "Half the Sky should submit a proposal explaining the goal, the activities, the items to buy, the training needs and salary and other expenses, together with how much Half the Sky will be obligated to pay. He personally brings proposal to Guangdong capital city, Guangzhou, for approval. He suggests the way of cooperation is we wire the money to him, then he wire to the institution, let them do the work."

ZZ went on, her expression unchanging, her voice lowered only slightly. "I explained the purpose of Half the Sky is not simply to donate money but to share love and training. When I listen to him, it seems that for the volunteers to come in October is difficult, but not impossible. Anyway, there is no point for him to go to Guangzhou. That part is nonsense."

I stood up.

"Thank you, President Red Sun Liu, for the information and advice. We will certainly think this over carefully and make a decision about this difficult situation as soon as possible."

We smiled and shook hands all around. I murmured to ZZ, "Tell Old Yang to meet us in the morning. We're going to Guangzhou."

That night, while ZZ pleaded with Madame Miao and Old Yang to join us on an emergency trip to Guangzhou, I wrote letters to the highest-ranking officials among our very small arsenal of influential friends, begging for their help. The sponsors' money was in the bank; the volunteers' tickets had been bought. We couldn't lose Guangdong.

Guangzhou, Guangdong Province

By the time ZZ, Madame Miao, Old Yang, and I checked into a hotel in Guangzhou, the letters had been translated and hand-delivered, and phone calls had been made. Over the next twelve hours, we shuttled back and forth between hotel rooms and government offices, pleading with every government official who'd talk with us. ZZ and Madame Miao worked the phones. Old Yang complained about how hard his job was.

"If you would quit reporting in and asking for approval at every step, it wouldn't be so hard," Madame Miao said.

"You don't understand," he grunted from behind his hand.

"I understand your boss is not helping," she said.

"If you let him control the funds, he will be responsible if there are any problems like this," said Old Yang.

Then all three were talking at once, outshouting one another in the Chinese style of friendly debate. Everybody talks; nobody listens. No hard feelings.

Finally Old Yang got back on the phone, muttered into it a bit, then looked up with a shrug.

"Mrs. Wu, the division chief, says that the two sites are not suitable," he said.

So much for our dear friend "Call me Jane."

"Tell Jane we would be happy if her boss selected different sites," I said.

"Her boss is out of the country," Old Yang said.

"Then who's making these decisions?!"

"Mrs. Wu says that Guangdong Province isn't ready."

"But is it all up to *Jane*?" I asked.

And the shouting started all over again. Miao chimed in with news about a letter from the Ministry of Civil Affairs (*our ministry!*) to all institutions forbidding the establishment of any new foreign programs. Then there was something about American spies, but Miao said that none of it applied to Half the Sky anyway because we were already approved partners with the government. ZZ called Jane. Finally, perhaps just to make us go away, Jane said we couldn't have an answer until after the National Holiday.

That weeklong holiday was two weeks away. Our volunteers were scheduled to fly in just two weeks after that. Unlike yours truly, most Americans don't blithely hop on airplanes bound for China at a moment's notice. Plans had been made—and they were set in concrete.

"SO DO THEY love us or hate us, Norman? I'm confused—and it's not just jet lag," I said.

In town on one of his monthly adoption trips, Norman invited ZZ and me for *yexiao*—Guangzhou's *famous* midnight breakfast. Breakfast at midnight?—why not? My body clock was permanently out of whack by now anyway.

"The problem has nothing to do with Half the Sky," he said. "It is quite serious."

Then he rattled off a whole new story in Chinese. ZZ grunted a few times but didn't translate. Not fit for foreign consumption, I gathered. I didn't press until we'd waved goodbye to Norman and our cab door was safely shut.

"So?"

"A short time ago, an American couple received a referral for a baby in the southern area. When the couple traveled to meet their new daughter, they were given a different child."

"It happens," I said. "Maybe the first baby didn't survive?"

"This couple was upset and suspicious. They took their complaint to the U.S. Consulate in Guangzhou. The Consulate start investigation. The Chinese government then also start investigation."

"So the orphanages are closed for the investigation?"

"For now, the whole province is closed to adoption," ZZ said.

"And closed to Half the Sky," I said.

"That is not clear. After the holiday we will know. It may be that we can come to Guangdong but to different part of the province."

"Ugh. Okay. I'll have to tell the volunteers. And the sponsors. And the board."

"In such situation, it is best don't say too much," ZZ said.

"But they think they're coming back to help their own children's orphanages," I said.

"It may be, at the time of adoption, that the parents of the first baby came to the orphanage to get her," ZZ said.

"You mean the birth parents changed their minds?"

"Maybe they never abandon her after all."

"She was kidnapped?"

"It is not certain. Maybe stolen by family member. Maybe sold to be a wife or servant. And maybe there have been other problems in the area. We cannot know. It is better not to worry the volunteer families."

I sat silent in a dark cab somewhere in China. Completely lost. *What was I doing in this place? This China. Kidnapped. Stolen. Sold. Thrown away. Those little girls . . . their dear faces.*

"ZZ? Norman always takes adopting families to the Temple of Six Banyans to have their new daughters blessed. Do you think anybody would be awake there now?"

"No."

"Can we try?"

"Certainly."

At the Temple of Six Banyans, we woke the night watchman, a wizened monk with not many teeth. He listened to ZZ, then turned and walked away. ZZ took my arm, and we followed him inside.

We found a small, carved-stone Guanyin in a rear chamber of the temple. I knelt on the cushion before the goddess.

"Hello again," I whispered. "Okay, now we really do need some help."

Before I boarded the plane for California, ZZ and I stopped in the jade market. We purchased a little dark-green jade Guanyin. I wore it always after that. One year I returned to the Temple of the Six Banyans and had my little Guanyin blessed by the monks. It was probably overkill, but, as ZZ told me once, "If heaven drops a date, be sure to have your mouth open."

ONCE HOME, I cautiously informed the board, sponsors, and volunteers that there was a problem in Guangdong Province but that we were still trying. ZZ toiled through the holiday. She brought wine and fruit to the homes of important people. The officials wouldn't say yes or no. It was all too familiar.

"Is there any other way you can move them, ZZ?" I fretted on the phone, twisting the little Guanyin on my neck.

"We say, 'Can you help the grass grow by tugging on it?'" ZZ said.

"I don't get it."

"You say, 'Even when you pull him to the well, you can't make the horse drink the water.'"

By the end of the holiday, there was still no definitive news. I couldn't keep people in the dark any longer. I first contacted the sponsors and board. Then I wrote to the volunteers and told them that Guangdong was off.

I do understand the importance of this trip to many of you who have children from Yangdong and Huazhou, and I'm so sorry to have to make this decision. It may be small comfort, but I have an alternative proposal to make:

Many of us have nonrefundable plane tickets and other paid-for reservations. What if we travel as planned, meet in Guangzhou as planned, and then Half the Sky takes you to work

on another new site in another new province? Think of it as a
travel adventure! You may not know where you're going until
you're already there, but I guarantee that you'll be helping kids
who need our programs as much as the kids in Guangdong. . . .

They were crushed. Almost every person on the crew had volunteered for the Guangdong build specifically so that they could visit and help the orphanages that had once housed their daughters. Not everybody was in Big Picture mode. Still, every one of them stood by us, as did one of the two sponsoring families.

The very next day, ZZ called to tell me that we had permission to work in Chenzhou, Hunan Province, a struggling orphanage that we'd visited early in the year. Perched at the juncture of three provinces—Hunan, Jiangxi, and Guangdong—the town of Chenzhou received children left behind by migrant workers on their way to find work in the far south. Somehow, despite the poverty and sorry conditions, the little orphanage community of 135 girl-children (as usual in those days, not a single boy) did have a special sort of charm. I was delighted that Chenzhou would be our fallback, but now we had a new problem. Our policy was to have two years' worth of funding committed before opening a new center. We never wanted to open a program that we might have to close for lack of funds. And we didn't have enough to support work at this new, larger center.

I made an emergency plea to our supporters and explained our dilemma. There were children who needed us; we had the opportunity to help, but we couldn't do it without them. Once again, our Half the Sky family rallied in a big way. They donated more than enough for us to set up shop in Chenzhou.

But now the board of directors was on edge. Terri wrote to our newest member, her friend Evelyn. She confided that, while she'd still lead the build, my fumbling in Guangdong and my public plea for funding for the new site was frustrating and embarrassing. I'd upset our volunteers and the Guangdong sponsors and probably all our supporters. I was endangering everything we'd built. Evelyn accidentally sent her commiserating reply to all fourteen of us on the board. Apart from Dick, who was always ready to rush to my defense, the other members were silent. Maybe they thought Terri was right.

Chenzhou, Hunan

The old fortune-teller wore a red Nike baseball cap and at least three layers of sweaters, all with tattered sleeves. I watched her practiced fingers sort through the plastic-covered flat sticks of bamboo. She was calm. As if she saw foreigners in her tiny cement-block apartment every day. The Chenzhou orphanage director, a nervous little man with hair like unmowed grass, had told me about her the morning we arrived, and I'd begged to go see her at once.

"She is the *most famous* fortune-teller in China," said the Chenzhou director, as he lit one cigarette off another. "High-ranking officials come from Beijing to see her."

"Really? Fantastic." I fanned the smoke from my face.

"Of course, everyone knows Chenzhou is magical because it is the *famous* Eighteenth Blessed Land—the place that gave birth to nine immortals and two Buddhas!"

The fortune-teller laid a handful of bamboo sticks on a red board painted with Chinese characters. Then she placed a cardboard circle over them and asked me to rotate it. Then again. At her direction, I selected some sticks. Then more.

"It is *Yijing Bagua* . . . most powerful method," ZZ said as we watched the fortune-teller sort and re-sort with endless patience.

"She was a doctor," said her gentle, bucktoothed husband. "I was a teacher. But in 1957, I was branded a rightist. The students turned against me. I could not teach. She could not work. So she began to study *Yijing*."

The fortune-teller smiled at me.

"*Chun*. It is good," she said, "but you must be patient. *Chun* means difficulty at the beginning. Rain and thunder. Don't be intimidated by the storm. We must remain firmly centered within. Perseverance furthers. Persevere, but not too much. Know when to retreat. Small perseverance brings good fortune."

It poured every day we worked in Chenzhou. ZZ told me that the Chinese believe rain is lucky. The paint wouldn't dry, but we kept on painting. Small perseverance.

LIKE MANY ORPHAN homes in smaller towns, the Chenzhou welfare institution began as a home for old folks. In large cities, before *Jiefang* (China's 1949 "Liberation"), orphanages were more often run by foreign missionaries and continued to be fairly well maintained post-revolution. This was not such a place.

Our volunteer crew arrived at a dumpy little compound that was brimful of extremely *senior* senior citizens, assorted ragamuffins, and over one hundred scrawny but adorable baby girls. The place was falling apart and far too small for its swelling population. The crew fell in love, and I think it was mutual. By the end of the week, we were one big family.

Ancient balding ladies grinned from their dark little rooms each morning as we traipsed by in the rain. "Rain is good luck," they trilled daily.

One toothless old gent routinely shouted instructions to the crew as they passed; he must have been a factory boss once upon a time. Nobody, not even the locals, understood a word he said.

• • •

DESPITE THE CONSTANT downpour, each afternoon the eight Chenzhou "big girls," eight to thirteen years old or so, splashed their way over to what would become our new preschool to practice their English on the volunteers.

"Hello! How are you today? My name is—" And they'd fall apart with giggles. The director would come and whisk the girls away whenever he caught them with the foreigners, but the girls would dart back the moment he was gone.

They helped paint and sometimes brought babies and toddlers for the volunteer crew to cuddle. Even though those big girls couldn't understand a word said to them, they just couldn't seem to get enough of the room full of foreign mommies—and vice versa.

Shibi, a blind girl of about nine, had never been to school, and although the new preschool was designed for younger children, she adored it. It was her first chance to experience a school of any sort. She spent her days with the volunteers, making little Play-Doh figurines and textured collages from feathers and shells.

Yaya, a quiet child, maybe thirteen, latched onto one volunteer family, a single mom and her young daughter. She spent every free moment helping the mom paint walls and assemble toys or teaching songs to the daughter. The child of itinerant scavengers who, we were told, left their daughter behind as they made their way south to Guangdong, Yaya seemed to remember what family felt like. Hungry for love, she savored each moment with the foreigners.

A few months later, when she was in our Big Sisters program and doing well, our staff in Chenzhou told us that Yaya's parents returned to claim her. The orphanage never heard from her again.

•　•　•

WHEN THE TRAINING and the rooms were finished, the little ones were decked out in dress-up clothes and given new dollies and treats. We all packed into the courtyard for a farewell celebration. After speeches and the usual entertainments, the big girls stood before us in two somber little rows. They began to sing softly.

The song was "Mama Hao." All Chinese children learn it. It's meant to be a song for China, the Motherland. But at the moment, *Mama* was all that mattered. We watched in aching silence as tears ran down the children's faces and stung at our own eyes.

Only Mama is the best in the world.
When a child has a Mama, she feels treasured.
In Mama's arms is endless happiness.
A child with no Mama is no more than a weed.
With no Mama's arms
Where can happiness lie?

We'd spiffed up the rooms, brought books and art supplies, and trained new mentors for the older children. But all of us—caregivers and directors and officials and volunteers—knew that there was little we could do to fix what hurt those big little girls the most.

There'd been no need to worry about the volunteer crew we'd spirited off to the "wrong orphanage." Once they met the children of Chenzhou, none were sorry that the winds of fate (and maybe the breath of Guanyin) had blown us there. It was the best possible outcome. It seemed to me that no obstacle was insurmountable when so many hearts were in the right place.

Of course, my theory would be tested.

Chapter 10

Push One Pumpkin Under Water, Another Pops Up

按下葫芦浮起瓢

Spring 2003

Subject: Bugs and Battles

Dear Hunan Volunteers,

    I imagine you've been following the news in the last couple of days. It seems that we're truly on the brink of war in Iraq and also that there's a dastardly form of pneumonia raging through parts of Southeast and East Asia and possibly spreading beyond.

    I've posted the latest World Health Organization info below. Thus far, in Mainland China, only the southern Guangdong region has been affected and even that may not be the same disease. However, since no one seems to be able to get a handle on this outbreak, we want to pay close attention.

    You will, of course, make your own decision about whether or not this is a wise time to travel and/or whether or not this is a wise time to go to that part of the world. I just want to tell you, as you consider the options over the coming days, that if you choose to cancel, you won't be letting anyone down. We will still go to those sites and we will hire people to do the work.

Please make the decision that's right for you and your family without further worry.

I leave for China in the morning. Wishing you peace and good health!

Jenny

None among our volunteers opted to stay home. We had a full crew: twelve adults and twelve children. Our builds by now were hugely popular among adoptive families—we had to turn many away. Only our official build leaders, Terri and Daniel, declined to join us. Now that their friend Evelyn had joined the board, those three were turning into my very own Greek e-mail chorus. After the Guangdong fiasco and our last-minute trip to Chenzhou, special as it was, they were flabbergasted to see me pushing ahead with yet another build in less than perfect circumstances. As Half the Sky's leader, the chorus sang in unison, I was "stubborn and hopeless."

Our bus lurched along the congested road to Shaoyang, a backwater town in Hunan Province. There was a major slowdown on the new expressway. Too big to scoot in and out of emergency lanes and embankments as cars did, we trailed obediently behind the line of big blue trucks loaded with goods of every sort: massive steel cable coils and fragrant onions and bamboo scaffolding and not-so-fragrant pigs.

Maya (now seven and already a veteran crew member) turned away in revulsion when she saw the pile of live pigs in the next lane, squashed in wire crates, their rumps and snouts pressed against each other and the frames of their confines.

"I hate this place, this China!" she said, closing her eyes tight. "I'm a pig too."

"Sweetie, you don't hate China," I said. "You just feel bad for the pigs. Me too."

"Year of the Pig," Dick said. "One of my two favorite years. Think we should give up spareribs?"

"Spareribs is pig?"

He nodded. Maya squirmed off his lap.

"I'm gonna play with my friends."

"Careful!" I reached but couldn't grab her as she scooted toward the back of the bus. Anya, who'd just turned five, was sprawled across my chest, sound asleep.

"You can worry all you want about that flu bug," Dick said, twisting to watch his daughter go. "What scares me is the traffic in this country. And no seat belts. Maya, sit down!"

Carol Kemble, an enthusiastic regular volunteer on our builds, was Terri's designated substitute crew leader. It was our good fortune. Her ebullience and energy (and her curly white-blond hair!) were magnets for little children; they'd never seen anyone like her. She loved them right back. And her delight was infectious. Few on the crew failed to respond to Carol's warmth. Many remained pals even years later, when she became our chief fundraiser.

Now her two daughters, Tai and Ava, were giggling in the rear of the bus with a little flock of new friends, all born in China. Maya put the pigs out of mind and joined the party.

I used the break to catch up on unread e-mails from home. Most of the notes were from supporters wishing they could be with us and cheering us on. I saved the board mail for last.

"Do you think I'm *patently inadequate*?" I asked Dick.

"It never occurred to me," he said. "Why?"

"That's what Terri says."

"Well, I love you anyway."

It all was unfortunate and confusing and felt contrary to the spirit of Half the Sky and our undeniable progress and impact. But it was not going to slow us down.

•   •   •

"WELCOME TO SHAOYANG!"

Mrs. Gu, an owlish Civil Affairs representative, climbed into our bus outside the city gate. Two men in dark glasses, windbreakers, and matching crew cuts followed her and hunkered into the front seats. They didn't smile. They didn't say a word. Mrs. Gu didn't introduce them, but we were used to that.

Mrs. Gu barked an order at all of us and then perched on the jump seat beside the driver, waiting for something.

"She says everyone must close their window shades," said ZZ.

"What for?" I asked.

"She just says that. Close the shades."

"But could she tell us why?"

The two crew-cut men stood up and turned toward the volunteers.

"Carol, please tell the volunteers to close their window shades," I said.

Ever agreeable, Carol (bless her heart for that attitude!) raised her eyebrows with an anticipatory grin. *Here comes a China moment.* Our builds were full of them.

"Okay . . . sure."

She moved along the aisle. The passengers pulled their shades. They looked at one another and at Carol, puzzled. She shrugged.

"I'm not sure we should tell the rest to the families," ZZ said to me.

"What rest?"

She whispered what Mrs. Gu had just passed along.

"Okay, folks," I said, standing in the aisle, holding on to a seat with one hand. "There's been a change of plans. Here's the story—as much as I think I understand.

"You all know that the U.S. has just invaded Iraq. Well, it seems Shaoyang City is composed of nine counties. Two of them are Muslim, with a total population of over one million. There are one hundred thousand young Muslim men between eighteen and thirty-five. They all want to go to Iraq to fight the Americans.

"Yesterday, twenty of their representatives marched on the city government building and demanded passports and permission to go. The permission was denied. So now they've gone to the highest Muslim cleric in China, and he is petitioning Beijing on their behalf. They are very determined and very angry.

"We are the only foreigners in town. And, of course, the only Americans.

"The city government is concerned about our safety. They want to keep our presence quiet—hence the window shades. And instead of the hotel, we're going to be honored guests at a special government compound."

"All right!" said one of the volunteers. "This should be great."

"It should be interesting," said Dick.

Now, as our blindfolded bus bumped along, Mrs. Gu recited the history of Shaoyang. ZZ didn't bother to translate for the volunteers. Most were dozing now—nothing to look at—and anyway she knew they'd inevitably hear the same spiel later on.

"What's Shaoyang famous for, Mrs. Gu?" I asked to be polite.

"Shaoyang? Shaoyang is *most famous* for garbage," Mrs. Gu said.

"Really?"

"There's no place for it. It just piles up."

I peeked through the window shades. She was right.

Besides the usual piles of dirt, trenches, dust, and little kids peeing on the side of the road like in every small rural town in China, there was garbage everywhere—plastic bags and food containers and plastic soda bottles and dented cooking-oil tins. Most places I'd been, outside of the big cities, had a litter problem. But this place was a giant landfill.

"China wasn't like this before Liberation," ZZ said, taking a peek and clucking at the mess. "The whole country was spotless. Now everyone pays attention to other things."

Just ahead, in the rubble of the road, lay a strange, lumpy black bundle. Traffic was weaving around it, and as the bus got closer, I saw the bundle move. A hand and arm, black with filth, reached up. An old woman stepped into the street, approached the bundle . . . and into the extended hand dropped a piece of bread.

The bus moved on. I turned quickly to make sure the children hadn't seen. That hand belonged to a human being, a beggar, lying in the dirt. I closed my eyes. "I hate this place," I whispered to no one.

I think, just for a second, I meant the whole country, not just Shaoyang. I knew I sounded just like my seven-year-old.

ON THE FAR side of town, we stopped in front of a lushly land-scaped gated compound. Six military guards stood out front, as-sault rifles poised, but thankfully not aimed, in both hands. While our bus waited for clearance, I inspected the troops. Scrawny country boys, really—their uniforms too big, their trousers bunched around slender waists. Still, I figured they knew how to use those guns. We were probably safe from any angry Muslim uprising. They saluted when we passed through the gates.

Inside, the compound looked like all other government retreat-hotels in China. Places where officials went for cadre school and conferences and could drink *baijiu,* smoke, and play mahjong into the wee hours. I'd stayed in quite a few such places run by provin-cial Civil Affairs Bureaus. They were okay. The beds were always like rocks, though.

We all climbed from the bus, eager to shake off the road and settle in to our new digs. Carol slung her backpack onto her shoulder with a jaunty grin, grabbed a huge duffel bag with her remaining hand, and—kids and volunteers trailing—followed the hotel manager to the residence unit to dole out our assigned rooms.

The place must have been used as some sort of detention center in the past, judging by the room the girls and I had been assigned. There were mold splotches and, I'm pretty sure, bloodstains on the walls. The carpets were slightly damp with something that may have backed up from a drain somewhere. I feared that our room might be the best of the bunch.

Within five minutes, Carol appeared in the doorway, distraught. This was not our ever-jolly girl. "I can't do this!" she wailed. "I have my kids with me. How can I let them get under those covers? And I can't bring myself to walk into the bathroom. This is the most horrific place I've ever been!"

We looked at our four little daughters now merrily jumping off the wooden ledge of a bed onto the squishy rug. For them it was all an adventure. I put my arm around Carol's shoulder.

"Let's see how your crew is doing," I suggested. "Maybe we can scout out some better rooms."

We walked down the gloomy hallway, lit only by the occasional blue fluorescent.

"Carol, we can do this," I said.

"Okay . . . I know," she said. She took a breath, dug deep. "Sure we can. Just another China moment, right?"

And she flashed that electric grin. I gave her a hug. "Thank you."

We gathered the volunteers and led them toward the dining hall. They were amazingly upbeat about the accommodations. They'd never been on a build before. They were delighted with everything. They were exactly where they wanted to be, doing what they wanted to do.

Mrs. Gu anxiously watched us approach.

"Will the rooms be all right?"

"Oh yes, Mrs. Gu," I said. "They're just fine. Our volunteer families are extremely grateful for your concern."

Dear Board,

  We've arrived and had our first day of work here at Shaoyang. Teacher and nanny training have both begun. The city officials and orphanage staff are wonderful. However, there is a war-related situation here that I want to share with you. . . .

A response appeared immediately. It was 2:00 A.M. in California.

Jenny,

  You must shut this trip down and get people on a plane to Shanghai. . . . I had no idea there was an enormous Muslim population and I don't know how it wasn't taken into account, but now that you know there is tremendous hostility, it's time for everyone to leave. The leadership needed here is to get people to a relatively SAFE location, NOW.
                                        Terri

At dinnertime—army food, served cafeteria-style—I talked to the volunteers. They had no interest in leaving. They felt completely safe and welcome. They were determined to finish the work they came to do.

COMPARED TO OUR government accommodations, Shaoyang orphanage was a sanctuary. Up a quiet lane on the outskirts of town, the orphanage grounds were divided by a tranquil canal edged with weeping willows. The children's building was spartan but clean. The halls were silent. The children's eyes were dull, incurious, but by now we knew we could find the sparkle.

Carol led her volunteers to a room stacked with painting and cleaning supplies, cartons of toys, and piles of bikes and books. She outlined the work schedule. First clear out the rooms; then clean them thoroughly. (She may have been feeling particularly hygienic at the moment. We weren't always so meticulous.)

The volunteers tied bandannas around their heads, donned gloves, and went to work. They spent their first morning scrubbing down walls and swabbing floors. Their children helped on occasion but spent most of their time turning the reception room into a fort/art gallery—watched over by the ever-patient Feng *Ayi*, official crew babysitter.

ZZ and the orphanage staff did the necessary shopping. I wasn't allowed to leave the grounds. It was just as well: I was to devote great chunks of each day on the computer in my own little war room (a corner of the toy-storage room), following WHO and CDC reports, adoption travel updates, embassy alerts, and all the news I could find on the web—and of course, responding to multiple e-mails from my irate board trio.

Carol is confident that we can finish work here in Shaoyang by Friday. It seems they all want to continue on to Baling for the second build. I'll know for certain tomorrow. We have told the volunteers that they will not be letting anyone down if they choose to go home early. We have workers on standby to do the job. No one wants to leave.

We've called Baling to inquire about the Muslim population in that area. There is no large Muslim population, angry or otherwise. Everyone is very eager for us to come.

Jenny,

Read this article. Staying put is really not an option here. I find it completely irresponsible to throw caution to the wind, under these conditions.

MYSTERY DISEASE MAY HAVE SPREAD ON PLANE

HONG KONG (AP)—*Adding to fears that a deadly flu-like illness is being spread by air travelers, Hong Kong officials said Tuesday nine tourists apparently came down with the deadly disease after another passenger infected them on a flight to Beijing. . . .*

Terri

Each night after work, as we were being bused back, curtains drawn, to the compound, I read the latest SARS story aloud to the volunteers.

"Even more reason to stay off airplanes and enjoy lovely Shaoyang," said one.

"If we could see it," said another.

We were captives. No sightseeing. No shopping. No distractions.

"I don't think I saw you all afternoon," I said to Dick on the second day.

He confessed that his inner photographer had gotten the better of him. He couldn't just paint orphanage walls in limbo with a whole unexplored Chinese landscape at his back. Having just begun working on *Mei Mei, Little Sister,* his book of photo portraits of orphaned girls and the twist of fate that had affected all of our lives, he just couldn't resist a quick look at the town. So he'd set out quietly with his camera.

Not far from the orphanage gate, he'd encountered a very pregnant young woman sitting on the broken pavement. Her head hung down; a roughly drawn cardboard sign was at her feet. A young schoolboy stopped and read the sign to Dick in broken English. "Please give money so I don't must abandon my child when it born."

Dick gave what he had and took a photo. A man appeared from the gathering crowd and began to rant. The young woman raised her head and screamed back. The boy said, "The man said she fake. Rags stuffing belly. The woman said no fake. She tells you go away. You making her trouble."

The man angrily grabbed the woman's arm and yanked her to her feet, sending her stumbling and shuffling away. Suddenly feeling worse than helpless, Dick backed off and turned in the opposite direction, wondering what he had done . . . what new grief he might have caused.

"Honey, certain people on our board would have your head if they heard that sorry tale," I said.

"It gets worse. After a while, I felt somebody behind me—like a shadow, but far off. I was being tailed."

"Oh no."

"I turn around. It's a guy in a sharkskin suit and wraparound sunglasses. He's wobbling along on a little Vespa. When I stop, he stops; he puts a foot down to steady himself and then he starts yelling at me."

"Oh geez."

"I just don't think this guy is an angry Muslim. Is it about the pregnant girl? Maybe he's trying to sell me something? But whatever he's selling, I don't want it. So I say, '*Buyao!* Don't want!' I walk off. But the guy keeps following me and shouting."

I groaned. I could see it. My over-six-foot tawny-haired husband with only one Chinese word to his name, arguing on the streets of a town with a hundred thousand young men who were itching for battle.

"Then the guy pulls out a cell phone, makes a call, and tries to give it to me. He pushes it at me. He won't go away. Finally I take it. I hear a girl trying to speak English. I can't understand a word, but I can guess. I've stayed in enough two-star hotels in China."

"The guy's a pimp," I said.

"That's what I figure. One of those midnight wakeup calls. 'Mister like a massage?' Now I explode, start yelling back at the guy in English. He drives off."

"Thank God," I said.

"Five minutes later, he's back—"

"Uh-oh."

"—in a van this time. He flags me down. The back door slides open. There's this girl inside. She doesn't look like a hooker. She says she's from the orphanage, that they've been trying to tell me I shouldn't be out walking. It's too dangerous."

"Oh honey. What did you do?"

"I got in the van. At the orphanage gate, the director and staff came out to greet me like I'd just crossed a minefield. I asked ZZ to apologize. Over and over again. She told me they'd been worried sick about me. I felt rotten. I'll stay at the orphanage tomorrow."

"Good plan."

Good morning, Board,

The work in Shaoyang is finished. This morning is for cleanup and then, in the afternoon, the volunteers will give a party for the children. The training will also be completed today. Tomorrow (Saturday) the volunteers and trainers will bus to our second build in Baling.

Yesterday I spoke to the U.S. Embassy in Beijing as they have consular jurisdiction over Hunan Province. They have had no reports of problems and there are no warnings or alerts for the province. They faxed me the current warnings about SARS and possible terrorism in China. Both were a week old and the information about SARS was far from current. We are staying up to the minute via various Internet sites—in particular, WHO and CDC.

We are purchasing high-grade N95 mouth masks for the volunteers in the event that any of them wish to use them in the airport or on flights. Currently the barriers are reported effective. We are avoiding crowded, closed areas.

Leaving no stone unturned, everyone on the crew has also received a bottle of special Chinese vinegar cure and a box of Chinese herb preventative.

Each day I update the volunteers and remind them that we do not need them to travel to Baling and that we cannot be responsible for their protection. They all know that they'll be required to sign an additional liability waiver before they can travel to Baling and all are completely willing—in the words of one, "without hesitation."

I won't respond to Terri and Daniel's remarks about my blind determination, poor leadership, or the mess that the organization is in. Perhaps we can discuss these issues at a less busy time.

Jenny

THE ROOMS WERE painted. The shelves were lined with books and toys. The nannies and teachers were trained. We all—volunteers, children, and orphanage staff, all wearing Half the Sky T-shirts—assembled in front of the children's building for our traditional group photo.

As the merry crowd made its way back inside to the new preschool for music and treats and balloons and, best of all, to explore the dress-up box, I detoured one last time into the war room,

now just empty toy boxes and me. I sat on the floor and opened
my laptop.

I no longer looked forward to booting up. There was always
something waiting for me. On the other side of the ocean, fingertips must have been poised above keyboards, ready to pounce.

>*BOARD, YOU NEED TO RESPOND TO THIS SITUATION! We*
>*can override Jenny's decision to stay.*
>
>*Jenny, read those advisories and evacuate all nonessential*
>*personnel!!!*
>
>>*Evelyn*

I swallowed hard. I leaned against a wall, closed my eyes, and
listened to the distant merriment. Over the music, I could hear
children laughing.

I opened my eyes and typed.

>*Dear Evelyn,*
>
>*If you read my e-mails, you will know that I have not made a*
>*decision to stay. There is nothing to override. What I have said*
>*repeatedly is that I cannot force people to leave China. Neither*
>*can this board. I can and will continue to give them the WHO,*
>*CDC, and embassy materials I've mentioned. I will also tell*
>*them about your concerns again.*
>
>>*Jenny*

The Greek chorus was hovering in cyberspace. The words flew
back at me:

>*Jenny:*
>
>*Now you can tell the volunteers that one Board Member has*
>*resigned over this.*

My fellow Board Members: It is with great anger and sadness that I must resign from the Board. We all admire entrepreneurs who can bring their vision to fruition. But the same tenacity and drive that turns an entrepreneur's dream into reality more often than not brings a company down. I am afraid Half the Sky is in such jeopardy. . . . Half the Sky is still run by one person. I am not a rubber stamp.

Evelyn

Terri, my once-dear pal and cofounder, leaped back into the fray.

AM I TALKING TO THE WALLS HERE??!!!
I'll state it once more, as I told you our pediatrician said at the beginning of the week: GET YOUR PEOPLE OUT OF THERE!
Terri

I PACKED UP my laptop and walked down the now-bright halls toward the music. I stopped in the doorway of the Infant Nurture Center and watched the newly trained nannies curled on cushioned floor mats, cuddling babies unfamiliar with real human contact.

One eager nanny tried to encourage her small charge to use the pull-up bar at the mirrored wall. The baby tried but couldn't grip; she plopped back on the floor. Both nanny and baby laughed out loud. For the child, it was maybe her first laugh ever. Then the mirror caught her eye. She reached out to touch the little smiling face in it. Her own. She stared. Captivated.

I leaned against the doorjamb. The nanny gave her love so easily. She'd already reached this baby girl. One day the baby would leave, and her nanny's heart would break . . . but then be healed by opening to another little stranger. I felt my chest tighten with an unwieldy mix of joy and sadness. Tears began to fall for no good reason and for every good reason. *I'll give you something to cry about.* Right then, I was the happiest and saddest person on earth. I wiped my tears away and followed the party music.

INSIDE THE NEW preschool, all was joyful chaos. Little girls with feather boas and sunglasses madly pedaling shiny trikes. A volunteer teaching a blind child to make music on the electronic keyboard. A toddler in the arms of her teacher, trying to figure out how to put little plastic shoes on the baby doll. In the reading corner, ZZ was settled on the sofa, reading a story to an enthralled trio of little girls.

"ZZ, do you have that Sharpie?" I asked.

I turned toward a freshly painted wall and climbed on a lavender chair. I wrote, as I always did, BUILT WITH LOVE AND HOPE.

Then ZZ wrote the message in Chinese. Finally, as they always did, the volunteers and new teachers and new nannies gathered and passed the Sharpie around, signing the wall with their own names and hometowns and happy wishes for the children.

Chapter 11

One Who Is Drowning Will Not Be Troubled by a Little Rain

曾溺水者何惧风雨

"Look folks," I said as our bus left Shaoyang, "I know you're tired of hearing about this, but if you insist on continuing with us to Baling, will you please write a note to our board and tell them why?"

No problem!

Hi Board from ZZ,

Thanks for your concerns for all of us working in China's institutions at this critical moment. . . . Fortunately, there is not a single SARS case in Hunan. People enjoy their weekend. Children are flying kites in the square with a beautiful warm weather. We can certainly feel that spring has arrived! We all wish and doing our best to make families returning home safe!

. . . I made the decision to stay because I believe so strongly in the work of the Foundation. This is a personal decision that I made completely on my own. . . .

Jackie (Nanny Trainer)

. . . The greater risk is probably the plane ride home (including the in-China flight, where the seats are very close

together). Whether we leave now, or next week, we still have to get on the planes to fly home. In fact, the risk of flying could be less by next week, as people become more aware of what is going on. . . .

Although I am not an epidemiologist but rather an anesthesiologist, I do not perceive there is any increased risk (or at the most minimal) of staying another week. All of life is a risk. We took a risk in embarking on this journey in the first place, and I do not think the risk has changed all that much.
Cynthia (Volunteer)

Every one of our crew wrote to the board. There was no response. And so we forged on.

A CARTON OF 3M N95 mouth masks, the most protective and last available in China (ZZ had managed to convince a hospital in Shanghai to share) was waiting for us when our bus stopped in Changsha, the provincial capital of Hunan, for lunch. After a celebratory banquet, ZZ distributed the masks and the Hunan Provincial Civil Affairs team passed out new bottles of best local brand flu-killing vinegar to all. Our volunteers vowed to wear their masks in crowded places and to drink their vinegar religiously (except for the kids, who absolutely refused the vinegar but adored the masks). Then we reboarded the bus, now bound for Baling.

In truth, I would have returned to Baling alone if I'd had to. I knew some little girls were waiting for us there—in the dark.

Jingli

Ba Jingli, female, was born on January 3, 1996; found at the gate of Baling City Social Welfare Institution on May 3, 1996, with a bottle, two suits of clothing, and a bag of diapers. She had a round face and black hair, with misshapen lower limbs. She was reported to Baling City Security Bureau on that day. The police couldn't find her parents and relatives, so placed her in Baling City Institution. We hope she can conquer the serious illness and have a peaceful, happy, and lucky life.

I first saw Jingli in the fall of 2002 when I visited her orphanage as a prospective program site. I always tried to scout potential sites well in advance of selection—in part to assess the need, but equally, to scope out the director and staff. It hadn't taken long to learn that the success of our programs would depend on those people.

Based on the obvious criteria, Baling was not a place I would have chosen. The Baling orphanage director reminded me of the worst kind of Hollywood agent, right down to the black shirts, quirky bright neckties, and slicked-back hair. But it wasn't the garb—Director "Slick" stood too close and was a butt-grabber, and he charged adoptive parents five hundred dollars for a homemade DVD about his orphanage. And maybe it was just me, but I had a hunch the man was a baby-broker.

I'd seen the signs before. Row after row of beautiful, healthy baby girls, all less than a year old—perfect for adoption. No older kids. No special needs. He walked me through the baby rooms as if they were auto showrooms. Only after he'd hurried off to take a call from the mayor (making sure we knew who was calling), and left us with a young office administrator, did we find the rest of the Baling story.

"*Nihao,*" I said to the office administrator. "What's your name?"

"Luo."

"ZZ, please ask Ms. Luo where the older children are. There must be some. Explain that Half the Sky would like to build a beautiful preschool here in Baling for the older children. But we must meet them first."

I'm sure that ZZ put it better, for Ms. Luo made a phone call and motioned for us to follow her to the yard behind the children's building.

It was a low, small concrete building. Out front, in the pounded dirt courtyard, a couple of women were providing rehabilitation massage for two small boys with cerebral palsy. The women seemed to be expecting us and beamed happily as we watched them set upon their tasks with vigor, bending and stretching spastic little limbs.

I edged toward the worn wooden doorway. Miss Luo tried to stop me. Too late. I was inside.

The only light came from one small window. The walls were dank and dirty. The air musty. The little children were lined up against the wall on small chairs or benches. There were maybe twenty of them, from about four to ten years old. All had special needs. They weren't tied. They *knew* to just sit. This was how they spent their days. All day, every day.

I can see the image even now. A still photograph. Near darkness, eyes looking at me. . . . A little girl whose face was burned off. A toddler who looked healthy, alert, and confused, as if she'd been dropped at the wrong bus stop. Another child, limp, almost translucent—she seemed to have no bones.

And especially, I see Jingli. Perhaps six or seven, she sat obediently alone on her plastic mini-chair, against the wall, away from the other kids. Her hair had been cropped not too long before. I see scabs on her scalp where the clippers had missed and bruises on her thin arms. Her lower legs are twisted. Her feet are askew; they look useless. But she sits composed, her little hands folded in her lap. And she has a fire in her eyes that glows even in that horror we came to call the Root Cellar.

I promised those girls I'd come back. I thought of Jingli every day until the day we returned.

•   •   •

A SHOWMAN ALL the way, Director Slick provided us a police escort, complete with sirens, the entire two and a half hour drive from Changsha to Baling. Leave it to him to also provide an adorable, chipper English-speaking greeter to deliver the requisite bus monologue on an ear-piercing loudspeaker:

"Hello, Half the Sky! Welcome! Baling lies in northeast Hunan Province on the eastern shore of Dongting Lake, the second-largest freshwater lake in all of China. Dongting Lake is on the boundary between Hunan and Hubei Province to the north. Do you know, the word 'Hunan' means 'south of lake,' 'Hubei' means 'north of lake'?

"Baling is *famous* for many things, including Baling Tower, which is three stories of wood constructed with not a single nail! Inside, you may read a tribute to Baling written in Song dynasty by *famous* poet Fan Zhongyan.

"Speaking of poets, in 278 BC, when his country's capital was captured in war, Qu Yuan, the father of Chinese poetry, walked into Dongting Lake carrying a huge rock and drowned himself!"

We checked into a posh lakeside resort, clearly a spot for high-ranking Communist Party officials to take their ease. After our Shaoyang experience, the volunteers were ecstatic. Within minutes, the gleaming lobby was emptied of people and luggage, and hot showers were flowing.

"LISTEN TO THIS: 'Today the Rolling Stones announced that their first-ever concerts in China—in Hong Kong, Shanghai, and Beijing—are cancelled because of the SARS epidemic.'"

"You mean *Keith Richards* is scared?" Dick said, toweling Anya dry postbath. I showed him the article.

"Okay, *now* I'm scared."

"Ha."

"Think about it. All the stuff that guy has done to his body, and he's scared to come to China?"

DIRECTOR SLICK HAD a dream, and he couldn't wait to share it with the foreigners. He was building a hotel!

Not just any hotel—this would be a place for foreign adoptive families to come and stay. They could bring their children back to visit their hometown. And best of all, it was right on the grounds of the orphanage.

He'd hinted at this little project earlier, when I first visited. But now he had something to show. So, before we were allowed to take the volunteers to visit the children (the very idea bored him), we all had to go and see Slick's dream hotel.

The orphanage was at the end of a narrow lane. As our bus squeezed toward it, Slick's fantasy was unmistakable. Still under construction, it towered over everything else in the neighborhood. Yet there had been no sign of it on my last visit, only a few months earlier.

We followed Slick into the lobby, floorless and still coated with plaster dust. He showed off his massive cut-crystal chandelier. We didn't know how to react. So he took us into the one already-working elevator. The doors opened onto an elegantly finished floor of rooms. We walked around.

"Wow!" I said.

"You like it?" asked Slick.

"How many floors like this will your hotel have?"

"Eleven!" he said.

"Fantastic," I said. All I could see was Jingli . . . her eyes, shining in darkness. "May we use two of them? One for the preschool and one for the infant center? And the preschoolers can have their dormitory on the preschool floor? This one is nice."

I imagined the Root Cellar kids riding trikes down these gleaming hallways.

"But—" Slick said. "I see. Oh . . ."

"I think he can't say why not," said ZZ.

"I'll bet he used adoption money to build this place," Dick muttered. "What can he say?" Already my husband didn't care for Slick. Now he started addressing Slick as Director Motherfucker. I prayed that Slick was as ignorant of English as it appeared.

Slick made a phone call. Carol and I wandered around making plans for our newest preschool, every room with a private bath!

ZZ found us happily plotting in one of the suites. "The director says that Half the Sky is welcome to use these two floors for programs," she reported. "He says that was always his intention, and this is why he wants to show you first thing. He hopes you like it."

"Hooray! Please tell him we *do* like it. Very much."

BY THE SECOND day Slick ignored us completely, except at banquet time. So I took Dick to see the Root Cellar. He saw Jingli. Those eyes.

Quietly, we took pictures, just as we always did before we began our programs. There was no way we would let these children be left out. The place was so dark that we took the kids outside one by one to photograph them. We asked the lone *ayi* to carry the ones who couldn't walk.

Jingli shuffled out the door, her bum legs going every which way. *All my byself.* She allowed Dick to place her against the crumbly wall, watching his every move—lest anyone doubt, the child was fully in control of the situation. With absolute presence and calm, she permitted him to take her picture. Her eyes were blazing. Who was this girl?

•   •   •

BY THE FOURTH day Slick had pretty much vanished. I think we were a disappointment. No money to be made; no junkets to America to angle for. We seemed to have the posh lakeside resort all to ourselves. Just as well, because the littlest crew members were getting stir-crazy. The lobby rang with squeals and giggles. Hide-and-seekers darted every which way, ever-smiling *ayi*s in pursuit.

As we were about to board the bus bound for the orphanage that day, Anya tried a fancy slip-slide-dive-under-the-flower-display-table maneuver, then shrieked with sudden pain.

"It broke! It broke!"

She screamed. Then louder still. We ran.

"I heard it broke! My leg . . . my leg!!!"

She couldn't stand. And then we wouldn't let her try. This was not a five-year-old tantrum. We needed a doctor.

After forever, the only ambulance in town pulled up outside. It was a little converted van of some sort. And it was grimy—must have been used for something else during the off-hours. The attendants lifted out an old army stretcher and placed Anya, still howling in fear and pain and unanchored to anything except my hand, on the floor of the van.

I crawled in after her. "But Madam . . . !" they said. Then Dick squeezed in too. We held on to Anya and each other and anything else we could find. ZZ followed in a cab.

The van had a siren, but still it bumbled through traffic. Every jolt was agony. We soothed Anya down to a whimper and moan.

"There's gonna be sick people in that hospital," Dick said. "Maybe even one with SARS."

"We have no choice."

"I'm sorry, Mommy!" wailed Anya.

"Shh, baby," we both said. "It's okay. Don't worry. It's all going to be okay."

Give me her pain . . . let me feel the hurt so she doesn't. . . .

When he was six, my son, Aaron, raced his bike into the street from between parked cars smack into an oncoming car. A single mom, sick with guilt and fear, I rode in the back of the ambulance clutching his hand, looking at the broken femur protruding from my baby's leg. "I'm sorry, Mommy!" he cried. "I rode between the parked cars . . . you told me never—"

It's okay, baby; don't worry. Give me my baby's pain.

I was every parent who ever watched her child suffer. There was no doubt that Anya Xinmei—who once bit and pinched and spit at me—was my precious little girl now and for all time. I don't remember when that changed.

THE CORRIDORS OF Baling People's Hospital No. 1 were even worse than Dick had imagined. The benches and any available wall space were thick with waiting patients. Most were in bad shape. Some were coughing. Some were gasping. Some were hacking and spitting. Some were doing all that and more.

When they saw the little girl arrive on a stretcher attached to two pasty-faced foreigners, all patients who were the least bit mobile crowded in for a look. We tried to herd them back, clear a path, keep the hackers away from our whimpering baby. Anya started wailing again.

The attendants set her down on the floor.

"No way!" I said.

Now Dick was frantic. "I'm getting her out of here!" He bent to lift Anya himself. She reached for him—she screamed.

ZZ barked at the attendants. "Pick the stretcher up and turn around!"

Somehow they did, and she marched the whole little traumatized bunch of us back outside. We found a quiet spot on the lawn and told the attendants to set the stretcher down.

"Tell the doctor to come to us," ZZ said. And there we waited.

In about forty-five minutes, they returned. We must go inside for x-rays. But we could go through the back tunnel entrance.

The tunnel was . . . well, a tunnel. The x-ray room was straight out of Stephen King.

Against one wall leaned a massive split log. The face of it was covered in dried (but not too long ago) blood. The door was closed, securing us inside.

Bloody handprints, these deep brown with age, ran the full length of the door.

Dick and I did our best to block Anya's view, squeezing her hands and holding our breath as the big machine did its thing, probably showering us all with rays.

Anya's leg was fractured. We went back through the tunnel to wait outside for the chief of orthopedic surgery to finish up his current OR duties. When he was available, the chief built Anya's cast himself—the old-fashioned plaster-of-Paris way, smoothing each layer with practiced alabaster hands.

"May we take a picture together?" he asked. Of course, we did.

Peering out the taxi window at the hospital as we drove off, I swore I could hear Terri: *"AM I TALKING TO THE WALLS HERE??!!!"*

WE RETURNED TO Slick's dream hotel for the final party. Everybody on the crew signed Anya's cast.

Then, calmly as we could—as if such things happened every day at the orphanage in Baling—we led and carried the Root Cellar kids to see their new preschool. They all looked pretty shell-shocked under wizard hats and wedding veils and tiaras as they clutched their juice and cookies. The volunteers turned on the music. They blew up balloons and gently batted them through the air. One by one, the balloons began to bounce back and, before too long, there were even some smiles. It was just a start, but it felt great to see the beginning of a new life for Jingli and her sisters.

And then, during the night, while we enjoyed a deep, exhausted sleep on our luxurious beds, Terri resigned from the board.

To the Board,

I can't bring myself to continue on with the foundation after seeing the absence of procedure on the part of the executive director toward this board. . . . I completely believe in the mission of Half the Sky. I have had a wonderful time helping this organization become a reality. There have been many remarkable adventures and I will certainly miss them.

This has been a very difficult decision to make, but I have no regrets here and I'd like to keep it that way, so please accept this as my letter of resignation.

Respectfully, Terri

A couple of weeks later, Daniel also resigned in solidarity. I couldn't pretend that I would miss the angry e-mails, but still I felt sad to see them go. They'd stood by Half the Sky even when it was clear they didn't trust my ways. Now I'd gone too far, and so lost two good friends. We've never spoken since.

Always before, when criticism stung me, when I wasn't good enough in somebody's eyes, I would assume that my critics must be right. Then I would find a way to make my own exit—to slip away from my failures, just as I'd slipped away from my childhood.

This time, I wasn't about to leave. In fact, I was even more de-termined to push on. This wasn't just about me. We were making quiet thunder now, and while maybe the heavens didn't hear us yet, more and more people on earth sure did. I could feel the ex-citement of discovery and new resolve whenever Half the Sky came to a new place. I could see lives turning around. I couldn't walk away from what felt so right for those little girls. It was the first time in my life that I stood up to bullies.

I confess, however, that when I reported back to what remained of our board, I never told them about Anya's broken leg and People's Hospital No. 1 of Baling.

Wait for Roast Duck to Fly into Mouth, Wait a Long Time

守株待兔

Berkeley, California
Christmas 2003

On the eve of the lunar New Year, northern Chinese families gather together and make vegetable *jiaozi*. The delicious boiled dumplings are then famously enjoyed on the first day of the New Year. They taste best (in my opinion) with black vinegar, hot sauce, and cold beer. Since ZZ—now beloved Zhang *Ayi* (Auntie Zhang) to our girls—was visiting us for the Christmas holidays, we figured why wait? We had an early *jiaozi* party. ZZ was the master chef and teacher—a role she's since played many times for little girls and their earnest, clumsy *laowai* parents. Every guest had a go at rolling at least a few dumplings.

Besides our grown kids (who adored their young siblings) and their families, our local staff, and friends, we invited our newly evolved board (only Dana, Carolyn, and Dick remained from the original) to join us. It was one of those count-your-blessings days. We had it all. But in my heart, I couldn't wait to get back to China.

Now the guests were gone; ZZ and the rest of our big family slept. Despite our efforts well into the wee hours, the house was still covered in flour. Floors, counters, even crannies we might not discover for months. Dick and I fried up some potstickers and enjoyed the rare quiet.

"It was fun," I said. "Do you know, that's the first party we've had in five years?"

"Wonder why," Dick said, not really wondering.

"Half the Sky, right? All I do is work twenty-four/seven. I miss other kids' birthday parties, and I even missed Anya's preschool Back to School Night. Our house is full of people on telephones, and you make more post office runs than Santa Claus."

"Did I say anything?"

"No. I can do my own guilt."

"Another potsticker?"

"Uh-uh. *Chibaole*—I'm stuffed. So what if we moved to China? All of us."

"I guess it was only a matter of time," he said.

I poked at the last few potstickers with my chopsticks. Skewered one. Looked up at my soul mate. I'm pretty sure he was smiling just a bit.

"You've said yourself that a cameraman can live anywhere. It would be a fantastic experience for the girls. And we'd all be together. We always wanted our life together to be an adventure."

"We've succeeded," he said.

"It'd just be for a year. But think what we could accomplish!"

"You don't have to *carpe diem* me, Jenny. Lay it out."

I drizzled a little vinegar lake around the lone potsticker. Added a spoonful of *lajiao,* hot chili. Too much *lajiao,* just the way I like it. I poked the potsticker into the hot spot.

Well, who do you think you are, Miss Priss? (That would be my mother talking.)

So what makes you think you can make a dent in the mess in somebody else's country? (That would be me.)

Patently inadequate. (The Greek chorus stirs in its grave.)

Okay. Well. Despite SARS, an angry board, reluctant government officials, and a constant scramble for funds, nobody could deny we were making progress. Real progress. By the end of 2003, just three years after the first Half the Sky preschool opened, we were operating our programs in thirteen orphanages and had three hundred–plus employees—most of them teachers and nannies. In an effort to spread the word that we had at least a partial solution to offer, we'd just held our first semipublic event in Hefei: Half the Sky's Fifth Anniversary Conference on Nurture and Education in China's State-Run Orphanages. Incredibly, a hundred orphanage directors and welfare officials accepted our invitation. Even CBS News and CNN showed up, and their stories had aired just before the holidays.

"Well," I said, "I just can't help thinking that if we had a real office in Beijing, instead of ZZ's apartment—and if we could be working right alongside our government partners and not just when I'm in town—we'd be more credible; we could find more supporters and reach more kids."

"How many are we reaching now? I can't keep up," he said.

"Maybe two thousand."

"And how many are you after?"

"I dunno. They say there's maybe a million."

The sun was just coming up. Dick poured some coffee. The kitchen was new. We'd spent the past couple of years living in a construction zone so we could have it. Outside, in pinkish light, through big storefront-type windows, we could see our garden: fruit trees, vegetables, old roses, herbs, a tree we'd hauled up from Southern California. The irrigation system Dick had made by hand, turning all his fingertips blue with plumber's gunk. Twenty-seven valves. Raised beds—one of them full of baby asparagus that would produce for fifty years.

"It would just be for a year," I said.

"Did you ever dream Half the Sky could reach so many kids?"

"Never."

"Why can't two thousand be enough?"

Dick swears he would never have said that. I *thought* he did. Probably I said it to myself.

I dissected the last potsticker with chopsticks. Herded all the filling bits into their own little circle on my plate.

"I don't know."

Dick put his arms around me.

"Well, the good news is—we'll see a lot more of you in China," he said.

ZZ MADE HER *famous* congee (rice porridge, or *zhou* in Chinese) for breakfast. My girls could live happily on congee alone. They and their nephew, our seven-year-old grandson, Colin, were blissful in their jammies, slurping it up with little porcelain spoons.

"Zhang *Ayi*," I said to ZZ, "remember the congee we had in Beihai?"

"Mmm . . . the one with the worms? Delicious."

Three spoons stopped midair. Three children froze.

"Tell us, Mommy," Maya said.

"Okay, so, it was lunchtime in Beihai—"

"In China?" asked Anya.

"Yep. Beihai's sort of a funky beach town in the south, in Guangxi Province. Before lunch, we strolled through a great big seafood market in front of the restaurant so the Beihai orphanage director could pick out our food. Giant octopi and squid were smooshed against glass boxes that were too small to hold them. And there were like *acres* of fish that were straight out of Dr. Seuss. And there was a hundred-year-old tortoise who looked like he'd rather be dead than in that place."

"Did you eat the tortoise?" Anya asked.

"Nope," I said. "I don't think he was for sale. But to tell you the truth, none of it looked like lunch to me. Anyway, so then we went inside.

"From the dining room window, we could see Vietnam, which was very cool. After a while they brought us a bowl of congee. That was fine with me. I was tired of banquets and fancy food. Then the Beihai director explained what we were eating. What did he say, ZZ?"

ZZ smiled. "He is so proud. He says, 'Beihai *shachangchong* is our *most famous* dish! These ones are wild from Lower Dragon Pool Village—very rare!' And then your mom ask me what we are eating."

"Zhang *Ayi* said, 'You don't want to know.' So I glared at her until she told me."

"Okay, so I tell her, '*Shachangchong* is sand worm or maggot,'" said ZZ.

"Yuck!!!" said the three children.

ZZ said, "First you turn them inside out to get rid of the sand. Then you dry and fry with oil and salt. Yummy!"

"Zhang *Ayi*!" screeched Anya.

"Did you eat them, Mommy?" Maya asked.

"Well, I wanted to be polite . . ."

"Eeeyewwwww," shrieked the chorus.

I threw up my hands in disappointment. "But then my phone rang. I had to take the call."

Actually, I was *going* to taste the things; I swear I was. What I didn't tell the kids was that it was Carol on the phone. Since Terri's departure, she was our official building director. And she was crying.

It was late summer, a few months after the SARS scare. While ZZ and I scouted future sites in Guangxi Province, I'd sent Carol back to Baling with our building assistant, Mr. Ji, to do a check on the progress of our new programs in Slick's would-be hotel. It was her first site visit alone. Now she was sobbing into her cell phone. The words tumbled out.

"The toys are gone. The shelves are empty! The children are no-where—maybe back in the Root Cellar! Director Slick made me . . . pose for a photo with him in our beautiful rooms. He must have sold all the toys. He put his hand on my butt!"

"Where are you now?"

"I locked myself in the bathroom! What do I do?"

"You wash your face. You walk out the door. You ask Mr. Ji to help you hail a cab. Carol, we'll fix this, I promise. The children will have their school. One little battle in a very big war. Don't say goodbye to Slick. Pretend he's just not there. Invisible."

"I'm really sorry."

"You are not the one who needs to apologize, kiddo. Go on. Wash and walk. I can stay with you on the phone if you want."

"No. I can do this."

"That's right. You can do it. Just walk."

I SHRUGGED AT my grossed-out little audience. "So when I came back to the lunch table, the congee had been cleared away. Worms and all."

The children collapsed with relief.

"When we live in China, I'm not eating worms," Maya said. "No way."

"Who says we're going to live in China?" I asked.

ZZ changed the subject. "Who wants to help me clear the table?"

•   •   •

FIVE MONTHS LATER, my family moved to Beijing. We left our beautiful old farmhouse in the Berkeley hills in the care of neighbors who were doing their own major remodel and needed temporary quarters. Our U.S. staff of three moved out of my basement and into a little office by the Berkeley railroad tracks.

When I told the new board our plan, no one flinched. They were even enthusiastic. It felt beyond great to have the board at my back again. "We're like a dot-com startup," one said. "Moving out of the basement at last."

Dick had a shooting job that would tie him up until late August. I had three new children's centers to build in May. We'd rendezvous in Beijing when our work was done. I pulled the girls out of school, set up e-mail accounts for them so they could stay connected with their U.S. friends, and we took off for our new lives, each of us clutching just a backpack full of precious possessions.

Part Two

Guoji Youren
(Foreign Friend)
国际友人

Dear Lady,

I am so happy to write to you. I am Ailin. I am 12 years old. I live in Hefei Children's Home. I study in a middle. I am the girl who you help, though I don't know your name. I'm sorry to that. But this time, if you say your name, I think I can remember it and remember it forever, for I have the honor to take part in Half the Sky.

Your love moved me deeply. I will try my best to make what you did worthy. I represent all the children to say very much Thank You.

Wish you happy forever.

Ailin

Chapter 13

Why Scratch an Itch from Outside the Boot?

为何隔靴搔痒?

Beijing

Summer 2004

We rented an apartment in Beijing, half a block from the North Korean Embassy, across the street from barracks that housed the Chinese military embassy guards. Every morning at 5:00 A.M. the troops sang patriotic tunes. They dried cabbage and socks on the roof. Whenever we ran across to Jenny Lou's, the expat grocery, to buy crusty German bread, or strolled over to Yabaolu, the Russian market, past the fur-coat stores and the pink-haired ladies, to buy mittens or frying pans, we dodged little platoons of mechanical soldiers, rigid and brisk, marching to keep watch over the embassies or marching back to the barracks to cabbage and noodles.

Our apartment compound was full of families, both local Chinese and longtime expats. Our girls had instant friends. With our neighbors' help we found an *ayi* to look after our home and lives. We loved Gao *Ayi* at once. She was openhearted, playful, and semiefficient—a round-faced beauty who was way too smart to be anybody's servant—she'd just had some bad breaks in life. Gao hated to cook and wasn't much good at cleaning, but she was wild about our girls, so we were content.

We might well have begun living the cliché of privileged expats in Asia at that point, but I couldn't wait to get back to work. Before we'd fully unpacked, ZZ, my girls, and I raced off to Jiangxi Province to meet up with a new crew of volunteers.

Nanchang, Jiangxi Province

The provincial party secretary of Jiangxi had the worst case of tobacco teeth I'd seen in China, yet his dining room was palatial; the banquet was sumptuous—replete with shark's fin soup and other fare made from costly endangered creatures. I watched my girls, just a few years away from institutional slop, wolfing the delicacies (no worms!) down. I poked around the edges. I resolved to become a vegetarian.

We had come to open centers in the provincial capital, Nanchang, and two other cities in southern China's Jiangxi Province. The year before, the Nanchang orphanage director—a tall, effervescent lady who wore bright-blue contact lenses and teetered on the highest possible high heels with the pointiest possible canoe-shaped toes—attended our conference in Hefei and, tottering on her pointy toes, she'd bubbled: "You must come to my institution! I also have studied early childhood education! You are doing just what I am trying to do in Nanchang! But the children here in Hefei are much smarter! Much stronger! This can only be Half the Sky programs! So exciting I am almost dizzy!"

"Maybe you should change your shoes," ZZ said.

The Jiangxi provincial government was exceptionally accommodating as well. This was a first. We'd never seen such cooperation! It turned out that an intern in our Berkeley office, a girl who rarely said a word and never smiled, was the party secretary's daughter.

A fly landed on the party secretary's forehead, just above his left eye. It sat there. He didn't flick it off. He thanked us for taking care of his daughter. (Who knew?) He offered us whatever we needed in his province.

"I suggest you try the shark's fin soup," ZZ said to me. "It's delicious. Very rare and expensive. A sign of friendship and respect."

"I think there's a boycott in the United States," I said.

"In China, we need friends," ZZ said. "We are always honest, of course. But we don't always speak. Without friends, we can do nothing."

I ate it.

ONCE THE WORK in Nanchang was under way, ZZ and I prepared to leave the build for a couple of days.

Led by Wen, Janice, and Carol, our volunteer crews and trainers no longer needed ZZ and me hovering over them as they accomplished the Half the Sky miracle. Janice and Wen always left the new nannies and teachers inspired and ready to begin their work transforming children's lives. Carol, now our full-time building director, was a superb crew leader; she certainly didn't need our help mixing paint or assembling trikes. Maya and Anya were now seasoned crew hands—happy to reconnect with old friends while slapping a bit of paint here and there, mostly on themselves. Feng *Ayi* and her helpers entertained the little girls when they tired of painting the walls and each other. Once we'd squared away any necessary issues—"We really need to knock down this wall"; "We can't afford to buy uniforms for the whole institution"; "We need to convert your office into a reading room"; "Sorry, we just don't purchase motor vehicles"—ZZ and I were free to go off and explore potential new sites. But first, we had to make a quick trip to Shanghai.

A brief stop, with a not-so-brief backstory.

I hadn't been able to get little Jingli of the Root Cellar out of my mind. After much probing, we'd learned that she had spina bifida and that, once upon a time, she'd had surgery to "detether" her spine, but it had been botched and now scar tissue was causing further nerve damage, ruining any hope she'd ever be continent. Even as we continued our work to improve conditions at her orphanage in Baling, I knew we had to get Jingli out of there . . . and out of China.

I contacted everyone I knew who might help find a place back home where she could be treated. I figured that once we got her out of the country, we'd find a way to get her a family. Others had done the same for children with complex medical needs that might be better treated outside China. But, after many inquiries, it became clear that her case wasn't unique enough to appeal to a U.S. hospital. Spina bifida is common—it was Jingli who was not.

Medical care was outside Half the Sky's purview. I was dead set against succumbing to the "mission drift" that I'd been warned weakened many nonprofits. We just couldn't do it all. Certainly, there was need everywhere you looked; it was hard to refuse to help. Adoptive parents asked. Orphanage directors asked. But time and time again, we forced ourselves to say, "Sorry, Half the Sky can't send a donation to your child's orphanage to buy diapers. Sorry, Half the Sky can't pay for a surgery or an ambulance or a study trip to America. We develop and operate programs to provide family-like nurture and enrichment for orphaned children. We don't give money; we give programs. That is *all* we do."

Back in that hotel room after my first visit to the orphanage in Shijiazhuang in 1999—that night I fell apart—I'd decided that helping a few children here and there just wasn't good enough when thousands were hurting. I was out to change a whole broken child welfare system. I was going to move a bureaucratic mountain aside and write a whole new story for forgotten children. Quietly.

And despite the doubters (there still were plenty), I didn't think I was fooling myself. It would never be easy; it was China after all.

But we were absolutely making progress. In our small way, we were beginning to fill a pressing need. Still, we were alone in our work, and that mountain was looming large. "Stay on mission" was my mantra. So I figured I'd have to find somebody else to help Jingli.

By now, the international adoption exodus from China was nearing its peak—more than fourteen thousand children in 2005 (95 percent of them little girls). There were now a number of parent-led charities offering orphanages donations of cash for goods, foster care, and medical services. I contacted an American group that was said to be funding orphan surgeries in-country. They told me yes, they could pay for surgery for Jingli; then, after several weeks, but with no explanation, they told me no, they could not. Then, finally, they told me that they could cover 3,000 *yuan* (365 dollars in those days)—a tenth of the actual cost. Perhaps the orphanage director would cover the rest?

China had already begun to teach me patience, but only when I saw no other solution. We had to help Jingli *now* if we could. We arranged for a new surgery in Shanghai; Dick and I would pay for it ourselves.

Shanghai

Jingli and an *ayi* from Baling arrived at Shanghai Children's Medical Center early that morning. They were having a hard time being seen, let alone treated. Funded by the American medical NGO Project Hope, the hospital was state-of-the-art. It offered the best pediatric care in the country. As long as you could pay.

We found Jingli and the *ayi* slumped against a wall in a waiting room full of screaming babies and exhausted parents. Jingli was wan and bone-thin. Her eyes took up half her face. This place was more terrifying than the Root Cellar.

"*Ayi* says Jingli got very excited about going to Shanghai and did not sleep the whole night on the train," ZZ explained. "In the car, she just looked out of the window all the time and got carsick due to all these excitements. Now they been standing here all morning."

"How do we get her out of here?"

"We must show your foreign face," ZZ said.

In less than twenty minutes, Jingli was in a hospital bed in a semiprivate room. I loved and hated having that kind of power. I'd never seen reverse racism before. China, *Zhongguo*, literally means Middle Country—the center of the world. But the pecking order—at least at that time and in my experience—told another story. Pale-faced Americans, for whatever reason, seemed to out-rank everyone, especially the Chinese. It seemed to me China had the world's biggest inferiority/superiority complex.

Anyway, right then I was thinking of Jingli. I took full advan-tage of my unearned status when the chief of neurosurgery en-tered the room wearing scrubs.

"Thank you for agreeing to see us, Doctor," I said. "We are so sorry to interrupt your busy schedule, but we were told that it might be difficult for this little girl to receive the detethering sur-gery she's supposed to have today. We scheduled it for her some weeks ago, but now there's some problem about too many on the waiting list. So I wondered if it's because the hospital believes that the child is an orphan and doesn't have family to pay?"

I'd learned that even the best surgeons in China make their paltry living through fees for surgeries. They can't afford to take charity cases. The doctor was flustered.

I jumped in again. "I just wanted to assure you, Doctor, that Jingli is my child, and my husband and I will pay for her surgery. Today!"

"She is your daughter?"

I smiled at Jingli, limp on the clean white hospital bed. I ruffled her greasy hair. She looked like she'd just dropped in from another planet.

"Yes. Well, she's one of my many daughters."

I took her pale hand and gave it a squeeze. "*Keyi*—it's okay," I whispered.

ZZ explained to the doctor about Half the Sky and about how we consider ourselves all one big family.

"Jenny has many thousands of children," she said. "She really means it."

She told the whole story. Her eyes teared up. (They always did.) The good doctor looked a little weepy too.

"Of course, we will take the very best care of your daughter, Mrs. Jenny," said the chief of neurosurgery. That was all we needed to hear. I held Jingli's hand until the doctor left the room.

Then we headed for the airport. Now I steeled myself to shake things up in a whole new province, Henan. By a sad twist of fate, it had more troubles than most.

Somewhere in Henan Province

Mr. Hu, director of the Henan Province welfare department, cracked the car window. "Do you mind if I smoke?"

I'd almost recovered from another lunch banquet cigarette headache. But I really wanted Mr. Hu to like me. I said it was okay.

The driver sped south along the expressway from the capital, Zhengzhou, in the north to Xinyang in the south. The landscape of Henan was flat, featureless, any signs of life concealed behind a dull-green ribbon of highway flora. There were no other cars. No other people. Except . . . every kilometer or so, a not-quite-life-size concrete police sentinel standing at rigid attention, keeping an eye on things. These little fellows looked oddly foreign—too much nose.

"This doesn't feel like China," I said. "Aren't there any people in Henan?"

"Ninety-eight million," said Mr. Hu. "More than any other province. They just can't afford the tolls."

Mr. Hu told us that Henan is where Chinese civilization began.

"In south of Henan, in Zhoukou, there is the tomb of Fuxi, who they say is the forefather of us all. It was the capital of the Three Emperors: Sky, Earth, Man. And Laozi, the founding father of Taoism, was born there too."

"What a proud heritage!"

"Yes. Now it is famous only for disasters: floods, famine, poverty, and AIDS."

There was my opening. My heart sped. I bit my tongue. I'd been trying to figure out a way to work in this province since 2002, when I'd first read Elisabeth Rosenthal's stories in the *New York Times:*

ZHENGZHOU (*NEW YORK TIMES*)—AIDS is creating an explosion of destitute orphans here in China's rural heartland and is driving large numbers of families into such dire poverty that they can no longer afford to feed or clothe, much less educate, their children. . . .

Wang Beibei, 10, a star pupil from Suixian, a county in northern Henan, was expelled from third grade last year after school officials discovered that her father had died of AIDS.

"They were afraid to let me in, and my friends stopped playing with me," she said. . . . In June, Beibei's mother died of AIDS. School is out of the question. There is no one to work the family's land, and she and her brother struggle just to look out for each other. "My brother cooks for me, and we eat noodles. We have no money for eggs or meat."

I knew we had to find a way to try to help. Sure, these weren't abandoned baby girls, but orphans were orphans. The hurt was the same. When I asked ZZ to make some calls to our few friends in high places, we quickly learned that the subject was closed. Off-limits. There were no AIDS orphans in Henan. In fact, according to the authorities, there was no AIDS in China.

So we asked permission to set up Half the Sky centers in "ordinary" orphanages in Henan Province—for just normal, everyday, abandoned kids. Old Yang told us that was impossible. He said the province was closed to foreigners.

Guanyin, my favorite goddess, must have been listening. A few months later, and with no explanation, Old Yang was again replaced by dear Mr. Shi, our first and best friend at the Social Workers Association. Mr. Shi somehow wangled permission for us to visit a small group of Henan orphanages and possibly open centers. He said he must particularly recommend Luoyang.

"But why Luoyang?" I asked ZZ. I knew they were getting plenty of foreign aid. Even the Gates Foundation was helping Luoyang.

"It's China," she said.

Despite the fact that Luoyang was the only place in the entire province that wasn't struggling to keep its doors open and tummies full, there was no avoiding it—the Luoyang director had both *guanxi* and *chutzpah*. So we would choose Luoyang, to make the officials happy, and then one other place—one deep in the heart of AIDS country. Then, somehow without succumbing to mission drift, we would find a way to reach the children who didn't exist.

I knew by now that the next step must be to make friends—local friends, preferably in high places. Mr. Shi introduced us to the director of the provincial welfare department, Mr. Hu. Our first Henan friend turned out to be our best. He was a gem. "Many Chinese even think all Henan people are thieves, criminals," Mr. Hu was saying.

ZZ whispered, "Yes, they do."

"Instead, we are victims of misfortune. Constant misfortune."

He lit a new cigarette from the butt of one still burning. I rolled my eyes at ZZ. Grabbed my throat.

"Mr. Hu, you shouldn't smoke so much," ZZ said.

"It's not good for me, I know. But it's part of my wife's free benefits. She works at a cigarette factory. I try to stop. Not successful."

He turned to look at me. "Does the smoke bother you?"

"Oh no." My eyes stung and my head throbbed, but I really wanted to keep my only friend in Henan happy.

Now, as we neared Xinyang, the landscape turned greener, the heat more intense. I could see mountains rising in the west. "Xinyang is a tea-growing area," said Mr. Hu. "Xinyang *Maojian* green tea—one of the top ten China *famous* teas."

"It is the place I was sent during Cultural Revolution," ZZ said quietly, looking out the window.

"Xinyang is where you came?" I took her hand. I knew that was the time she'd had to leave behind her baby boy when he was only six months old and, like other young intellectuals of her generation, go "down to the countryside" to learn about the roots of communism from the farmers. She'd slept on a dirt *kang* (communal bed) and moved from house to house, working in rice paddies with leeches clinging to her legs. The farmers thought she was useless. The only food was a watery porridge sprinkled with a few grains of millet. She didn't complain; her hosts ate the same.

Her breasts ached until the milk dried, and even after, she dreamed each night about her tiny son, her first and only child. She was away from him for almost a year. She was still haunted by that . . . abandoning her baby to come to this place.

TO ME, XINYANG looked like yet another smallish Chinese city struggling to come into the twenty-first century. To my foreign eyes, these cities all looked the same: a patchwork of single-story, tired-looking shops selling cell phones and dresses, a couple of McDonald's and KFC look-alikes, assorted tiny cafés with grimy windows, a block where merchants sold only giant coils of wire, another block of only used electrical parts, another of funeral wreaths, the occasional shiny new department store (still under construction), and a China Unicom tower. The government buildings, each on its own block, were always the most impressive.

"It was completely different then," ZZ said.

A woman bicycled past, wearing a visor and a filmy "butterfly" scarf floating over her shoulders to shelter her pale skin from the sun. A small boy, perched on the crossbar, peered from between her arms. A young family cruised by on a motor scooter, baba and mama sharing the single seat, baby in the basket.

We turned off the main drag onto a rough road leading to the orphanage on the sleepy outskirts of town. These were more like village streets, the few houses and shops more ramshackle. I tried to imagine a young ZZ arriving here thirty-five years before.

"Not even like this," ZZ said, reading my mind. "It was much more rural. Primitive. They had nothing."

AT THE ORPHANAGE gate, we were greeted by Director Feng, a cheerful, open-faced farm boy who clearly relished his job. As we walked through the sad little rooms of his orphanage, he was kind to the children and truly eager to help them. With no one to train his team in how to do anything like running a children's home, Director Feng had put his ample good energy and rural know-how into designing gadgets to make the children's lives more bearable. He'd cooked up hoists for kids with cerebral palsy and gizmos to correctly angle bottles into baby mouths.

Still, and as usual, the children were pretty much on their own. Nobody was holding or playing or talking with them. Every child I saw that bright summer day languished in bed. Except one.

She lived in a beat-up old baby stroller that wasn't going anywhere. She was about three years old. She had lost both her feet. Both of them cut off. Her name was Baobao.

I lifted her from the stroller and sat her on my lap. She allowed me to hold her close. Not tense or fearful—just unaccustomed to any sort of intimacy. She gazed at me with a sort of foggy curiosity.

Baobao

She'd been abandoned at the gate of Xinyang Central Hospital. The police report says that she was severely burned; both lower legs had turned black. She was dying. The doctors kept her alive, but her burns were so bad that one-third of each lower leg had to be amputated. Baobao spent eight months in the hospital, including the Spring Festival (the Chinese New Year holiday), when everybody who *could* went home. The nurses took turns looking after her. When I met her, she had just arrived at the Xinyang orphanage. Like so many of the children, the rest of Baobao's story was a blank.

"You are a very brave girl, Baobao," I told her. "We're coming back to help you."

I peered up at Mr. Hu. "I think Director Feng is wonderful, don't you, Mr. Hu? There is a great warm feeling about this place. They only need some training. If you are agreeable, we'd like to work here in Xinyang."

"I can see that is true," he said. He ruffled Baobao's stubbly hair.

IT WAS MY first (and only) Chinese "camping experience." We wouldn't actually sleep in the place, my hosts explained, but the Xinyang officials wanted to give us China's "*famous* camping in nature" treat. (I don't think there was much camping going on in China in those days.) First we drove through a mountain resort area, one of the country's four *most famous* resorts. Before every gorgeous view spot, there was a billboard with a cheesy inflated rendition of what we were about to see, along with a sales pitch for something irrelevant—cigarettes or skin lightener or a villa by a lake that didn't actually exist in China but looked suspiciously like Switzerland.

And then we bumped along an endless dirt road in black night. As far as I could tell in the darkness, there was no sign that anything like camping had ever occurred anywhere in the vicinity. Somehow we arrived just in time for dinner.

It was an outdoor kitchen on the shores of a reservoir—also *famous*. Bare electric lightbulbs were strung from assorted tree branches. We sat at a big round table covered with sticky oilcloth. It was a hot and humid night. Countless flying things batted themselves against the lightbulbs and the dinner guests. Cicadas screeched in the trees—deafening. But the food was great and the ice-cold bottles of local beer, a gift from the gods.

"Do they have cicadas in America?" shouted Mr. Hu.

"Not where I come from—not in San Francisco," I shouted back.

"The cicada lives underground in larval stage for sixteen years," he said, leaning in closer so we could hear him over the din of cicada romance. "Then it pushes to the surface, develops wings, and flies to the trees. From the trees, it sings for six days. And then it dies."

"A strange and sort of beautiful life," I said.

"Not over," he said. "Then we eat it."

"We do?"

I looked down at the crunchy, formerly delicious nugget poised between my chopsticks. Set it down quietly. Sipped and sloshed the icy beer.

"Mr. Hu, this morning when you told me about the bad fortune of Zhoukou, you mentioned the problem of AIDS. Do you think there are children, AIDS orphans, who might need help?"

"Oh yes. Many. It is sad. Our provincial government is working on the problem." He explained that the government plan was to spruce up the hardest-hit villages, adding clean wells and clinics and methane digesters to turn pig manure into gas. And then take the children away.

"Expert teams are working in many villages already," he said. "And we are moving all the children who've lost both parents into special new housing. And the grandparents too, if they are still living. They are called Sunshine Villages! Nineteen are under construction right now!"

"You mean like orphanages? And so the children have to leave their own village?"

"Of course, if the grandparents are healthy and not too old, the children can stay in their own home. No one else will take them."

"Not the aunts and uncles?"

"Often they are sick too. If they are not sick, some will take the children just to get the land." He stopped eating. Lit a cigarette. "It is not an easy life in the countryside," he said.

"Mr. Hu, will you take us to see some of those children?"

He didn't answer for a long time.

"This is difficult," he said slowly, blowing smoke into the night. Just us and the bugs. "We know Half the Sky. We know your heart is good and you help many children. We welcome your help here in Henan. But . . . this is difficult—"

I waited.

"Foreigners are not allowed in the villages," he said finally. "The people are embarrassed. They are very poor. The AIDS, it came from selling blood, you understand. It was a way to build a new roof, educate their children—they didn't know."

They didn't know that their blood would be drawn into a centrifuge to extract blood products to sell to pharmaceutical companies. They didn't know that their good blood would be mixed with bad blood lurking in the already-used needles and centrifuge equipment—blood tainted with HIV—and then passed back into their own clean bodies. They knew only that each time they sold their blood, they received fifty *yuan* . . . six dollars. So they went back again and again. Now they could pay school fees, pay their debts, patch the mud walls of their homes. They shared what they knew with their sisters and brothers and even their aging parents.

And then some began to get sick with fever and sores. A few died. The lucrative blood stations, some of which, although they were official Red Cross stations, were owned by the relatives of a high-ranking provincial official, quietly shut down.

Over the years, more and more villagers got sick. They could no longer work, so they sold their few possessions. Their children stopped attending school; they couldn't pay. They stayed at home and took care of their parents as best they could. Many of the children were still very young. They knew that the blood money had been used to give them an education and a better life. Knowing that, they watched their parents die.

"I wonder," I said quietly, "if children like that, who have known only family life, village life, will be okay in those Sunshine Villages. They have already lost so much."

"Yes," he said. His eyes were glistening in the dark. "And I do understand you wish to help. You must be patient."

AT DAWN WE drove back to the Zhengzhou airport. Our Air China flight to Nanchang was canceled. The only remaining flight that day between Henan and Jiangxi, two "underdeveloped" provinces, would be on a forty-seat Dash 8 turboprop.

"Would you like to wait and take the Air China flight tomorrow?" ZZ asked hopefully. She was not a fan of small planes. But

I needed to get back to our build in Nanchang to hold my little daughters.

The plane looked old and tired. With some trepidation (well, a lot on ZZ's part), we squeezed into the last two seats.

We taxied. We stopped.

"There's a problem with the brakes," said a voice on the intercom. "Please wait a moment." A few seconds passed. We taxied again. Now I was worried we were going to take off with bad brakes. We stopped again. Two flight attendants passed out boxes of some sort of green juice. They had enough for only six rows. I was in row seven, ZZ in ten. I was debating using my foreign status to get a green juice for ZZ, when suddenly everyone stood and started getting off the plane.

I followed the crowd and climbed down the flimsy air-stairs. We all stood in a huddle in the shade of an engine and wing, watching a lone mechanic trying to fix the brakes. Some of the passengers were right next to a propeller that was still lazily coming to a halt. I tried not to look at them until I was certain the thing had completely stopped.

"I'm sorry, ZZ," I said. "I guess we should have waited for the big plane."

"*Mei wenti,*" she said. "No problem. *Eating bitter* is Chinese way."

Ten minutes passed. Most of the passengers were squatting now. Some shared fruit and watermelon seeds.

"Must eat bitter to taste the sweet," ZZ said.

We stood under the plane wing for almost an hour. Not a single passenger complained.

FINALLY BACK IN Jiangxi Province, I scooped my beautiful little daughters into my arms. I thought about Jingli and Baobao, hurting and alone. I thought about the children in Henan, their parents gone for blood money.

Children eating bitter.

"You two are the most precious gifts in my life," I said. "How can I be so lucky?"

"Mommy, that's a big squeeze," Anya said. "Don't squeeze our dinner out."

"I just love you so much."

"We do too, Mommy," Maya said.

"*Wo ai ni,*" Anya said.

"Anya said *Wo ai ni* to Feng *Ayi,* and she told us Chinese people never say 'I love you' like that to children," Maya said.

"Really?" I said. "Well, *Wo ai ni* anyway. *Wo ai ni* big-time. Forever and ever."

IN THE MORNING, I went along with the volunteers to Lushan National Park to see my second of four *most famous* resorts in China. After checking out the posh villa where Chiang Kai-shek, and later Mao, liked to cool off in summertime, we spiraled slowly up the mountain road behind a line of tour buses. More billboards. Ford Motors, then some giant swimsuited babes on surfboards—not a clue what they were selling. When we'd gone as far as we could go, we climbed one thousand steps to the Rock of One Thousand Clouds to see the Three Ancient Trees, planted by monks fifteen hundred years before. We washed our hands in a lucky stream and threw coins in the Cave of the Immortals.

My two little girls lit incense and said a prayer to Guanyin to thank her for helping us to help the orphans. I knew I was utterly and completely blessed.

Chapter 14

A Sparrow Sings, Not Because It Has an Answer, but Because It Has a Song

不鸣则已　一鸣惊人

Beijing

Autumn 2004

Once back in Beijing, it was time to find a real office for Half the Sky. ZZ's living room would no longer do. My first choice was right in the heart of Ritan Park, "Temple of the Sun." The place I had in mind was a modest imperial changing room dating only from the 1950s but fashioned after the original 1530 model. It was empty, dust-covered, and storybook elegant. Perfect. Across the courtyard, a little company of some sort had an office. Why couldn't we do the same?

"Well," said ZZ, "there is no air-conditioning. There is no toilet. There is no water."

"But look at those roof tiles, ZZ. And the painted ceiling—magical! Half the Sky should live in the Temple of the Sun!" I was clearly still in movie mode.

We ended up a few blocks away in Jianguomenwai Diplomatic Residence Compound—Jianwai for short. There were a number of more pleasant, less Soviet-looking options even before Olympic fever rebuilt the city, but the location (just blocks from Tiananmen Square) and the rents (fair) were incentive enough to keep the place fully occupied. After the Cultural Revolution and during the period of "opening and reform," all foreigners *had* to live in a place like Jianwai—especially anybody connected with the media. Chinese had not been allowed entry without a special permit. Now Jianwai was home to assorted foreign media, international NGOs, and embassy staff from all over the world. Anachronistically and for no good reason I could think of, our Chinese staff still needed a pass to enter. Foreign faces zipped right past the guards. Some things about China weren't changing fast enough.

Around the time our new Beijing office opened for business with two actual employees, the Ministry of Civil Affairs announced that foreign organizations like Half the Sky could soon be actually, legally registered. This was a big deal!

Despite the fact that we were now running seventeen children's centers inside government orphanages, that we partnered with government agencies, and that we paid the salaries of about 450 Chinese citizens, officially we (like the AIDS orphans) didn't exist. Even as our government partners were beginning to trust us and depend on us to deliver on our promises, Half the Sky along with all other foreign NGOs in China inhabited a gray zone—no bank accounts or employees or any sort of legal anything. Our office lease was in my name, our bank account in ZZ's. All we had built could be shut down on a whim and at a moment's notice.

When official registration began on June 1, 2004, ZZ was among the very first on the very first day to submit our application. She made friends with the man who ran the NGO registration department. She called him every week and brought him sweets on the holidays. For four years. That's how long it took before the first foreign NGO was, in fact, registered in China. Unfortunately, it wasn't Half the Sky. It was Bill Gates's.

"*Perseverance furthers*—right, ZZ?" I said.

"Fools in a hurry drink with chopsticks," she said.

DICK AND I had this idea that if our year in China was really going to benefit our girls, we must, as much as possible, make sure they had a genuine Chinese experience. We wanted to give them the gift of their Chinese culture so that they would never feel that it had been taken away from them. The obvious first step was to enroll them in a real Chinese school.

At Fangcaodi Primary, a government-run school with an "international track" and impressive reputation, Anya, who was six, bravely tackled first grade. Maya, then eight, entered second grade for the second time because her Mandarin language skills were nonexistent. Within a week, she'd learned to despise everything about school. Chinese primary education at its most traditional is probably not much more nurturing than an orphanage. At Fangcaodi, the name of the student with the worst homework (usually our girls) was written on the blackboard each day. Sit on your hands or your knuckles got rapped. Ask no questions. But when the teacher left the room, the boys ran over the tops of the desks and beat up on the girls.

After the first day, when ZZ explained to our girls that when the teacher tells you, "*Ni bu hao*," which means, "You are bad," it doesn't really mean you are a bad person, teary-eyed Anya swallowed hard, then seemed resigned. She trudged back to school. She didn't know that big-kid school could be otherwise.

But Maya cried every morning and begged to stay home. She cried at bedtime too. Nothing could comfort her. So, there we were, trying to make life better for a million kids who had nobody, while ruining the life of the child who'd inspired it all.

We called every international school in Beijing. The semester was already under way; there were no openings—and we had no *guanxi*. Maya would have to become a grade school dropout.

"How about gymnastics?" ZZ suggested. "I think we can get Maya into Shichahai, the government sports school. She can learn half-day gymnastics, half-day academics. Maybe she can become Olympic star!"

Maya was ecstatic. She was free! And so we hired a home-schooling tutor to teach her Chinese and math in the afternoons, and Maya devoted her mornings to learning handsprings and lay-outs with China's future champions.

Our girl was not destined to become one of them. In zealous preparation for the Beijing Olympics, still four years away, little Chinese gymnasts at Shichahai were driven to peak performance hour after hour by unrelenting trainers. But Maya was a foreigner now; she was given foreign treatment. She was allowed to sit when she got tired, to give up when she failed. As the children around her ignored their blisters and bruises and struggled for excellence and dreams of Olympic glory for China—their parents sacrificing their only child (even the six-year-olds were boarders)—our little girl watched from the sidelines.

Wuqiao County, Hebei Province

Wuqiao County's claim to fame was acrobatics. Dick was head-ing there, just a three-hour train ride south of Beijing, to shoot a photo story. We all went along; maybe the young athletes would inspire our budding gymnast.

WELCOME TO WUQIAO—FAMOUS HOMETOWN OF CHINESE ACROBATICS! said a string of giant roadside billboards. Behind the signs, Wuqiao seemed to be a mix of barren fields, small farms, and assorted rundown acrobatic schools in barnlike buildings.

We were expected at the *most famous* school. The principal greeted us in her reception room. She told us that her family had been training acrobats for two thousand years. "Ours is the best and biggest acrobat school in China," she said. "People send their children from all over the world to live and study here. Some begin when they are just four years old."

Anya squeezed my hand tighter. I picked her up and gave her a hug. "Don't worry, she doesn't mean you. You guys are coming home with us. Always."

While Dick shot, we watched some children spinning plates on their feet. A couple of girls were bending themselves into pretzels. We watched tiny jugglers, and human pyramids made up of exchange students from Africa.

At the second school, Maya had a turn at practicing Chinese yoyo and received one as a gift. She handed the prize over to her little sister and turned to us. "Can we go home now?"

"Had enough?" Dick asked. "Sure, just a few more minutes."

"Home to America," she said.

"Hey, how about Circus World?" said Dick. "I heard you can actually ride on a tiger there."

"A real one?" asked Maya.

"I want to! I'm a tiger!" Anya said.

At Circus World, we watched an obese performing mouse climb a ladder and walk a tightrope in his own mini-world, complete with pagoda. Dick, eager to cheer Maya up, agreed to be shot out of a canon. At the Funny Zoo, Anya had her picture taken on a real (and pathetic, not funny) tiger.

Months later, we would manage to move the girls to an international school. They would both love it. And that would be the end of Maya's Olympics career.

OUR BEIJING HOME was just a block from Ritan Park. Early each morning, after a breakfast of congee and heart-stopping deep-fried dough sticks, we walked to the park.

Despite tortured-looking sawed-off trees and fake rockeries with mucky koi ponds, parks in China feel like the country at its most heartfelt and personal and somehow spiritual. Time and progress blissfully come to a standstill. Wherever you are in that vast, almost always polluted, almost always chaotic land, at 7:00 A.M. you will find a peaceful retreat full of people doing their own thing—some performing morning exercises that require banging on tree trunks, groups of ladies dancing with fans, aging *taiji* warriors thrusting swords in slow-motion battles, players of *jianzi* (a shuttlecock game played with feet) and the ancient *erhu*, with its two mournful strings. Some folks stroll alone, beating their chests, vocalizing into the treetops.

Old men shuffle the paths in pairs and threesomes, each carrying a tiny bird swinging in its covered bamboo cage. When they arrive at their favorite spot, the men arrange the delicate cages to hang from low branches and uncover them so the birds can see each other. Then the men sit and smoke and play checkers and argue while their little birds chirp out melodious birdie gossip.

I was coming to see my journey in China as something like wending through one of those gardens. There were no straight routes, only winding paths and zigzag galleries and bridges to pavilions and towers and vistas designed to draw attention and distract one from one's worldly cares. But always in the distance was something—an artificial mountain peak, a *most excellent and magnificent* specimen—that seemed almost out of reach, yet not quite. If you kept your eyes on it, if you kept wending along the paths and didn't let yourself be seduced by the Listening to the Rain Pavilion or the Hall of Distant Fragrances, it seemed you could get there. If you could just stay focused.

Easier said than done. It was never the closed orphanage doors that obscured my view and drew me off course. It wasn't the endless bureaucracy, the fear of the unknown, the now-familiar China Smile. I'd just find another path, my eyes always on the prize. The challenge for me was to not get caught up in the lives of individual children. Each of them was like my siren call to mission drift. I understood all about that mountain in the middle, how I had to keep moving toward it. But the more I came to know the children, the more I ached for every one of them. And although I tried not to, sometimes I just had to pause along the way.

One of our new expat friends in Beijing ran an organization that arranged medical care for local orphans. She told me that an American orthopedic surgeon would soon be coming to treat some of her kids. I told her about Jingli, who was now back in Baling.

After the Shanghai surgery, Jingli had gained some bowel control, nothing else. No further treatment had been suggested. I wondered if her gait could be improved—if something could be done for those floppy feet. And was she allowed to be with the other kids now? After attending our happy little preschool each day, was she sent back to the Root Cellar?

"Do you think your doctor friend would see Jingli?" I asked. "Maybe there's something more we could do."

A week later, Jingli arrived in Beijing, accompanied by an *ayi* from the orphanage and by Director Slick's wife, who it turned out was the orphanage "doctor." Mrs. Slick gave no indication of ever having examined Jingli or of knowing anything about spina bifida or even about medicine. She was, however, very attractive.

The American surgeon told us that Jingli had no bone deformity and that she'd healed as well as could be expected from surgery. Certainly her gait could be improved; Jingli needed to be fitted for AFOs—ankle/foot braces—and after she'd been wearing them for a couple of years and her legs were accustomed to being straight, she might benefit from tendon surgery.

We all sat at dinner that night—Jingli's escorts, my family, ZZ.

"Can she even get AFOs in Baling?" I asked.

Mrs. Slick didn't know. ZZ doubted it.

"We'll keep her here, then, with the *ayi*. Just until the braces are ready. She'll have to miss some school."

"That's no problem. She doesn't go to school," said Mrs. Slick.

We all looked at her.

"She's eight years old now. She graduated from Half the Sky preschool. No disabled children can be admitted to our community schools in Baling."

Dick and I looked at each other.

"Well, then," Dick said, "we'll just keep her here with us and get her what she needs."

"That's not possible," said Mrs. Slick. "We must follow procedures—"

"Of course, Mrs. Slick," I said quickly. "We also respect procedures. She must stay in Beijing until she is fitted for the AFOs. Certainly, you and your *ayi* will stay too. We'll extend your time at the hotel. Let's wait and discuss the next step after Jingli's had her AFO appointment."

"But I can't stay—"

"Oh, what a pity," I said, smiling at Dick. "Then I suggest Jingli stay at our home! What do you think, girls?"

"Yes!" the girls chimed.

"We're never sending her back to the Root Cellar," Dick said quietly.

"Never," I said.

JINGLI TOOK ONE look at our Beijing apartment, at the white Ikea sofa and the white Ikea chair, and refused to sit. She was terrified of soiling those (to her eyes) pristine surfaces. We tried to tell her it was okay. She stood firm on her wobbly little legs. We brought wooden chairs into the living room and all sat on them together. Still she stood. We asked Gao *Ayi* to run out and buy Pull-Ups or diapers—whatever she could find to fit a big girl. For the first of a thousand times, we told Jingli, "Please don't worry. For this time, we are your family and this is your home. We all take care of each other, and we will take care of you."

Jingli's eyes shone, but she didn't smile.

We showed her the girls' bedroom. "I'm not going to sleep on the floor," she said. "If you make me do that, I want to go back to Baling."

"Of course, you don't have to sleep on the floor, Jingli! You can sleep here with Maya or, if you want, back at the hotel with Mrs. Slick and your *ayi* tonight. And tomorrow we'll buy you a bed," I said.

"With a blanket?" she said.

"Yes . . . definitely with a blanket."

"I'll stay here," she said.

This child was a survivor.

"JENNY, *KUAI LAI*," Gao *Ayi* called from the bathroom.

She was giving Jingli a bath. When I opened the door, she looked up at me in distress.

Jingli's little bottom, her entire genital area, was a mass of red, oozing sores, deep and surely painful. The poor child had been sitting in her own waste for months, maybe years.

An angry lump rose in my throat. My breath caught. I closed my eyes. Behind my closed lids I saw Anya's burned feet, the diaper scars . . . all the hungry, tied babies . . . their blank little faces. I felt the anger burning in my chest. *Don't. It solves nothing. Let it go. What is changing is that I can do something now. I can help.*

It was the last time rage swallowed me. It has paid fleeting visits since, but never lingers more than a heartbeat. Sadness, though, seems to be forever.

I tried to smile in a reassuring way. "We'll fix it. *Mingtian*, tomorrow, I promise."

First thing the next morning, ZZ and I took Jingli to Beijing Union Hospital. We were prescribed salve and antibiotics and told to park Jingli under bright lights for two hours each day. The last suggestion seemed impractical for an eight-year-old who was long overdue to start living her life; we decided to aim a warm hairdryer at the affected area twice a day instead. It worked great and Jingli thought it was hilarious. The scars, of course, would be there always.

ON THE WAY home, ZZ called Director Slick and somehow managed to convince him to let Jingli stay with us in Beijing and to submit her dossier for adoption. We'd take care of her until she was matched with a family. Slick doubted that any family would want such damaged goods. Still, he bragged, he had special *guanxi* with the vice director of CCAA. They were old army buddies. He would see what could be done. ZZ complimented him on his considerable influence. "How fortunate that Jingli's life is in the hands of such an important man," she told him.

Mrs. Slick and the Baling *ayi* went home. And Jingli became, at least for now, our daughter. Gao *Ayi*, who'd been working only during the day, now moved in with us to care for Jingli full-time. The Bowen household was, yet again, complete: five females—six counting ZZ, whom I rarely let out of my sight—and Dick.

A WEEK LATER, our visit to the orthotics and prosthetics department at Bo'Ai Orthopedic Hospital reminded me of the prop shops from my theater days. The room was covered in plaster dust. Plaster-of-Paris hands and feet were strewn on tabletops. Assorted artificial limbs and braces and buckles and crutches rested everywhere—leaning against chairs, littering the floors and every other possible surface.

A giant wall case displayed orthotics and prosthetics behind smudged glass doors. Jingli's favorites were the hands and fingers—every size and shape imaginable, and looking almost real. The doctor himself had an artificial leg; he took his work seriously. A whole team swarmed around Jingli, measuring and conferring. She was enthralled by the attention.

Just then, a flurry of excitement! Baobao, my little footless friend from the Xinyang orphanage, was escorted in the door by her Half the Sky preschool teacher and an *ayi*.

"Baobao!" I whooped.

"It's really Baobao's appointment time," ZZ said. "I thought we can share. *Nihao! Nihao,* Baobao!"

Baobao was tottering proudly on two new prosthetic feet covered by bright red boots. Forever free of her stroller, she was smiling—glowing with happiness. A whole new girl.

After a big welcome, Baobao was plunked in a chair. The *ayi* removed her feet. "They still hurt her," the *ayi* said. "But she doesn't want to take them off."

"Let's take a look," said the doctor.

"Zhang *Ayi,*" Jingli said, "I want to go."

"But Jingli, they haven't finished the plaster mold yet. *Deng yi huir,* wait a bit," ZZ said.

I saw the tears fall. "Jingli, what's wrong?"

"I don't want my feet cut off," she said, her eyes on Baobao.

Then Baobao started to cry too. I sat down on the plaster-coated floor and took both sobbing little girls into my lap. "Oh ZZ, please explain to them."

"Where can I begin?"

•   •   •

FANGCAODI PRIMARY SCHOOL refused to admit Jingli, officially because she didn't have the proper *hukou* (residence permit), but privately they told us that no school in Beijing would accept a handicapped child. We decided to homeschool her along with our little gymnast.

Life settled into a new normal. I began to quietly browse the adoption e-mail lists, looking for special voices, the right parents for a most special child. I wished it could be us—that we could give Jingli the time and care she needed and deserved. But I was never home. We lived in a place where she couldn't even go to school. We were not the ones.

Still, Jingli was soon entirely at home. When Dick traveled for work, he'd call daily and talk to all of his girls. Jingli was always first to the phone, even though they couldn't understand a word the other said. At night the phone rang and Jingli ran dripping wet and naked from the bath, calling out, "*Baba ShuShu!*—Uncle Daddy! My talk!"

When he was in town, Dick took the girls "fishing" for goldfish in Ritan Park using crackers for bait. Jingli loved it—the one sport where she could excel. She'd fish all day if allowed and didn't mind a bit when, at the end of each outing, Dick made her dump her entire catch back into the pond.

We had rented a piano.

"Jingli, how would you like to take piano lessons?"

"I don't want."

"You might love it. You can't know unless you try."

"I don't want try."

"But why not?"

"I don't know how make music."

"Well, that's what a piano teacher does: teaches you how."

"Oh. I think about it."

It didn't matter; we never found a decent teacher. So Anya took tap-dance lessons. Maya practiced splits and backbends. Jingli started learning "English with Mickey Mouse."

WHILE DICK STILL took the occasional shooting job, he was beginning to reconsider his own life choices. He completed his book of photographic portraits, *Mei Mei, Little Sister.* Then, in a Beijing library, he discovered the world's first telling of the Cinderella story, written in AD 768, and he began to dream a film, *Cinderella Moon*—a movie to be shot in China, in Chinese. Like the girls, he was finding his way.

And so was I. Even as my family struggled to adapt to new lives, I was almost instantly more at home in Beijing than I'd ever been during fifteen years of edgewise living in Hollywood. I missed nothing about those days. Maybe for the first time ever, my life made perfect sense.

I'd started taking Mandarin lessons in my nonexistent spare time, but I traveled so much that I missed just about every class. Although I began picking up the language slowly through constant exposure, I never learned beyond kindergarten Chinese; I could grasp the gist, but never the nuance. After a while, I decided things were just right the way they were. ZZ made me sound far better than I could ever hope to manage as a non-native speaker; and in meetings, officials spoke freely, assuming there was no way the foreigner understood.

Despite the fact that I could barely direct a taxi to my house, for now, at least, I felt whole, integrated—family, work, heart. Peaceful in this chaotic place.

Maybe the adventure would last more than a year.

•　　•　　•

CHINA CELEBRATES TWO "Golden Weeks" each year: the Chinese New Year Spring Festival and October 1, China's National Day. All China travels during a Golden Week. Our first opportunity to join the hordes came on the October holiday in 2004. We would have loved to explore Asia a bit, but since, as a ward of the state, Jingli couldn't leave the country, we opted for Sanya—a beach resort at the very southern tip of China, on Hainan Island.

On departure morning, Jingli refused breakfast. She stood by the window all morning while we ran around packing forgotten items and zipping suitcases. "What are you doing?" Uncle Daddy asked her.

"I waiting for airplane."

"Oh, Jingli baby, the airplane doesn't come to our house. We have to go to it."

Why should this child know of airports?

When we arrived in Sanya, Jingli was in paradise. As if the plane ride weren't magnificent enough, now she saw the ocean for the first time. She was stunned that there could be such a thing.

She tossed off her new AFOs and staggered through the sand, falling and laughing. She rode on Uncle Daddy's shoulders into the waves. She shrieked when a macaque stole her bag of peanuts at Monkey Island. She danced the hula-hula with showgirls from the Philippines. She paddled around the big pool in her star-shaped floaty wearing shocking-pink goggles, singing "*Wo youyong!*—I'm swimming!"

It was as if the Root Cellar had never existed.

SOON AFTER THE holiday, Slick called. He was coming to Beijing and had arranged a lunch with the CCAA vice director to discuss Jingli's case. ZZ and I were to join them. I must bring Jingli.

She didn't believe me when I told her that I wasn't giving her back to Slick. In a last-ditch effort to stay home, she started blurting out her secrets.

"In that orphanage, they don't let me drink water. They don't want me to wet. They make me sleep on floor."

I squeezed her hand. "You never have to go back there, Jingli. Remember, I promised. I *promised*. We are just going to have lunch with the director. He wants to see how well you're doing. You can tell him about Sanya and *youyong*."

"In that orphanage, when I go to Little Sisters school, everything is nice and the teachers are nice, but at night, after school, the *ayi*s hit the children, especially the little ones. And pinch them. And whip them in the bathroom."

I climbed into the back of the cab, took Jingli on my lap, and kissed her teary cheeks. I was a traitor, taking her to see Slick. I didn't know a way out.

"I'm so sorry that happened, Jingli. You are finished with that bad place. Please trust me."

"When I make mistake and pee in my clothes, the *ayi*s don't let me have clean ones. They don't want to do laundry all the time. Then I am smelly. Why you not send me to Shanghai?"

"Shanghai?"

"I like Shanghai. There I have operation in hospital, and after that operation, no one dares hit me."

Jingli was silent at lunch. She ate nothing. I didn't force her. Slick and the CCAA vice director didn't notice. They were too busy sharing army stories. When we said goodbye, I gave them each a bottle of brandy. I asked casually if I could help find Jingli the right family. The vice director said that, as long as the prospective parents were qualified to adopt a Chinese child, the choice was mine. ZZ and I silently cheered and got out of there before he could change his mind.

"Why can't I stay with Jenny Mama and Uncle Daddy?" Jingli asked ZZ in the cab.

"This not the family that is meant to be yours," ZZ said, trying to sound upbeat. "Someone very wonderful is waiting for you. Now Jenny Mama can find the best family."

Jingli blinked back tears. She turned away and looked out the window. She was quiet for a long time. Then . . .

"I do *not* want to go back to the orphanage. My new mama must be Jenny Mama's friend—not a stranger. My new family must have other children so I don't feel lonely. And I want to go to America so I can have a horse and salt on the ground."

ZZ stopped translating. "Salt?" she asked.

"Maya showed me a picture of America. She was sliding down a hill of salt."

"Snow? Jingli, I'm going to do my best to find exactly that family," I said.

With an aching heart, I began to look in earnest for Jingli's family.

A couple of months after our lunch, Slick called ZZ and told her he was in trouble. He didn't explain, but he wanted to know if we might have a job for Mrs. Slick, the doctor. ZZ told him we had no openings. Although Half the Sky already had been able to raise the standards of care at Baling, the place took a dramatic leap forward when Slick disappeared shortly after that call. We never saw him or his wife again.

FATE, AND SOME persistence on my part, brought Jingli the perfect family, and it was not us. She would have the siblings she wanted—two of them adopted from China. Her future parents were devoted to their kids. They dearly wanted to complete their family with an older child who had special needs and could use some extra loving. They couldn't have been more perfect. Except *we* were her family too.

As it began to sink in that we were going to lose her soon, Dick and I found ourselves rattled and depressed. We kept the news a secret while Jingli's new family waited for approval. We couldn't imagine life without her.

For our first and last Christmas together, we shopped at the Russian market. We found a cheesy little artificial tree with multicolored flashing mini-lights embedded in its branches. On Christmas Day, after our three girls raced around the courtyard on their new bikes, we flew to Hong Kong. We saw *The Nutcracker* at the Hong Kong Ballet. We had high tea at the Peninsula Hotel. We took a bus tour of Hong Kong run by Splendid Tours. We ditched the rest of the Splendid Tour group somewhere in Stanley Market, and from then on we called ourselves the Splendids.

And Jingli was a Splendid, through and through. She was family. Even when she left us, that would never change.

Chapter 15

Eat the Wind, Swallow Bitterness

忍气吞声

Gaoyou, Jiangsu Province
Spring 2005

Gaoyou, a not-too-large city in eastern China's Jiangsu Province, was perfect casting. It had tree-lined streets and the friendly warmth of a small town (population less than a million!). Every morning the street-sweeping truck woke us up with "Happy Birthday" and "Jingle Bells." The place felt the opposite of orphanage, and that was just what I was seeking for our nineteenth site and the inaugural home of our fourth and final Half the Sky program, the Family Village.

By 2005, international adoption had become big business. Healthy babies and young children were easily finding new homes, in China or outside. They rarely stayed in our programs for long. But unless adopting families specifically requested otherwise, CCAA, in those days, was careful to offer foreigners only children they considered healthy or with minor, correctable special needs. And while a few bold Chinese were willing to go against tradition and beyond bloodlines to adopt a child, they had no interest in one who appeared less than perfect.

So what would happen to the children whose physical or developmental special needs were *not* minor and could *not* be repaired?

We could see that there were more and more such new arrivals all the time—children given up by parents who'd run out of options, who couldn't afford medical care or expensive therapies. Children, like the rest, abandoned due to desperate circumstance. Most were doomed to live their lives in institutions.

The Family Village program would offer *permanent* families in government-supplied housing on or near orphanage grounds. The children would grow up outside the institution and inside loving families but would still participate in Half the Sky programs. I couldn't imagine a better way to give them a second chance at a happy childhood.

WE WERE THE first Western guests to stay at Gaoyou's new "international" hotel. Before the volunteers arrived, we bought toasters and coffee pots and taught the cooks how to make omelets and toast and scrambled eggs.

At the orphanage, we renovated a dilapidated outpatient clinic, turning it into sparkling new family apartments complete with bright-colored prefab kitchens and a Little Sisters Preschool down the hall. We built a bridge from the preschool to the new Infant Nurture Center. It was Half the Sky's first real construction project; we'd done only simple renovations before.

Our new Family Village program director, "Jade Dawn" Zhang (the newly retired director of the Hefei orphanage), spent a month in Gaoyou, interviewing parents from the community. All were married couples, devoted parents who'd raised their allotted one child and now had empty nests and a longing for more family. There were dozens of applicants; she chose thirteen couples for training. Then, after training, medical checks, and ZZ interrogation, we narrowed that down to six wonderful couples who happily moved out of their homes and opened their hearts to four children of strangers—twenty-four children altogether—all with special needs. We paid the stay-at-home parent a small stipend. The other parent continued to work outside the home. Each couple promised to raise their four new children until they were adults.

On matching day, Jade Dawn Zhang led the children and their *ayi*s into a reception room where the twelve parents anxiously waited. She stood at the head of the table, a small, solid woman who had a way of taking over a room. She held up a plastic basket and grinned. "Our new families," she announced. Then she closed her eyes and . . . ever so slowly . . . snagged a slip of paper and unfolded it.

"Family of Wang Chunli and Yang Yueming," she read. Two trembling people stood.

"Your first new daughter is Weiping."

Weiping's *ayi* took her by the hand and led her to meet the Wangs. Weiping was five years old. She had round button eyes and a spiky orphanage haircut. Cerebral palsy gave her an awkward gait, but as her new mama and baba took her into their arms, she was transformed in their eyes. She was perfect.

And so it went. One by one, until each of the twenty-four children had looked into the eyes of a kind stranger whom they could soon call their very own mama or baba. In China, where tradition was held dear and deep, nothing like Half the Sky's Family Village had been imagined before. In fact, there may be nothing quite like it in the world.

GAOYOU DIRECTOR NI had been nervous all month. There were all these excited new families to settle and this construction project going on day and night. Soon his sleepy little orphanage was going to be overrun with foreign volunteers. And on top of that, at the last minute he'd been told that Half the Sky was bringing in the foreign media.

It was true, CNN and *Newsweek* and a few others were coming, but we had permission, more or less. Or at least we had advice from our friends in the Jiangsu government that it would take too long to get official permission and the build would be long over, so the journalists should just show up as if they were volunteers. When the big day finally came and we were all gathered—new teachers, new nannies, new parents, trainers, foreigners, and assorted journalists—to celebrate our nineteenth children's center and first Family Village along with the children of Gaoyou, Director Ni, who was gaunt to begin with, looked as if he'd lost ten pounds.

The man barely spoke to anyone. I tried to discourage the reporters from asking him any questions. I feared he'd keel over. The *Newsweek* journalist asked one of the new fathers, a radiologist who already had a nineteen-year-old son, why he had made the decision to add such a difficult second chapter to his life.

"We have been good parents," the man said. "Our son has done well. He is in university now. He doesn't need us anymore. There is . . . a hole in my heart. These children—I have known them only a short while, but . . . my new children fill that hole."

Director Ni's taut shoulders seemed to relax just a bit.

Xinyang, Henan Province

The following month, Mr. Hu invited us to return to Henan. Besides the faint hope that he'd made some progress on the AIDS front, I looked forward to visiting our new centers in that province. Although we had a growing team of program directors and field supervisors and trainers working to raise and maintain quality at all of our sites, and although we received quarterly reports on every child, there was nothing quite like a site visit to help me stay connected with our work.

Xinyang Director Feng had delivered. Often a new center would struggle in the early months as the teachers, nannies, and youth mentors worked to create a family-like environment while quietly integrating themselves into daily orphanage life. Under the best directors and over time, the new nurturing child-centered atmosphere would spread beyond the Half the Sky programs throughout the institution. It was already happening in Xinyang.

We visited the infant nurture rooms and watched Half the Sky nannies on the floor, playing with and cuddling the babies. No one even noticed we were there. The babies not in arms were busy crawling or toddling about, exploring their world; the nannies were busy watching the babies. The once-silent rooms were now full of life.

Just as I walked into the preschool, I saw Baobao's chubby cheeks disappear in a cloud of pouf as her teacher slipped a lavender chiffon dress-up gown over her head. What emerged in front of the mirror was a princess. Bright eyes and a sudden, stunned smile. Now a diamond-studded tiara atop scraggly, starting-to-grow hair. Baobao looked down and fingered the filmy fabric of her gown. She looked up. She gazed at the mirror in absolute wonder. *This gorgeous girl is me, Baobao!*

Baobao saw us watching her in the mirror and waved happily. She turned toward us with excitement. "*Ayi, nihao! Ayi,* see my dress! Do you want to see my flower?"

We did. She took our hands and led us to a windowsill lined with flowerpots. From each sprouted a tiny seedling. She found the pot marked with her name and proudly held it high. "What is it, Baobao?" ZZ asked.

"Flower seeds! *Hao chi* [good food]!" she said. Now Director Feng was like one of the kids; he jumped in, even more excited than Baobao. "Come, let us show you the sunflower wall! See, the photos show the children planting the seedlings outside, then tending the garden. Now here's a chart where they mark how the seedlings grew."

"We ate sunflower seeds at snack time one day," Baobao's teacher said. "The children wondered where the seeds come from, so we started a garden. While our seeds were growing in the garden, we learned the parts of the plant and made drawings and sang sunflower songs and talked about what makes plants grow."

"When we harvested the seeds," said Director Feng, "the children decided to eat only some and to plant the rest. Look how their drawings have become more complex over time. Even growing up in the countryside and working on the land, I did not learn so much!"

"I don't know who is more proud," Baobao's teacher said, laughing, "the children or Director Feng."

"Half the Sky has brought our children great good," Director Feng said. "Even the little babies are stronger and more confident. I *am* proud. And I'm proud of our Baobao!"

"*Ayi,*" Baobao said, tugging on my shirt. "You want to see me ride my bike?"

"Sure!"

I watched Baobao, still in lavender chiffon, zipping around on her trike. I watched her give rides to her schoolmates, her face glowing with the thrill of sport. It was almost impossible to believe that this was the footless waif I had lifted from a broken stroller only a year before.

A few years later, Baobao's new American mother, an amputee herself, would tell me, "She is fearless! She will try anything— skating, running, swimming, biking, or kickball. Anything! And our little girl is beautiful, confident, and full of love. She is the kindest child I've ever known."

Like a child who had been loved all her life.

•   •   •

MR. HU CAME for us at lunchtime. He explained to Director Feng that he would take us sightseeing. *Sightseeing?* I glanced at ZZ. She shook her head.

"Don't worry," she murmured. "Just follow." Of course I did.

The road to the village was carpeted with sheaves of wheat, spread over the road by wily farmers who enlisted passing cars and trucks to ease their workload. Mr. Hu's driver dutifully rolled over miles of drying grain. Here and there, farmers winnowed with giant two-pronged forks as the car passed, tossing the separated wheat chaff in the air.

The fields outside the car window were brown, flat, stubbled with waste. Still, there was an air of timeless order about the place. A row of evenly planted narrow trees lined either side of the road. Their trunks had been painted white once, now long-faded. Ghosts of what had been.

At one nondescript spot in the road, a car waited. We stopped. Three men in the standard uniform of local officials—short-sleeved shirt (black or white), black belt (silver buckle, black-leather cellphone case), black shoes, lit cigarette—stepped out to greet Mr. Hu warmly. We rolled down the car windows. The men looked at my foreign face and said hello with a wary smile.

As we followed the local officials' car up a dirt road toward the village—a cluster of scraggy trees and mud houses—I thought of the leaflet thrust into my hand when I first came to Henan. Someone had translated an anonymous villager's plea into English:

Have you heard the blood plague that is surrounding our village? . . .

Because of our own ignorance, public health department's setting up so many plasma collection stations and the national propaganda on "taking pride of donating blood" and the slogan of "donating blood to save lives of the injured," our innocent peasants reached out their strong arms from years of hard labor. Their freshly red blood streamed into the collection stations and in turn they received "fees of nutrition" to compensate their blood losses. . . . These benevolent and innocent peasants always have dug their food from the earth. Who has pushed us into the valley of death? . . .

The young peasants died one after another leaving seventy-year-old parents and still breast-fed babies behind. Some victims hung themselves, threw themselves into the wells or took poison, unable to cope with the pain and suffering. Those who have stayed in bed for a long time moaned and cursed for relief: "God, please let me die, I can't take it anymore." These scenes were unbearably chilling and it made this village of only orphans and elderly without support.

Whose fault this blood plague is . . . ? And who is there to sympathize us . . . ? People of our village wish to thank you with our deepest gratitude.

WE CLIMBED OUT of the car. Assorted mongrels ambled over to check us out with halfhearted barks. Right behind them were the village officials—two men in the same basic local officials' garb, except scruffier and with an extra coating of dust.

We were expected. Mr. Hu explained that we wanted to help the children and wanted to see their situation. The village officials thanked us and shook our hands and we followed them toward a nearby home. No ceremonies here.

I'm pretty sure I was the first foreigner they'd seen in that place, and they were curious to have a look, but there seemed to be no fear or paranoia. They were just like villagers I'd met all over China: friendly, eager to share their lives and to know about mine.

One young woman proudly showed me her chubby baby boy;

two little girls tagged behind me, giggling and running away each time I turned to peek at them. I tried to take a picture of a scrawny, shirtless old fellow, bronze from countless hours of labor in the fields. He waved me away. "No pictures, no pictures."

"I'm sorry," I said, and hastily put my camera away.

"It's okay," ZZ said. "The old man is embarrassed he's lost some teeth."

I reached out to shake the old man's hand. "*Duibuqi*, I'm sorry," I said. "I wanted to take a photo because you are a handsome man."

"All right, then. All right." And he posed.

I snapped a quick shot and caught up with the officials. I'd forgotten where I was. This place was charming. Just another village somewhere in China. Life goes on—no cloud of death as I'd imagined.

That changed when we entered the first courtyard.

IT WAS BARREN, save for an anorexic pig, hunched motionless in a too-small pen that was dark and shrouded with torn burlap. A lone, tired-looking chicken patrolled the hard ground, halfheartedly pecking at what seemed to be nothing more than dirt.

Although clearly long-neglected, the broad-faced brick home with a carved wooden lintel must have once commanded respect in the village. Standing at almost military attention before the door, perhaps the saddest family I had ever seen: two grandparents, a young father, and three children.

The grandparents both looked ancient, but ZZ said they were likely younger than sixty. Their eyes were red with fatigue and sorrow—as if they'd borne all the pain and suffering a human being can endure.

Behind them lurked their son . . . or what remained of him. Disheveled, gaunt, haunted—he didn't seem to know where he was or why he was standing there. Mr. Hu told us he was sick with AIDS and dementia. I prayed that they hadn't taken the man from his bed to greet us.

"His wife died only a few months ago," Mr. Hu said. "In this area, more women sold their blood than men. Even after the sickness came. They believed that as long as they menstruated each month, they were all right."

There were two girls, perhaps ten and seven, and a boy about five. It was clear that everything this family had left was being given to the children. Despite their poverty, the children looked well fed. Their hair was combed; their faces and hands, washed. Their clothes were almost clean. Someone cared. The two littlest ones looked on timidly—probably frightened of me. The big girl looked resigned.

I was sure she could be no more than ten. No hint yet of approaching puberty. Yet it seemed only a matter of time before these three lost the grownups in their lives. Ready or not, she would be the woman of the family. No hopes and dreams for her.

What could we do for these children?

THEN A FAMILY of four—mother sick (father dead), again two girls, and then the long-awaited boy.

The mom had not been tested; there were no antiretroviral (ARV) drugs available here yet. She didn't know there were such things. She was too sick to work the land. Her eldest girl, not yet twelve, had dropped out of school to care for the family.

"Is there no help from the government, Mr. Hu?"

"While the mother lives, the local government provides eight *yuan* each month."

Less than a dollar.

"We have many such families," he said. "Almost twenty thousand in the province, twenty-three in this village alone. We are trying to get more subsidy for them."

A local official chimed in. "Only true orphans can be helped. When the mother is gone, the government will take care of her children. They'll be better off then."

Don't say that in front of her! I felt sick. A fraud.

Better off without her. The mother stood mute, chastened for being alive. I longed to help them. *What could I possibly have to offer here? Was this mission drift? I couldn't remember the rules.*

My foreign self got the best of me. I put my arms around the mother. She stiffened even more in my arms. The entire room tensed. Chinese people don't do that. They don't hold strangers.

"What is your name?" I asked the mother.

"Rao," she said.

Now what? I had to do something.

"Mrs. Rao, we would like to help your children stay in school," I found myself saying. "If you agree to let your daughter return to school, we will offer support of 500 *yuan* each month for your family."

Sixty dollars—a fortune in this place. I handed her the first installment. She cried. I cried. ZZ cried. Even Mr. Hu got teary-eyed. I told ZZ that my family would cover the costs if we couldn't find support somewhere for AIDS-affected kids. I didn't know what else to do. I'd never felt so helpless in my life.

WE VISITED ANOTHER village . . . and another. Wherever we went, the villagers knew Mr. Hu. They greeted me like I was somebody special. Someone who could help make it better. I felt worse and worse.

Zhoukou, maybe the most dismal town I'd ever seen, was the place that Mr. Hu had told us was the cradle of Chinese civilization. As we drove along the barren main drag—past a man who appeared to be dying in a doorway, past a cluster of scraggy adolescent boys practicing martial arts with cigarettes dangling from their mouths—the fellow from Zhoukou Civil Affairs repeated the claim. He embellished a bit: "The ancient city Pingliangtai is over 4,600 years old—oldest city in China!"

"It's here?" I asked, noting the toilet paper peddler stationed in front of our hotel. I wondered if we should stop and buy some.

"Here in Zhoukou!"

"May we visit?"

"Oh, it's gone."

"Are there ruins or anything?"

He shrugged. "Here is Zhoukou Guest House. You must be very tired. We will eat now."

THERE WERE AT least six new faces at dinner, all of them male—lower-level county officials. I'm pretty sure there was no such thing as a female official in this part of China.

I sat at the mayor's side. He had studied English in university twenty-four years earlier and wanted to see what he could remember. Nothing, as far as I could tell—not that it mattered. After we discussed the reason for my visit, and how much we really wanted to do whatever we could to help the children, but couldn't possibly afford to contribute four million *yuan* to help Zhoukou finish construction of a new civic center that had been partially funded by a Hong Kong businessman who had *guanxi* with the vice party secretary but ran out of money, the mayor lost interest in talking to me.

The rest of the evening disintegrated into a *baijiu*- and cigarette-fueled argument about which county had the most AIDS cases. It was the opposite of a government cover-up. Each of my dinner partners was claiming top prize.

Quietly, beneath the smoke and din, ZZ suddenly turned to me.

"Jenny, there is one thing I should tell . . . ," she said, struggling for the right words. So unlike her. "Today . . . they say when you touch someone with . . . the AIDS sickness . . . you may yourself–"

"But . . . that isn't how you get it, ZZ. Ah, you are worried because I hugged Mrs. Rao?"

"Hu," she said. "It is Hu who worries about this."

"Let's take a walk," I said. "I'll explain what I know about the disease. You can share with Mr. Hu."

IN THE MORNING, Mr. Hu took us deeper into the backroads. "Now we will see a Sunshine Village for the AIDS orphans," he said.

"Mr. Hu, I appreciate from the bottom of my heart that you are making these difficult visits possible. I want to make sure you know that. I only hope that we can repay your trust by finding a way to help the children."

"You will," he said, lighting one cigarette from another. "You will."

The car turned into a whitewashed cluster of single-story red-roofed buildings. They looked like army barracks.

"It used to be just a home for old people," Mr. Hu said. "There is a primary school just a few hundred meters away. The children are welcomed there."

We got out of the car. Two local officials greeted us. ZZ and I followed Mr. Hu's cloud of smoke down a path lined with neatly clipped boxwood shrubs. The place was silent. Not even birds peeped.

We stopped at an open door.

Standing in military formation, wearing red, white, and black sports uniforms, were five somber rows of children, eight to thirteen years old. Forty-four children. When we walked into the room, they spoke in perfect unison.

"Good morning, Teacher Jenny. Welcome to our home."

I tried to smile. "Good morning, children. Thank you."

From somewhere, tinny music started to play. Still maintaining their formation, the children sang and danced. None of them smiled.

I could feel the China Smile fixing itself on my own face. We applauded. Then we all stood there, looking at each other. I knew I was supposed to say something. But I just couldn't. Finally I croaked, "Will you show me around your home?"

EACH OF THE dormitory rooms was nearly identical. Two narrow, hard beds with blond-wood headboards, each stamped in red characters that said, SHAODIAN SERVICE CENTER FOR THE ELDERLY. Between the two beds, two matching bedside tables with a single drawer. Atop the tables, two identical blue plastic electric fans and a shared hot water thermos. The girls' dorm rooms had bright-pink bedspreads with a bamboo mat and bamboo-covered pillow. Nothing else. The boys had the same in orange. The children were separated by age and gender. They did not live with their siblings or, if they survived, their grandparents.

"Who looks after the children?" I asked Mr. Hu later, as we walked to the car.

"A local farmer's wife comes each day to cook for them."

"That's it?" I said. "And the kids can never go back to their real homes?"

"Oh yes, they do. For holidays and at harvest time. If they have living relatives."

I SAT LIKE stone in the back of Mr. Hu's car. The road went on and on.

"It must be hard for them," I said finally. "Those children only know life in families. Even though they were poor, they had someone. I wish the siblings could live together."

Mr. Hu didn't answer. We drove on in silence and smoke.

I had no answers. I was lost here.

My California-sunshine-can-do attitude was gone. I slumped in my seat, depressed beyond words. The flat fields outside looked dead to me now.

After a long quiet while, the car stopped. We were nowhere, as far as I could tell. Mr. Hu got out and told us to follow him.

In the middle of a barren field, there was a truckload of gravel, several piles of brick, and a big green sign displaying an architectural rendering of a large military compound. At least I thought it was.

"Red Ribbon Family," read ZZ. "Sponsored by All-China Industrial and Commercial Federation."

"What is it, Mr. Hu?"

"Home for AIDS orphans," he said with a hopeful smile. "By next August, seventy-five orphans will live here. All of them are under ten years old."

"Little kids. In some sort of families?"

"There will be *ayi*s, of course. And a cook. And teachers for the school. Everything the children need—all here in one place."

"But—" I said. And then I couldn't hold the flood: I burst into tears. I sobbed. I embarrassed us both. I begged him to reconsider. "See, those little kids are traumatized, Mr. Hu. They watched their parents die. Now you—I don't mean *you*, but . . . well, somebody wants to take them from their brothers and sisters and leave them here with nobody to hold them at night and smile at them in the morning and . . . Look . . . Please let us help, Mr. Hu. . . . Oh, wait! I know . . . I know—Half the Sky . . . in Jiangsu Province, a town called Gaoyou—we're piloting a new program! Family Village! It's for orphans with disabilities—the ones who won't be adopted. A way for them to grow up in families. We could do the same thing here! I mean, I don't know how we can pay for it, but we'll figure it out—we always do—please, Mr. Hu—excuse me for this . . . damn crying. . . . What do you think?"

By now I was both crying and laughing—maybe a little bit

crazed. *We can do this!* Mr. Hu looked shaken. I am sure I never seemed more foreign to him than at that moment.

A WEEK LATER, the fax machine rattled in our Beijing office. ZZ translated as she read:

> The Henan Provincial Government has recently made a decision that they will not expand the building of Sunshine Villages, instead to accept the idea of foreign expert Jenny Bowen of Half the Sky to build the Sunshine Family.
>
> At the beginning it can start with temporarily renting houses from the families who've had both parents die—a courtyard with about five rooms. Each new family can foster five to six orphans. . . . Twenty foster parents, five teachers, and five staff have already been selected.

ZZ looked up and grinned. "It's a good start—do you think so?"

I jumped up and hugged her. "It's great; it's wonderful! But ZZ, I sure wish they wouldn't call me an *expert*. They know I'm not, right? Did *you* tell Mr. Hu I was an expert?"

"Certainly not. But why should it matter?" she said. "We say, 'Why add legs to the painting of a snake?'"

"Huh?"

"You say, 'Leave well enough alone.'"

WE SAID GOODBYE to our Jingli that summer. A month before she left us, she met her new family on the telephone. Although she'd known that they would find her one day, we didn't share the whole story with Jingli until just before they called. We waited because we didn't want her to worry. We didn't know if that was the right way . . . or if there *was* a right way. She'd been our daughter for nine months.

We gave her the box they sent—a dress that matched her new sister's, a stuffed animal, pretty hair things . . . most precious, a photo album introducing her new family.

We watched her brave little face as she heard her mother's voice for the first time. She didn't understand all the words, but she got the message. When it was all over and we had all cried, Jingli said, "I so much happy."

She moved to Pennsylvania and soon forgot how to speak Chinese. A few years later, the little girl who taught me that what is best in us may be hidden, but can never be destroyed, became my friend on Facebook.

Dear Jenny Mama:

I am sixteen years old now and about to turn seventeen. I know I'm getting old by the minute. Can't you believe it?! My life with my family is great. I love them no matter what but not always show it. Well, at least that's what my parents said. They think I should be a lawyer because I am good at arguing. One most important quality that is special about my family is that it is filled with love.

My favorite things to do during free time are pretty much anything that has to do with art. I'm not much of a sporty person. A lot of my friends are involved in some school sports. For wearing the brace, it's really hard for me to participate in the fun like everybody else does. At times I really wish I could run and be able to do those things like any of my peers can. I hate to admit things like the fact that it's really hard for me to make friends.

There are times where I do think about China. Sometimes I ponder at the thoughts of it. If you didn't take me into your family, will I still be in the orphanage? Who knows where I'll be? There are memories of China that connect me to there. There are shadows here and there about the orphanage I lived in. I have to say there's not one thing I missed about that place. I love my family to pieces.

> *Thank you out of my whole heart,*
> *Jingli*

Chapter 16

One Who Rides a Tiger Cannot Dismount

骑虎难下

Chongqing

Autumn 2005

The buses snaking in convoy through southwestern China's back-country were crowded with government officials, orphanage directors, a handful of directors of foreign adoption agencies—and ZZ and me. We were on our way to visit one of Chongqing's "model" orphanages, and then to board a ship and cruise down the Yangtze River. The occasion was China's First National Social Welfare Institute Child Care Training Conference. Either somebody in high places was finally beginning to pay attention to orphans, or this was one mighty expensive junket.

Whatever it was, Half the Sky had been invited! It was our very first invitation from the Chinese government. Even though they pretty much left us alone now, we still weren't legally registered, and nobody from the Ministry of Civil Affairs had officially en-dorsed what we were doing. If we were ever going to make a real dent in the problem, we needed the government on our side—a tall order for a foreign organization in China.

The invitation called me a "foreign expert." The title made me squirm, but if playing that role might get kids the love they needed, then that's who I'd try to be. Luckily, Dana Johnson, my board colleague and a *true* expert, had been invited to be the key-note speaker.

We arrived at the model orphanage. Its balconies were deco-rated with curtains of bright-green plastic bamboo leaves, kind of a happy karaoke feeling. Inside, the place looked like most other orphanages in China. Full of children left alone. What made it a model was Baby Bubbles.

Small groups of conference delegates squeezed in and out of the Baby Bubbles demonstration room. ZZ, Dana, and I squeezed in last. We all agreed: Baby Bubbles was certainly something new.

On one side of the bathroom-tiled room was a row of six bright lamps aimed at a long table. Under the lamps lay six naked babies. They were being gently and efficiently massaged by six *ayi*s in crisp white uniforms. On the other side of the room were six transparent inflated tubs—sort of double-decker inner tubes—filled with water.

Designed by an army doctor and patented by his friend (who happened to head the Chongqing office of CCAA), the tubs were decorated with cute baby designs and the Baby Bubbles logo. Inside each tub floated a naked baby girl with a dazed expression on her face, wearing a tiny inner tube around her neck.

The very tall, craggy-faced army doctor explained. "The water temperature is carefully controlled at twenty to twenty-five de-grees centigrade [about seventy-three Fahrenheit]. The infants float for five minutes each day. Then they are given massage for five minutes. These activities stimulate the developing brain."

The local CCAA official chimed in. "This doctor taught us to look at things in a scientific way. Now we are able to discover misbehavior at an early stage. If we do nothing, the children will become retarded. We should do our best to avoid producing re-tarded children by getting to them before six months of age. Such scientific early childhood education should be made available to all of our institutionalized children!"

The visiting directors all seemed to agree. There was a buzz in the room. I was having visions of babies drowning and polluted poopy water and electrocution by temperature-control device.

"Early childhood education?" I asked.

"Our research shows that stimulation makes the children more intelligent," said the army doctor.

"I've always thought that if I wanted to be a billionaire, I'd just set up a quack shop in China," Dana muttered under his breath.

"Remember the orgone box?" I asked, not quietly enough. I was referring to Wilhelm Reich's 1940 "energy accumulator," which had mysteriously captivated Western intellectuals but had ultimately sent Reich to prison. The army doctor gave me a look.

I realized too late that he probably understood English. He probably even knew who Wilhelm Reich was.

The Yangtze River

Once we were all on board the ship, the first order of business was a banquet.

"You doubt our Baby Bubbles therapy."

I turned to the voice behind me in the buffet line and found myself looking at the army doctor's chest. I am not a tall person; we were standing too close. I looked around for ZZ. Although the army doctor was speaking decent English, I needed reinforcements. She was lost in the mob at the shellfish table, elbowing with the best of them.

"No! . . . Well . . . I think it's really interesting and . . . um . . . womblike." I backed away as much as I could.

"But you think it's laughable. What do *you* suggest we do?"

"Me? Oh, I'm certainly not an expert!"

"No?"

So what was I doing here?

"Well . . . I guess . . . um, I guess I think that the babies would benefit more if the money went into providing more caregivers.

I mean, five minutes of water time a day is—well, I'm sure the babies like the floating and especially the five minutes of attention they get from the *ayi*s at massage time. But if they had someone to cuddle and play with them all day instead, they'd get all the stimulation they needed and also might feel loved. Maybe even attached to their caregivers. Babies need that for healthy emotional development."

"I see," said the army doctor.

"But I suppose it wouldn't do much for the Baby Bubble business," I said.

"Do you think that Chinese people care only about getting rich?"

THE SHIP'S MAIN hall had been turned into a floating conference room. Through green-tinted picture windows, the narrow sculpted peaks along the Yangtze River Three Gorges drifted by in thick mist. . . . Iron Lock Pass, Water-Stealing Hole, Fragrance Stream . . .

Dana—Dr. Johnson—stood before government officials and orphanage directors, all diligently taking notes. He spoke with the calm assurance of an academic, his voice nonthreatening. He showed them slides of children in institutional care, none in China, all failing to thrive. Photos of tiny children who looked three or four but were actually in their teens.

"If a newborn infant enters an institution and stays for longer than six months," he said, "the risk of significant mental health problems increases. For longer than twelve months, he or she won't experience optimal growth. For longer than eighteen months, language will be affected. And for longer than twenty-four months, that child's cognitive abilities may be permanently compromised and interpersonal relationships will be impaired. Devoid of nurturing care, institutions steal a child's future."

The note-taking stopped. The room was silent. Dr. Johnson said, "The interventions developed by Half the Sky Foundation in China may provide our best hope."

My heart thumped. I tried to look like an expert. I secretly kind of hoped the army doctor was paying attention. But then it was over. CCAA Director Lu came to the podium and my mood took a dive. We were back in the world of *mu* of land and other somehow relevant statistics.

Chinese voices droned on. ZZ's quiet voice at my side interpreted anything she thought worthwhile . . .

"Orphans in institutions are vulnerable. They need special attention and care, the love and warmth of a family, and sensitive nurturing to ensure their healthy physical, emotional, and mental development," ZZ murmured.

Hey! I snapped alert. *I wrote that!*

"ZZ," I whispered. "Did the CCAA director just say that children need nurturing care? I mean, did he use the word *nurture?*"

"Yes."

"He's reading my lines, ZZ!" I whispered louder. "The words I say in meetings! Somebody's actually been listening!"

"Somebody important." She smiled. "You make him sound good."

Incredible. . . . The head of the CCAA was quoting me. Maybe they really did think I was an expert. So maybe it wasn't completely crazy to think that Half the Sky could change things in a big way.

But how? There were too many children. We would never be big enough to set up programs for them all. They'd have to wait forever.

But if the government got behind us, why couldn't we train others to develop the programs themselves? I'd always imagined that we would give it all to China one day. If we could train the whole country, that day might come sooner than I'd dreamed.

So why not? Why not train the whole country?

Oh, there you go again, Miss Priss, said the voice of my mother.

Patently inadequate, sighed the voice of Terri.

I looked around the room at my fellow delegates, some of them nodding off post-banquet.

But if we didn't at least try, who would?

"ZZ," I whispered.

"Yes?"

"New strategy."

"Yes?"

"No more one child at a time, or one orphanage at a time," I whispered. "The kids can't wait forever. We're going to take on China."

"Understood," she said.

THE PERKY TOUR guide spoke into a megaphone inches from my face. "Hello! These boat trackers you see used to be everywhere in the Three Gorges area."

We were touring Shennong Stream, a must-see on every Yangtze River cruise. All the delegates and their cameras had been transferred by ferry into small peapod-shaped boats manned by picturesque, ethnically clad singing oarsmen. The rocky cliffs on either side of the stream disappeared in clouds.

"In the time when there were no engine-driven ships, the boat trackers had to draw the boat with the tracking rope over their backs. They frequently encountered dangerous shoals and had to fight with winds and waves in the water. Therefore, they were naked. Now they wear clothes because a foreign tourist lady complained.

"Today some people think to attract more tourists, the ecological tourist site must have naked boat trackers again. The head of

the tracking team says, 'As long as tourists need it, and are willing to pay for it, we boat trackers are willing to go naked.' What
do you think, travelers?"

Hilarity ensued.

Director Zheng, that sour-faced pocket-protector of a man from
Maya's orphanage in Guangzhou, was squished beside ZZ. But
wonder of wonders, he was a changed fellow! He actually smiled.
He offered us cigarettes and then lit up himself. Then he invited
us to come to Guangzhou to set up programs.

"Guangzhou? You're sure?"

"Of course!"

"What about the province? Will Guangdong Province welcome
us?" I asked.

"Certainly!"

"What if we want to train the entire province?"

"Yes! Everybody wants Half the Sky programs!" Director Zheng
said.

So this was how it happened. Just like Hollywood—it can take a
lot of years to become an overnight sensation.

BACK ABOARD THE ship, all of the delegates signed a pledge that
promised:

> . . . through our common efforts, to let orphans and handi-
> capped children in social welfare institutions live in a richer
> and more stimulating environment of love, enjoy a standard
> of living best suited to their healthy growth, receive inspir-
> ing education and have their individuality and potential de-
> veloped fully so as to prepare the conditions and lay a good
> foundation for them to return to families and society.
>
> We solemnly take oath and propose to all social welfare

institutions and all people with loving hearts: Let us unite, irrespective of regions, states and races, and work hand in hand and shoulder to shoulder to realize our goal with full passions and determination and start a new stage of care for Chinese orphans and handicapped children.

We hereby sign this Joint Proposal for the Healthy Development of Children in Chinese Welfare Institutions.

I couldn't have said it better myself.

WE STOOD ON the overlook, gazing at the massive Three Gorges Dam project, the river rising slowly beyond. China vs. Mother Nature. Verdict still out.

CCAA Director Lu, who had never before spoken a single word to me, wandered over as if we were old friends. Just one big Hollywood party.

"I loved your talk," I said.

CCAA Director Lu shrugged modestly, as if nurturing orphans was just a little something he'd dreamed up. I took a deep breath.

"Director Lu, Half the Sky is eager to work with the government to train caregivers in our special approach to child nurture. We want to help you teach the whole country," I said.

Director Lu lit a cigarette, inhaled slowly, turned his head, and blew smoke at the dam below. I looked out through river mist and cigarette smoke at what would become the largest hydropower project in the world. The sheer audacity of it! Whole cities and towns and villages submerged, more than a million people resettled, wild rivers tamed. Environmental repercussions still unknown. The Chinese were capable of doing whatever they chose.

So why should I imagine that these people needed the help of a foreign do-gooder?

Still . . . he'd used my words.

It seemed forever before the director replied. "We will first do a survey on the status quo," he said. "Then publish operational guidelines to lay solid foundation for national trainings to follow."

Not precisely what I had in mind, but it was a start. Maybe.

"I'm delighted," I said.

"Total cost for the survey is 250,000 *yuan* [about 30,000 dollars]," he said.

"Of course, I'll have to ask our board," I said.

I looked out at China's 35 *billion*-dollar baby. And I wondered where we would find 30,000.

"All right, Director Lu," I said. "We'll be honored to help. Somehow."

As I left the viewing platform, I passed the army doctor, father of Baby Bubbles. He was mesmerized by the giant dam.

"I *don't* think the Chinese care only about getting rich," I said to him. "Not at all."

ON THE WAY home, I asked ZZ if she thought the CCAA director had said yes. She thought so, probably.

"Maybe that's as close as we'll ever get to hearing yes," I said. "Anyway, it's yes enough for now."

So I wrote a new plan. We'd jump on Director Zheng's invitation and open a center in Guangzhou. Then we'd train all of Guangdong Province. And so we would grow, province by province. We'd always try to begin in the capital and make it a training center for the rest. Perfect! I just had to figure out the money thing.

I knew that if we just kept moving forward, kept making miracles, one day the Chinese government would be ready and willing to take on the costs. But we weren't there yet. In truth, we were already struggling to support our twenty-four centers. I didn't think adoptive families could do much more. But how about big business?

By now there were plenty of foreign corporations prospering in China. There hadn't been much interest in helping Half the Sky when we'd tried before. Orphans didn't easily translate into profits. But with the government sort of on our side now, the time was ripe for convincing big business to do its part for China's future consumers.

A month later, just the way I imagined it, a large toy company actually agreed to sponsor our new centers in Guangzhou and Shenzhen!

Shenzhen, Guangdong Province
Spring 2006

Bruce, the toy company's cheery HR man, was on the phone.

"Jenny, can I get your last thoughts on tomorrow?"

And before I could reply, he rattled on, "At oh–nine hundred we will arrive and congregate in the assembly room. I think the Shenzhen director might want to say a three-minute welcome to us. We will have a party of twelve people including Martha, Guy Russo, and his wife. Remember, most critical is lots of photos of Guy and his wife giving gifts—and of course the children's reactions to them. Martha's expectation is that a camera is going off constantly—you gotta love her—and she wants quality close-ups in order to put together a great storyboard for McDonald's. Really pull at the heartstrings. By the way, I got Guy's title wrong—he's bigger than I thought. He's *president* for McDonald's Asia. The next highest in Asia is God."

Then he hung up. I was ready. This was not my first briefing. Bruce's boss, Martha, was the CEO of the Australian company that manufactured half of the toys at the bottom of McDonald's Happy Meals. They were in fierce competition with the American company that manufactured the other half. Most of the toys were made right there in Guangdong Province. Martha's business was heavily reliant on Happy Meals. She wanted to please McDonald's. I should take lots of photos of the boss and his wife hugging babies. It was a generous sponsorship—I was happy to oblige.

PEOPLE SEEING Half the Sky programs for the first time almost always cry. You can't see so many dozens of joyous and doted-upon little kids without feeling your own pleasure mixed with sadness. Sadness for where they came from, for why they have to be there. And, if you let your mind go there, sadness for the thousands who don't have it this good.

The guests visited the rooms, program by program, and as I dutifully captured the moments, I saw plenty of tears and laughter. Even Martha, in her purple Pucci separates, brushed a tear away as she shook the hand of an earnest tot who proudly shared her art.

But when I looked at the photos that night, to select the heart-tuggers for Bruce, I hesitated. Some of the photos of Guy and his wife, Deanne, seemed almost intimate in their connection to the children and to each other. I couldn't bring myself to lump them with the other publicity stills. I asked Bruce for permission to contact them first.

Well, the moment I spent some time with the Russos, I completely fell in love. Their hearts for children in trouble were enormous. Australians, they were now living in Hong Kong. Deanne, a former corporate executive, had quickly tired of the shopping and long lunches that often fill the life of a trailing spouse far from home. She soon became Half the Sky's top volunteer fundraiser. In time, Guy became chairman of our board. They were our first major corporate supporters and, in no time at all, dear friends.

And after corporations came royalty! At another new Half the Sky center, another celebration—this time sponsored by Ronald McDonald House Charities—we met that organization's goodwill ambassador, the duchess of York (who mostly wanted to know how she would go about adopting a Chinese baby).

Much more importantly, we next heard from representatives of the queen of Sweden. The World Childhood Foundation had been started by Sweden's Queen Sylvia to assist children at risk. They kindly agreed to sponsor our new center in Nanning, the steamy capital of Guangxi Province.

Nanning, Guangxi Province

Princess Madeleine, the Swedish queen's youngest daughter, was our program officer. Unlike at World Childhood project sites in other countries, nobody in China had a clue who she was. So, despite looking like a Disney princess come to life (truly!), in China Princess Madeleine could travel freely without paparazzi in pursuit. Still, the Swedish Embassy insisted on bodyguards. Two very tall and quiet gentlemen joined her on her visit to the Nanning Half the Sky center.

The Nanning director—let's call him Director "Big"—was a blustery retired army guy—a man's man. When our van pulled up at the orphanage, he ignored the princess completely and bellowed a warm welcome to the bodyguards.

As we entered each room to observe the programs and chat with the children, the bodyguards stationed themselves outside the door. Director Big kept running to the door to urge the men to come in. He tried to shove them, in that friendly Chinese way. The bodyguards smiled pleasantly and remained at their posts. They wouldn't budge. Big was perplexed.

Princess Madeleine complimented Director Big on the enthusiastic and engaged little girls, so obviously thriving in his Half the Sky programs. He wandered off before ZZ could translate.

We gathered in the reception room after our visit. The body-guards waited outside the door. Director Big sat in the room full of women, deflated and confused.

Anna De Geer, World Childhood's gracious representative, introduced the work of "Her Majesty, Queen Sylvia of Sweden," and described her efforts to assist children at risk. She said the queen had a special interest in protecting and empowering young girls. Director Big barely listened to the translation; his eyes were glazed and he wore the China Smile.

Anna then introduced "Her Highness, Princess Madeleine of Sweden, Duchess of Hälsingland and Gästrikland." As ZZ translated, Director Big saw, apparently for the first time, the stunning blond princess with her perfectly radiant smile. The old army guy blushed and shrank to half-size. He looked ten.

Someone once told me that the best way to handle meetings with creeps or adversaries or otherwise intimidating people is to envision them in their underwear. What works for me is to see them as the children they probably were. I'm rarely intimidated anymore. Big was now forever little.

Guangzhou, Guangdong Province

After our visit to Nanning, we returned to Guangzhou orphanage, Maya's first home, to see how our new programs were doing.

ZZ and I sat in the orphanage reception room where, eight years earlier, our Maya found her family. Everything was unchanged, yet entirely different. I felt strangely detached from the room and its history. What happened in that time when Maya was placed in my arms seemed to have happened somewhere else—in our own private limbo. This room, this orphanage, and its young residents were now part of who I had become.

Now, in that place that was just another orphanage reception room among the hundreds I'd seen, I thanked my new friend, Director Zheng, for allowing Half the Sky to come to his institution and congratulated him on the work his team had done so far. I told him I hoped that Guangzhou could become the training hub for the province.

"Under your leadership, Director Zheng, Guangzhou will become the model for Guangdong Province—in time maybe even the model for the entire southern region! Your programs will set the example for others, showing them that all children, even those with special needs, have potential to make something of their lives."

Zheng smiled modestly and sipped his tea. He looked into his teacup and said, "Of course, there are other children."

"Other children? You mean besides the two hundred or so in our programs?"

"Many more. In the other places."

And then he took us to see other buildings, other rooms elsewhere in the compound. Far from the place we'd met Maya. Too many children to count. Most had special needs. They sat on plastic stools or potty chairs or on rough wooden chairs with restraints. Others lay quietly in cribs in dim rooms. Some lay on the floor. Children perhaps six or seven, flat on their backs for the endless hours of their childhood. Not a single toy or book. Not even a scratchy TV this time. Just small children with blank faces.

I crouched before a frail child, maybe four, slumped in a battered wooden contraption—sort of a cross between a potty chair and a cage. She ignored me. She was focused on something in front of her. She moved her finger gently over a worn tray in what seemed to be intricate patterns. I looked around to find an *ayi,* to ask if she knew what the little girl was doing. There were none in the room.

"ZZ, will you see if she can speak?"

ZZ tried. The girl whispered without looking up.

"Cantonese . . . gibberish . . . *wakwak* or something."

Director Zheng said, "*Draw.* She's drawing."

"What is her name?" I asked.

Nobody knew. An *ayi* was summoned from another room.

"Her name is Lihua," the woman said.

Lihua

At 9:30 P.M. on June 24, 2001, policemen from Guangzhou Public Security Bureau took a baby dying with jaundice to the orphanage. The baby, born on June 17, 2001, was a girl weighing only two kilograms. The institution named her Lihua.

Under delicate care of the institution, Lihua's jaundice gradually faded away and she turned for the better. But shortly after this, she was attacked by a brain fever, which left her with lower limbs atrophy. She is brain-retarded and her legs are paralyzed.

With a lot of help from our friends, we doubled our plans for the new Guangzhou center. A year later, we doubled the size again. Lihua entered the Little Sisters Preschool in her new wheelchair.

At first, she was so shy that she would not even look at others. We tried hard to establish a bond with her. Then she discovered painting. She has a gift. Gradually, Lihua opened up and grew more confident, and we began to hear her words and laughter. She was fully enjoying the love and warmth of the big family.

Lihua worked very hard and her efforts paid off. The next year, she was allowed to go to primary school in our community. Half the Sky has a teacher to keep her company while attending school.

Her special talent in art was obvious, so Half the Sky hired a professional teacher for her. With the teacher's help, Lihua progressed significantly. When she was eight years old, she participated in the Jinlei Cup arts competition and won the silver medal.

Just before she entered primary school, Lihua became one of the first residents at Half the Sky's new Guangzhou Family Village, and as we did for all Half the Sky children, we received quarterly reports on her progress.

How are you, Auntie!? I'm Lihua. I am writing to you again. Are you happy?

At the orphanage, we held a "The Mid-Autumn Festival Performance" outside. My mother, younger brother, and I attended it. Uncle Zheng director bought much food for us to eat, such as moon cakes, pears, earthnuts, and apples. They were very delicious! There were shows performed, lantern riddle games, and clapping balloons. Here I have sent you a picture.

In my picture, the moon rises and the flowers in the garden are all in bloom. Two little girls are in the garden. They are so happy to see the beautiful moon that they dance. They wear pretty skirts with flowers like the garden. When they dance, the skirts will blow in the air. The girls wear high heels. They dance gracefully. My sisters and brothers and all the children in the house stick their heads out the window, watching us dancing happily.

Wish you happy every day!
Lihua

Now correctly diagnosed with polio, Lihua is learning to walk with assistance. And while she has physical challenges, to be sure, she is a brilliant young artist. She tells us she has never wanted anything more than to paint. And in her art, she can dance.

Our Lucky Star Is Shining

福星高照

Spring 2006

Big change was coming to China. In 2001, when China both won the Olympic bid and was admitted to the World Trade Organization, you could feel the pulse begin to quicken. The pace of progress increased every year. By 2005, construction cranes were appearing everywhere, even far from Beijing and Shanghai. Now change was ubiquitous and relentless.

Change. New buildings and high-speed expressways popped up "like bamboo shoots after spring rain." Beijing was torn down and rebuilt so fast and so often that old-timers got lost in their own neighborhoods.

China was morphing into New China at warp speed. Olympic fever gripped the entire nation. And it wasn't just about buildings and highways and Bird's Nests. New China meant new ideas, new money, new values, new dreams.

Even in our small domain—the world of disenfranchised children—keeping up with the changes and their accompanying tangle of contradictions was overwhelming. The ever-evolving situation was just about impossible to explain to our supporters.

The new affluence brought about a new middle class, which brought about a welcome slowdown in abandonment of healthy baby girls. Infertile middle-class families even began to consider adoption in a positive light. Healthy baby girls and those with mild special needs were now easily finding new families at home and overseas.

The new affluence also brought about the illegal but widespread use of ultrasound to determine gender. A million baby girls that should have been born in China were nowhere to be found.

And word about the government's well-intentioned Tomorrow Plan—a program to provide surgeries for orphans born with birth defects—was reaching the nation's poor. As medical costs soared and news of the plan spread, there was a dramatic increase in abandonment of children with special needs. Although the government's intention was to correct minor special needs so that more orphans would be adopted, rumors told a different story. Poverty-stricken parents who'd struggled to care for their severely disabled children were now abandoning those beloved children in hopes of getting them help.

In the big cities, the places that attracted China's floating population of migrant workers, children born of brief affairs or to poor couples who simply couldn't afford to be parents, were abandoned.

Prosperity brought disparity. And disparity brought crime. Some orphanages were filling with the children of prisoners—children of drug dealers, thieves, or dissidents. Orphanages across the river from North Korea were filled with stateless children whose mothers had defected but then had been caught and deported.

As the government cracked down on the growing numbers of child abduction and trafficking rings, big-city orphanages received children from distant provinces, almost impossible to reunite with desperately searching poor families—if, indeed, their parents had not sold them in the first place.

As for our family—the Splendids—there was no way we could leave China at the end of one year, or even two. As the situation for orphans grew ever more complicated, our great plan to train the nation and put Half the Sky out of business was fraught with obstacles. My resolve hadn't lessened one bit, but my Chinese garden, with its *most excellent and magnificent* mountain in the middle, was turning into a maze.

We sold our house in Berkeley.

ZZ and I were on the road almost nonstop. Besides running our programs in twenty-eight orphanages, watching small miracles happen for children every day, perpetually fundraising, and managing a growing team of field supervisors, teachers, youth mentors, foster parents, and nannies, we were working with our program directors to develop a comprehensive training curriculum for caregivers and a plan for training the places we would never reach. Neither of us took days off anymore.

OUR SECOND BEIJING apartment was number 142 on floor 14 of building 4 in the same diplomatic compound as our office. I knew enough by now to understand that all those fours just didn't bode well. Unlike the much sought after number eight, *ba* in Chinese, which sounds just like good fortune and happiness, four—*si*— sounds like the word for death. I wondered if I should pay a visit to Guanyin but decided that unlucky apartment numbers were too trivial, and who had time anyway? I was barely finding time to sleep in our new home, let alone figure out how to banish its bad juju.

Then *stuff* started happening.

First, we heard that Half the Sky was being investigated by the government. Orphanage directors started telling us not to come visit because the Public Security Bureau was in town investigating us. *What had happened to our government partnership?*

"Do you think it's our bad-luck apartment, ZZ?" I asked.

"I don't think so. Certainly not." But she didn't look so sure.

Then, on the May 1 holiday, we went to Gaoyou—the site of Half the Sky's first Family Village for children who are unlikely to be adopted—to join the families in celebrating the successful first year of their new lives. (Gaoyou is so far off the beaten track, I guess no one thought to investigate us there.)

It was a lovely event. Director Ni said a few words; I said even fewer. I asked the moms and dads if, after a year of family life, they had any concerns. One mother said, "Our only worry is that one day we may lose our children. We love them so much."

That was my worry too. I knew it wouldn't be up to me.

"I look at all your happy faces," I said, "and I feel so proud of what we've created together. This kind of family—our kind of family—is new . . . it's different, for sure. But it definitely isn't second-best. I dearly hope you and your beautiful children can stay together always."

We all posed for pictures, the children surrounded and cuddled by their doting parents. The fathers set off endless strings of firecrackers in the courtyard. When the building was thoroughly obliterated by smoke, we had a feast.

It was a joyous day—made even better because our dear friend, Mr. Hu from Henan, joined the party. He toured the new apartments and chatted with the families. "Now I understand," he said to me. "*This* is what children need."

And then his phone rang. When he hung up, his face had gone as gray as the smoky sky.

"I have to leave."

We found a quiet office to hide in. Mr. Hu and ZZ conferred in tense, low voices. I didn't understand a word. I cursed myself again for my pathetic Chinese.

"What's happened?" I blurted.

"That was the Henan Province party secretary," ZZ said. "He

asked why Mr. Hu was in Jiangsu. He said Hu must return at once."

"What does it mean?"

"We think someone has reported that he brought a foreigner to the AIDS villages. And there is something about the Internet. Something found with photographs."

I knew absolutely and with sudden dread what it was.

"ZZ, I feel sick. I used the Internet to send that report to the board about our visit to ask if we could seek funds for an AIDS Family Village project. It had photos."

ZZ's face turned as pale as Mr. Hu's.

Mr. Hu said, "My colleague at the department was sentenced to prison for four years for talking to the Chinese press. He gave only official statistics, nothing more. No matter—I was in the army for more than thirty years. There is nothing that I fear."

The two old survivors of the Cultural Revolution began discussing the best strategy. Don't rush back. Don't fly. Take the train. Arrive on Sunday. Call as soon as you know the score.

I closed my eyes and whispered, "If something happens to this dear man, I'll never forgive myself."

Mr. Hu left by slow train, bound for Henan.

BEIJING (*XINHUA*)—China declares all Living Buddhas must seek official permission before they reincarnate.

The minute we got back to Beijing, I asked ZZ if she could find some sort of feng shui master to give our bad-luck apartment a going-over.

"I know it's silly," I said. "But all those fours. What else can we do?"

The next day she brought us a Living Buddha.

The Living Buddha was a young monk with a buzz cut and a

cell phone. But even Dick had to admit he seemed to know his business.

He walked in the door and greeted us all with a charming smile. From his bag, he carefully removed a prayer book, beads, a small brass singing-bowl, a twig, and some rice.

The Living Buddha instructed us to arrange people and items of importance to us on the floor in a semicircle. The girls were at school, so we put out their photos. I also put out a Half the Sky brochure and my little jade Guanyin. I had nothing that belonged to Mr. Hu, so I added a small handful of Xinyang tea. Dick shrugged and contributed his camera.

The Living Buddha chanted for an hour. Every once in a while he struck the singing-bowl and a mellow hum would fill the air. He sprinkled water and rice around the apartment. He gave us little balls of stuff to eat that were both sweet and tasted of dirt.

While he was packing up, he invited us to visit his temple, a three-day donkey ride from Lhasa. "They look after orphans in that temple," he told us. He said our work is a blessing and we should have good fortune always.

BUT FROM OUR beloved Mr. Hu, there was only silence. I chewed on the fragrant dirt and worried.

Then, on Children's Day, June 1, 2006, President Hu Jintao visited the Beijing Children's Welfare Institution. President Hu played with the kids for a few minutes and, for the photo op, smiled benevolently at an adorable little girl who had cerebral palsy. Then he gave a speech:

China must increase its commitment to assisting disabled children and orphans. They are the weakest and neediest group in our society. They need care and love the most. Party committee and government at all levels must put these spe-

cial children in their hearts—improve their care and education. We must mobilize the whole society to share in care and
love for the orphans. We must bring them to the same level
as other children, to live and grow happily under the same
blue sky of the motherland.

It was an extraordinary statement from China's top leader. We
didn't know where it had come from or where it would lead.

Then, just an hour after we heard news of the speech, *our* Mr.
Hu called! He was jubilant about the message from Hu Jintao.

"He feels all things are possible now!" said ZZ.

"But ZZ, is he okay?"

"It seems he is well," she said. "He gave his report to the government. The Civil Affairs director says he thinks it will be all
right, but they wait for party secretary. Since someone has questioned Hu's activities, they need to find a way to make U-turn
before further approval to say yes."

"Yes to what?"

"To whether our Henan AIDS program will go on or stop."

"But—we don't have board approval for an AIDS program yet.
Or money."

"If party secretary says yes, it is better to have the program. If
not, the situation is quite difficult."

"Oh. Of course. We'll just . . . figure it out."

IN DECEMBER, JUST six months after the president's speech, the
Ministry of Civil Affairs announced China's Blue Sky Plan, a five-
year initiative dedicating two billion *yuan* (then about 245 million
dollars) to creating new children's welfare institutions that would
deliver improved care, education, and rehabilitation for orphaned
children across China.

In the New Year, ZZ and I were summoned to the Ministry of

Civil Affairs. A rare invitation from a ministry that seldom deals with *guoji youren*—foreign friends. Despite the recent auspicious turn of events, this couldn't bode well.

Bundled against icy wind, ZZ and I crossed through the middle of a broad Beijing street swarming with traffic, dodging cabs that I could swear were aiming for us. I never dared this trick on my own. ZZ darted across with the resolute calm of a longtime Beijinger. I had no choice but to follow.

On the other side, at the gates of the Ministry of Civil Affairs of the People's Republic of China, two gloved and overcoated military guards stood at attention.

I stood there too, wondering what was waiting for us beyond those gates. ZZ tugged me toward them. One of the guards shouted. I froze.

"Give me your ID," said ZZ.

The young guard studied my passport for a full minute. He made a phone call. Finally he pointed, stiff-armed, at the reception building.

A government drone sat embalmed behind dirty glass. ZZ handed her my passport and her ID card. The drone began painstakingly writing an essay, presumably on the background she found in my passport. ZZ sat me down.

"Foreigners don't usually come here," she said.

"Do you think this is about the investigation, ZZ?"

"They didn't say."

Her poker face made me nervous. I closed my eyes and tried to imagine a movie in which a well-intentioned woman from China goes to Washington and offers to help the government overhaul the American foster care system.

They'd just ignore her, assume she was a nutcase. They certainly wouldn't arrest her, would they? What if Mr. Hu wasn't really okay? Maybe someone told him to say he was? . . . I struggled to remember the sound of the Living Buddha chanting and the hum of his little singing-bowl.

"DO YOU REMEMBER me?" asked the man inside the ministry. He had a broad smile and round eyeglasses.

"Sure . . ."

"This is Section Chief Ma," ZZ said. "You met him when you first came to Beijing!"

"Oh yes, in 1999!"

Of course! He was my first government official. My first China Smile.

"1999," ZZ translated.

"1999," Section Chief Ma concurred.

That settled, tea was poured, and I was introduced to two women. Division Chief Gan was a faded beauty with a white-toothed grin and a girlish ponytail. Once upon a time, she must have been gorgeous.

"I was sent to the Film Academy," Mrs. Gan told me on another day. "I would have been selected to be a movie star, but I failed the acting test."

Her sidekick, Mrs. Gao, was plump and balding, with frizzy bits—too many cheap China perms.

Now everyone was smiling. I began to relax just a bit. I'd feel better when I knew why I was there.

After a suitable amount of chitchat, the three got down to business. Section Chief Ma explained that China had made great progress in the past few years toward two important goals: economic development and President Hu's plan for establishing a harmonious society, which would encourage social development. Certainly, concern for orphans was part of that plan.

"Certainly," I said.

"You have heard of the Blue Sky Plan?" Mrs. Gan asked.

"Yes, you plan to build new welfare institutions, right?"

"More than three hundred!" Mrs. Gan shouted.

"The children need facilities, but they also need service inside," said the more sedate Mrs. Gao.

The three then launched into a discussion of their plans. Soon ZZ joined in. I was forgotten. Things heated up—voices rose, soon everyone was shouting—all in a perfectly friendly way.

"There is one problem," said Section Chief Ma. He looked at me through his round eyeglasses. His smile was gone.

The chatter stopped. *Everyone* looked at me. Still clueless, I attempted the China Smile.

Section Chief Ma picked up a sheet of paper. He adjusted his glasses and read aloud: "On the afternoon of March 5, 2001, at the botanical gardens in Kunming, Jenny Bowen photographed young minority girls begging."

Everyone looked at me and waited. My smile may have wilted a bit.

"The Public Security Bureau wishes to know the purpose," said Section Chief Ma.

"2001?" I asked.

This was it? This was what would send me to the gulag? I remembered the policeman's hand on my camera lens. *Did I still have that photo?*

Whoosh! In a tornado of female fury, all three ladies leaped to my defense, all shouting at once.

"She was just a tourist!" "She liked the colors of the minority clothes!" "She is an ignorant foreigner!" "Certainly she would not think to publish such photographs!"

Then, as abruptly as it had begun, the storm subsided. No matter that two of the three women didn't even know me in 2001. Section Chief Ma wrote something and stamped it. ZZ patted my hand. It seemed that I was exonerated.

Mrs. Gao, the sedate one, turned to me. "We like Half the Sky," she said. "Your method comes from experience inside, not like other NGOs coming from a foreign place. Unsuitable for China."

"It should be like a joint venture," barked Mrs. Gan, the failed actress. "We do hardware; you do software. Not just new facilities, but service inside."

"With the Ministry of Civil Affairs in charge, of course," said Section Chief Ma. "And we will submit a joint annual report to the State Council and hold seminars on-site for high-level government officials."

"So . . . you mean Half the Sky could set up programs inside the new institutions?" I ventured.

"You decide how you want to proceed," said Section Chief Ma with a wave of his hand and his biggest smile yet.

"And maybe a national training center?" I asked.

"Make a proposal!"

"Does this mean that Half the Sky will now be registered?"

They ignored me without missing a beat.

"We can have a huge media event!" shouted Mrs. Gan. "And our own logo!"

Now the discussion turned to TV specials and the PR plan and which movie stars might be recruited, and in the excitement of it all, I was once again forgotten.

How did I get here? Where was this movie going? Had I completely lost control of the script?

TWO HOURS LATER, we exited the gates of the Ministry of Civil Affairs.

"ZZ, what just happened? Did I just dream that meeting up?"

"I don't think so. The ministry wants to be our partner. They say they need Half the Sky!"

Her smile was triumphant. That was all I needed to see. Before the pinch could come and wake me from the dream, I went home and spread the news.

Dear Half the Sky Family,

I have something extraordinary to share: In what will be its first-ever national partnership with a foreign NGO, the Ministry of Civil Affairs has invited Half the Sky to introduce its model and its four programs to orphaned children across China through a new government initiative called Blue Sky—a plan to build or renovate three hundred purpose-built children's homes offering a family-like environment along with education, rehabilitation, and nurturing care.

The government's idea is not to build more orphanages or to promote institutionalization over foster care or adoption. At the ministry I was told that every child belongs in a family and that will always be the priority.

We know, and we believe that the ministry understands, that the beautiful bright new buildings of Blue Sky don't really matter to the children. The children don't care if the walls are faded and the furniture is worn. What matters is that someone cares about them. That they are held and spoken to and feel safe. That they know they are loved. And Half the Sky has been entrusted with that tremendous task. What an amazing moment for all of us!

One orphanage director told me this: "Things are changing in China. The old idea that one must have a son to work the land and take care of you in your old age is slowly going away. Young people are leaving the land and going to the cities to work. Now it is rare in these smaller-city institutions that we receive healthy abandoned infants. But there are thousands of orphans living in small county-level institutions or living on the streets in our jurisdiction. Blue Sky will mean we can give those children loving care too."

So, in partnership with the Chinese government, I'm thrilled to tell you that our fall build in Wuhan will be the first of thirty-one Blue Sky / Half the Sky model children's centers—one in every province in China.

Nine years ago a small group of adoptive parents had a simple vision to make life better for the children they couldn't bring home. Look how far we've come! Who could have imagined?! I do believe we may well accomplish everything we've ever set out to do!

Thank you, all of you, for bringing us to this place.

OF COURSE, WE still had to figure out how we were going to pull it off. The ministry had assigned a grand total of two people to oversee the effort, Mrs. Gan and Mrs. Gao.

The two women did their best to show us everything there was to show about child welfare in China. The whole picture. We traveled the country together, from the southern tip of Guangdong to the North Korean border. The trust began to grow.

We developed our own Blue Sky plan to complete our written curriculum and to establish four or five model centers, offering provincial trainings in different provinces each year. World Childhood, the Swedish queen's charity, agreed to support our new plans with a multiyear capacity-building grant. JPMorgan Chase would support our first Blue Sky Center, in Wuhan, Mrs. Gan's hometown.

And sponsored by the Ford Foundation, in Shaodian Township, Henan, we quietly opened the first Family Village for children orphaned by AIDS. It was so successful that Premier Wen Jiabao led a delegation to visit it on World AIDS Day 2007.

Wuhan, Hubei Province

Autumn 2007

It is fair to say that the walls were rocking at the Wuhan orphanage as 160 children, 42 new nannies and teachers and foster parents, the orphanage staff, assorted Half the Sky staff and volunteers, Mrs. Gan, Mrs. Gao, and (it seemed) half the city and provincial governments celebrated China's brand-new, first-ever Blue Sky Center. Mrs. Gan gave interview upon interview, shouting over the music, flashing her gorgeous smile—our tireless media darling. I felt, for the first time, that the partnership was real. China was serious about helping its kids.

My cell phone rang. It was a reporter from the *China Daily,* the government's English-language newspaper. He said he was e-mailing me some questions about being the sole American elected to carry the Olympic torch on Chinese soil.

"Are you sure?"

In the run-up to the Olympics, *China Daily* and Lenovo had sponsored a contest for expats. The competitors had to explain why they would like to carry the torch inside China. Eight would win by popular vote. Of course, the fine print said that the government would make the final selection.

I am not a runner. But ZZ convinced me to enter. "What a great way to tell China about all of our forgotten orphans!"

That was all I needed to hear. I entered the contest:

I want to run for the children of China.

Mother to two girls adopted from Chinese welfare institutions, in 1998 I founded Half the Sky Foundation in order to enrich the lives and enhance the prospects of orphaned children in China. 2008 is our tenth anniversary!

My family moved to Beijing in 2004 to be closer to the work that has become the passion of our lives. Half the Sky offers its nurture and enrichment programs to children living in thirty-six orphanages across China.

This year, as part of China's Blue Sky Plan, Half the Sky was invited by the Ministry of Civil Affairs to introduce its life-changing programs to welfare institutions in every province in China. We are so honored!

If I were selected to carry the torch, I would run with the children—eight lovely children from our programs in eight different provinces. What an amazing experience that would be for them!

Now the reporter told me that I had been the top vote-getter and would definitely carry the torch.

Stunned, I hung up the phone and told the ladies. ZZ was ecstatic. Mrs. Gan and Mrs. Gao were beside themselves.

And the good fortune kept on coming. Just a short while later, I got yet another extraordinary phone call.

Ten years earlier, right around the time I was turning my life around to start Half the Sky, Jeff Skoll, first president of eBay and a soft-spoken billionaire with a vision, decided to turn his good fortune into something really big. He would use it to build a better world. He would solve "the world's most pressing problems" by betting on good people doing good things.

That second phone call was the Skoll Foundation telling me that we'd won the Skoll Award. Half the Sky would receive *one million dollars*. Along with a handful of other social entrepreneurs, I would accept the honor at the Skoll World Forum in Oxford, England. The award would be presented by former president Jimmy Carter.

There was no doubt in my mind that, at least for the moment, both Guanyin and the Living Buddha were playing on our team.

But China is the birthplace of *yin* and *yang*. Where there is light, there is sure to be dark.

Every Day Cannot Be a Feast of Lanterns

天下没有不散的宴席

Chinese New Year 2008

BEIJING (*GUARDIAN*)—Blizzards in China stranded hundreds of thousands of travelers today as forecasters warned more severe snowstorms were on their way. The harsh weather—said to be the worst for half a century in parts of the country—has destroyed homes and crops, shut major roads and rail lines, grounded flights and caused power blackouts. The China Meteorological Administration issued a red alert, the highest of its five ratings, warning central and eastern regions to expect more severe snow and ice storms. It has already wreaked havoc on a transport system facing its busiest time of year, with millions of workers preparing to return home for the Spring Festival (Chinese New Year). For many people, it is their only chance of the year to see their families. According to state news agency, Xinhua, the premier, Wen Jiabao, warned yesterday that lives were still at risk, adding, "The most difficult phase has not passed."

Even Guangzhou, usually balmy in winter, was caught in the bitter freeze. ZZ and I were trying to get out of town. On our taxi ride to the airport, we passed dozens, then hundreds of would-be travelers trudging along with cheap little suitcases and twine-wrapped plastic zipper bags stuffed with holiday gifts, headed for the train station. Our taxi edged around the station where, behind a police barricade, a mob of more than four hundred thousand migrant workers were already massed, pressing forward, elbowing one another, shouting, crying, some fainting in the desperate rush to push their way onto trains . . . most of which could go nowhere because power grids had collapsed.

WHEN WE FINALLY got to the Guangzhou airport, the scene there was chaotic too, but nothing like the train station. Our flight, along with most others, had been canceled.

An irate college student began shouting, demanding that the planes fly. The girl's pals hoisted her onto the ticket counter; she was red-faced with self-righteous fury. In seconds, that rowdy girl was joined by others, all screaming. The ticket clerks ignored them. A small contingent of soldiers in formation appeared from nowhere to quell the troublemakers. The kids didn't back down. They yelled at the soldiers and took pictures with their cell phones. The soldiers gently and relentlessly pushed forward. It seemed to go on and on, and then it fizzled into nothing.

Whether it was this unruly bunch (the privileged young beneficiaries of China's new economic miracle) or the frantic mob of migrants at the train station (the ones who'd made the miracle possible), maintaining China's "harmonious society" seemed to require constant vigilance. More and more all the time.

Eating bitterness did not come so easily anymore.

Unfazed by the commotion, ZZ pushed her way to the ticket counter. I found the quietest corner I could, called our Beijing office, and asked if they had any news about how our orphanages were faring in all this.

"It is snowing heavily in all central China," said Winnie, one of the office team. "We heard there are more than thirty railway stations shut down without electricity. There are power cuts in Hunan, Guizhou, and Jiangxi Provinces. Some institutions' power supply is not working. Our nannies and teachers are helping how they can."

"Okay. We're waiting for a plane in Guangzhou; it's probably four to five hours before we can fly. While I'm here, Winnie, will you and whoever hasn't gone home for the holiday try calling every institution we work with? If phones are down, try the local Civil Affairs office. Get a report on the weather situation. How are they keeping the children warm and dry? Do they have enough quilts, food, water? Is there anything Half the Sky can do? What is the plan for the holiday? Please send each of them our warmest wishes for the New Year and tell them that everyone is thinking about them and hoping for the best."

"You mean we can help with money? We can buy things for the orphanages?"

Our staff knew the rules. No mission drift.

"Well . . . ," I said. "It's family. They're in trouble."

"Of course," she said. "Thank you, Jenny."

WE MADE IT home and spent the next days working with the ministry to contact every orphanage that might be in distress. The more we called, the less it mattered whether they were Half the Sky sites, or that we didn't "do" disasters.

Everybody needed help—mostly water, fuel, food, disposable diapers, warm clothing, and bedding. Prices soared because no goods could be shipped and cold weather had ruined the winter crops. Wherever we could, we wired funds. In a few places where banks were closed due to power failures, we offered to reimburse any orphanage staff who gave cash to help the institutions while goods were still available in local stores.

"Chenzhou is in terrible trouble," reported Winnie. "It's listed as an official disaster area now. Even Premier Wen Jiabao is having trouble to go there. A giant power grid was destroyed by heavy snows, and the whole city has been dark for a week. Trains are not running because there is no power.

"Now the orphanage has to burn coal, but they are running out of it. Water has also been cut; now they get it from a natural well, which is, thank goodness, not frozen. Everyone including the older children helps to fetch water. All supermarkets and banks are closed. Even when staff has personal money to pay for baby food, diapers, and coal, things are getting hard to find and are very expensive. They have some food but are not sure how long this will last—maybe about five days. The local government is not able to give much support because they are now focused on dealing with transportation and electricity problems."

Dear Half the Sky Family,

Every year at this time we send you a note celebrating and welcoming the Lunar New Year. The Year of the Mouse promises prosperity (we hope!) and good fortune, and in 2008 there should be plenty to celebrate.

But in these days leading up to the holiday the weather has dealt China a heavy blow. You've probably heard about the millions of workers stranded all over the country, struggling to return home to their families for the Spring Festival holiday. But I don't know if you know how rough these days are for our children in welfare institutions, who, of course, have no families to go home to. Despite power outages and downed phone lines, our Beijing staff has been trying to reach all Half the Sky orphanages by whatever means possible and has talked with almost all.

Welfare institutions in south and central China are having the hardest time. This part of the country is simply not equipped to deal with extreme cold or heavy snow and ice. The most common critical problems are power outages, lack of safe drinking and cooking water, and lack of fuel, diapers, and public transportation. As conditions worsen, our nannies and teachers are remaining at the institutions day and night. They have given up the idea of going home to their own families for the holidays.

Gathering these reports together makes me think about how careful we have always been at Half the Sky to maintain our focus on nurture and education programs. Ours is not a medical or relief organization. There are many wonderful groups who do that work.

But now our family is in trouble. We need to break our own rule. I'm asking for your help.

I'd sent an urgent plea like this only once before—in 2002, when Guangdong Province turned us away at the last minute and I didn't know how to pay for moving our build to Chenzhou. Now, all these years later, it was the babies of Chenzhou—babies who hadn't even been born the last time we asked for help—who needed us the most. Once again, the world became a little smaller. Support rolled in.

Winnie called me at home that night. "So far, no train, plane, or car can reach Chenzhou. And they are now trying to borrow money from any possible resource to buy food, coal, and diapers. Twenty babies are sick, but the hospital is closed. They ask, can we please help in some way? The highway is closed but there should be other backroads. The Chenzhou director warns it is dangerous."

"Sounds interesting," Dick said. "I'll go."

"Are you sure?" I said, not entirely shocked.

My husband has a filmmaker's heart. He's shot on mountaintops and deserts and in every type of weather. He's shot underwater and from the open doors of helicopters (once, he later learned, without being tethered to anything). Such danger makes for gorgeous cinema. Guys like him will do anything to get the shot. I tried to explain all this to ZZ. She called Mrs. Gao at the ministry.

"The call is not very promising," ZZ said. "Gao called the Hunan Civil Affairs. Provincial director says they know Jenny and Half the Sky and they do appreciate the support for Hunan. They thank you especially for your concern for the children in the disaster. They want Gao to pass this message to you.

"As for Dick's kind wish, they also thank him, but due to the difficult situation and road, they cannot let him come. Even Premier Wen Jiabao must use helicopter to a nearby place and then followed by special cars accompanied by armed police to finally enter Chenzhou. No road is open. The Changsha airport is still not fully open, so they don't think Dick can go any farther even if he arrives in Changsha."

"Then we'll have to come up from the south," Dick said. "I'll get there from Guangzhou."

"Over the mountains?" I said. "I don't think I'll tell ZZ just yet."

"GAO CALLED ME just now," said ZZ the next morning. "Besides the new list of institution needs, she wants you to know that yesterday in Chenzhou, eleven workers died when they tried to repair power supply. She says now all roads are blocked and even *they* are asked not to go there at this time. Not to use the road in order to keep it safe since it is very slippery and very dangerous for driving. So they cannot help Dick to go there and they hope Dick is not going there at this time. Besides, they definitely do not want foreign friends to go there to protect the safety."

"So this is a definite no, ZZ?"

"Definite no."

"Dick is already in Guangzhou," I said. "He recruited our friend Miranda, a film production coordinator from Shanghai, to travel with him to Chenzhou. They're renting a truck and they will take it over the mountains tomorrow."

ZZ hesitated only for a moment.

"Okay, tell me how I can help," she said.

DICK AND MIRANDA set off from Guangzhou with a driver and a rented Jeep loaded with baby formula, candles, blankets, flashlights, batteries, quilts, and rice (in case the truck they'd arranged to pick up and load farther north couldn't get through). They stopped first to collect 100,000 *yuan* wired from Hong Kong at 2:00 A.M. by Mei, our finance director, to Mu, our Guangzhou nanny supervisor. It took three hours at the bank with ZZ on the phone from Beijing and Mei on the phone from Hong Kong to get the cash.

Miranda sweet-talked her way through police barricades, and in the foothills of snow-covered mountains, they met up with the waiting truck, did a whirlwind sweep of a local supermarket, and more than quadrupled their load of supplies—big boxes of infant formula, giant jugs of water, stacks of diapers, bags of coal, and piles of blankets. Just as they were pulling out of town, Dick spotted a lady selling brightly colored balloons on the street. He bought them all—it was a holiday, after all. When the balloon lady learned they were for orphans, she cut her price in half. And so had the blanket seller and the coal vendor.

DICK CALLED AS they started what was normally a two-hour drive to Chenzhou. And then he called again, seven hours later.

"It was all snow and black ice and crashed cars going over the mountain pass. We just now made it to Chenzhou."

Normally bustling with neon store lights, packed sidewalks, and chaotic traffic, most Chinese cities seem more alive and energy-filled at night than during the day. Not that night, Dick told me.

"It's so dark here," he said. "And unbelievably cold. A few cars, a few candles flickering in windows, but mostly just dark. I wonder what it's like for those babies to be in this kind of darkness. I hope they're sleeping."

When, at last, they pulled through the gates of the orphanage, they were greeted by forty jubilant Half the Sky nannies. Teachers and orphanage staff had taken the older children home with them, but the babies were sleeping inside. Nobody had known how Dick's rescue convoy could possibly make it, and yet "we knew Half the Sky would find a way," our nanny supervisor said.

Dear Half the Sky Family,

Tonight is Chinese New Year's Eve. Everyone in China who possibly can has gone home; all shops and offices are closed, no one answers the phone, the whole country is suddenly quiet.

The weather remains bitter cold but no serious snow is forecast now until the beginning of next week. For families in China, that's wonderful news, as relatives make their way from house to house with greetings and treats for the New Year.

I'm happy to tell you that, in Chenzhou, there is now at least a week's worth of food, two weeks' worth of coal, blankets, and diapers, and money to buy more. Although it's expected to take three to six months for the city to fully return to normal, we're so relieved that the children are safe and, at least for now, out of danger. My husband, Richard, who led the relief effort, wrote this when he got home last night:

As we make our way home, it's hard not to think about those little faces in the baby rooms staring up at me from beneath piles of blankets. I'm so happy they're warm, so happy they'll eat well, so happy they've got such dedicated Half the Sky nannies to attend to their needs. I wish they had parents.

As the stars of this little drama, they remained blissfully unaware of the countless worldwide threads, the amazing generosity of donors abroad, and their fellow Chinese who all contributed to this effort to make sure they would be okay now, so that someday they could thrive.

As I arrive home to my daughters and wife, I'm struck by the deeper meaning of this little adventure. I realize how, in my own way, I became infected with the spirit of Chinese New Year. This holiday that puts family first, that says get home at all costs, your family's waiting. I'm now sure that's what drove us up that mountain. Even if those little family members in Chenzhou didn't know they were awaiting our arrival.

Happy New Year from all of us at Half the Sky!

In less than a week, we'd publicly and completely broken our own rules. We'd bought generators and coal and blankets and milk powder and even a couple of washing machines. We'd raised over half a million dollars and given financial support to a hundred orphanages. With some trepidation, I wrote to the board, explaining why we may have strayed a bit and apologizing for not asking permission. Every one of them responded by giving us their full support and blessing. They understood. They even sent money! "Half the Sky is all about taking care of family," one said. If I was drifting from our mission, at least I wasn't doing it alone.

I failed to mention to the board that the Chinese government had told us *no* for the very first time. And that we had disobeyed.

Harbin, Heilongjiang Province
Spring 2008

In China's far north, up near the Russian border, a tiny baby girl struggled to breathe. Her bony chest heaved with the effort. I could see her heart pounding each time she exhaled. Each breath made a rattling sound. With fingertips I traced her little heart-shaped mouth, her blue lips. She made no effort to suckle. Only the next bit of air mattered.

She looked exhausted and alone. I feared that if I picked her up, I would kill her.

"Bad heart," said the head of the children's department. "Very complicated. There is nothing we can do."

I looked up at the bright walls of the Harbin orphanage, newly built with Blue Sky funding. Soon we would hear Half the Sky volunteers working and laughing down the hall. Harbin would become Half the Sky's thirty-eighth children's center and its third Blue Sky Model Center. The children here would begin to thrive. But, even now, with so much to be hopeful about, there was nothing we could do for this baby girl.

We can't do it all. We must stay focused on the mission. And yet . . .

In a country where more than three hundred thousand children were born each year with congenital heart disease, less than a quarter of them had access to medical care.

"She was surely abandoned by parents who had no other way to help her," ZZ said.

I watched that baby fighting for her life, and I began to wonder if, with all the good fortune we had been given, Half the Sky couldn't do more.

ZZ's phone rang. She listened for a very long time.

"We must return to Beijing," she said.

The Ministry of Civil Affairs, Beijing
The Next Day

ZZ, my ever-trusty barometer, was silent and expressionless as we were led through the hallways of the Ministry of Civil Affairs.

"Are you sure they didn't explain at all?" I asked again.

She shook her head.

We were ushered into a small, formal reception room. Red on red. Chairs and small sofas lined the walls. We waited.

Vice Minister Dou Yupei entered the room with his entourage of about ten or twelve—among them, Mrs. Gan and Mrs. Gao. The vice minister was not a very imposing figure. No taller than I am. A friendly chipmunk face with an extra chin or two. Upon his smallish shoulders rested responsibility for China's entire child welfare system.

We sat in the formal configuration. An interpreter sat behind the vice minister. Tea was poured.

The vice minister began by reciting Half the Sky's history in China. Reading off a page in front of him, he accurately listed the thirty-seven cities where we now had programs. Then there was a silence.

"In general, the Ministry of Civil Affairs wishes to commend Half the Sky on its important work for China's most vulnerable children," said Vice Minister Dou.

"We're honored," I said, waiting for the other shoe.

"We understand that your husband, Mr. Richard, undertook a difficult journey to Chenzhou during our Spring Festival storms."

Ah.

"Yes. Well . . . um . . . it wasn't too bad."

"Even Premier Wen Jiabao found it difficult to get to Chenzhou! With a military escort!"

"Oh . . . yes . . . well . . ."

"China has many problems," Vice Minister Dou went on. "We

are still developing, and there is much work yet to be done."

He smiled.

"We offer our sincere thanks for your love for the children and our hopes that we can continue our cooperation in the future. We are pleased to tell you that Half the Sky will be the featured story of our *Social Welfare* magazine next month! Now we shall take a picture for the cover."

That's it?

Someone appeared with a camera and began snapping. The vice minister smiled steadily for the camera and chattered away. "Usually, we do not expect foreign friends to give so much," he said. "You are like a Chinese! Of course, we know you have Chinese daughters. We find your story very moving. We also want to congratulate you on your registration."

Registration?

I looked at my pals. Gan, Gao, and ZZ all had giant grins plastered on their faces. *They knew!*

Not until the photo session was over did I recover my voice and my good manners.

"Vice Minister Dou . . . sir. On behalf of the many thousands who support our work, I thank you from my heart. You can count on Half the Sky!"

The vice minister left with his entourage. Gan escorted us outside. I felt dizzy.

"We have registration?"

ZZ swallowed me in a bear hug. "It's true! We worked so hard!"

"We're legal?"

"The third American NGO to be registered!" shouted Mrs. Gan. "First Bill Gates Foundation. Then Clinton. And then Half the Sky!"

For the first time, after ten years of operating in the shadows, we could legally open a bank account, legally hire staff. We were recognized. We existed.

"I almost shed tears," said ZZ, laughing and sniffling and wiping behind her glasses.

"Well," I said. "Wow! I guess we're really part of the family now."

"That's right!" ZZ said.

"Not 'the other kind'?"

"You're *zijiren,* one of us," she said.

And then the true test came.

Hongbai Town, Sichuan Province
May 12, 2008

One thousand miles from Beijing, in the mountains of Sichuan, a kindergarten class in an isolated township was waking from naptime. Sprawled or curled atop green painted desks, cozy under quilts from home, the children were just beginning to stir when the rumbling began.

Kailu

Four-year-old Kailu tried to sit up but couldn't. Everything was shaking, even the ground. The desk toppled, with Kailu clinging to it. She wiggled out from underneath. Everything around her was tumbling and cracking. The air was filled with dust and dirt and falling things. It was hard to see. The world was crashing and breaking and roaring loudly.

Somehow Kailu could hear Granny Yu, her teacher, cry out, "Children! This way! Run! The walls are falling! This way out!"

Kailu crawled through the heaving wreckage; wooden beams were starting to fall from the sky. Her hand touched something soft. She saw the face of her friend, Pingping, on the ground. Sleeping. She clutched Pingping's hand and looked around desperately.

"Granny Yu! I can't find my shoe!" Kailu cried, choking on dirt.

She tried to stand, pulling on Pingping, but now something was pinning her leg. Sudden strong arms grabbed Kailu around the chest, lifted her high, and held her tight. It hurt her tummy.

"My shoe . . . I lost it."

Granny Yu lurched forward, hugging the child, pushing through falling debris. Then something heavy fell and it was dark. The roaring sounds faded to nothing.

Part Three

Zijiren
(One of Us)
自己人

Forget the years, forget distinctions.
Leap into the boundless and make it your home!
ZHUANG ZI (369–286 BC)

C h a p t e r   1 9

If the Sky Falls on Me,
Let It Be My Quilt

天塌下来当被盖

May 2008

BEIJING (*GUARDIAN*)—The death toll from the most deadly earthquake to hit China in more than three decades today reached nearly 10,000 in Sichuan province alone, the state-run Xinhua news agency reported.

Worst hit was Sichuan province's Beichuan County, where a further 10,000 were feared injured and 80% of the buildings were flattened, including eight schools and one hospital. Photos posted on the Internet revealed arms and a torso sticking out of the wreckage of the school as dozens of people scrambled to free the students using small mechanical winches or their bare hands.

Even as the Ministry of Civil Affairs called asking for help, we were already on the phone, trying to reach the orphanages affected by the earthquake. We sent two of our Beijing staff, both Sichuan natives who could speak local dialects, to Chengdu, the provincial capital, to coordinate our efforts. No more questions about mission. Children were in trouble. Family helps family.

They needed tents, food, water, blankets, diapers, medicine. We called in favors from every business we thought might help us get supplies. Dick called a friend who ran a film production services company in Beijing and asked him to mobilize his team to help us with procuring goods, transport, and distribution. In an instant, we were "in production" on a massive scale.

Mrs. Gao called us from the ministry every few hours with updates on the children needing relief. Along with a plea for help, I began to send whatever information I had to our supporters. The world grew smaller still. Our family would have to grow larger.

We know that it is not only children in orphanages who are in trouble. We know that hundreds of children have been separated from their families, have lost their parents, are hurt, traumatized, and in pain. We know we must help.

There have been dozens of aftershocks, one reported to be as strong as 6.0. Children have again been evacuated from the Chengdu institution. They need tents.

Relief workers have arrived in the epicenter. The Ministry of Civil Affairs (this is the ministry that Half the Sky works with and also the agency responsible for disaster relief) has been unable to reach orphanages in the most affected areas: Mianyang, Zitong, Deyang, and Aba. While we've heard rumors about some of them, we won't pass on that information until we've made direct contact and verified.

Hongbai Town

Two days passed before soldiers finally marched into the little mountain town of Hongbai.

Like most of the buildings there, the kindergarten had collapsed. Parents and grandparents clawed at the twisted wreckage with bare hands, afraid to do further damage, calling plaintively for their children. Of more than eighty in the school, only about twenty had emerged before the building fell. Almost all had been rescued by their teachers, who had managed to pull another eight, still alive, from the rubble. Now the surviving teachers wept in the courtyard for the children they had failed. Beside them lay twelve small corpses, roughly covered. Alongside a few, parents wailed, clutching at the bodies in disbelief. The fate of forty children was still unknown.

The soldiers fanned out and gently pulled the parents away from the rubble. The parents protested. How could they leave their children? A child's head and arm stuck out of the debris. No one had come for him yet.

Some of the soldiers linked hands to form a blockade, holding the parents back.

"I hear someone in there!" a woman sobbed. "Please, children are still alive!"

"We can help them if you will let us do our work," one soldier said, choking back his own anguished tears. He looked no more than sixteen. The parents had no choice but to stand and watch as the soldiers moved carefully, all too slowly, across the mound of shattered lives.

A small voice sang from beneath the rubble:

Two tigers, two tigers,
Running so fast . . .

The soldiers moved in, cautiously removing heavy bricks and beams and twisted metal piece by piece.

One without ears,
One without a tail—
Very strange, very strange . . .

Finally they uncovered the cold body of Granny Yu. She was hunched over little Kailu, giving the child air and life.

Kailu didn't know that Granny Yu was crouched dead above her. She didn't know that her own leg was crushed and would soon be amputated. She didn't know that her own dear grandparents, the ones who cared for her while her parents worked far away, had died in their beds during afternoon nap.

Kailu blinked back dirt and squinted at the light. She peered up at the hazy faces of young soldiers and said, "Uncles, my friend Pingping is sleeping. Will you wake her up?"

Chengdu

It's Monday afternoon here in China. As I write this, the entire country just held three minutes of silence to commence a three-day period of national mourning. It began at 2:28 P.M., marking the very moment the massive quake struck in Wenchuan County, Sichuan. Flags flew at half-staff; the people wore white flowers and, heads bowed, held hands. Across the country, horns and sirens wailed in grief.

There are 32,477 people confirmed dead, more than 35,000 still missing.

Children in the institutions are all still well. We have now reached every affected orphanage, with the exception of Aba Tibetan-Qiang Autonomous Prefecture, where the orphanage is said to house fifty-two children. We will let you know as soon as we make contact.

Mianyang has become a major refugee center. Of the more than 20,000 refugees in the city's Jiuzhou Stadium, "scores" of them are young children. We are told, but this is not confirmed, that the entire center area of the stadium is reserved for toddlers and infants.

Perhaps today's most heartbreaking story was about some

of the seventy injured children who'd been carried down from the affected areas to West China Hospital in Chengdu. Most of the children were reunited with parents or relatives; some were even well enough to leave the hospital after treatment. But a few remained alone and unclaimed. They were required to sign their own consent forms so that the doctors could amputate their limbs to save their lives.

There were more reporters than doctors in the teeming West China Hospital corridors. Lights, mics, and cameras were focused on one ward where a *famous* television presenter was "counseling" a young boy who'd lost an arm, a leg, and his entire family.

A nearby high school had been commandeered to serve as temporary shelter for displaced children. ZZ and I found them there, curled on rows of cots, cuddling stuffed toys or gazing at photos, if they were lucky enough to have them. Meals and warm clothes provided, but no adults—all available volunteers were closer to the action.

Children alone with their sorrow. I began to see our role in all this. We were getting more information about children newly orphaned. Many hundreds, perhaps thousands more were separated from their families. All raw with trauma and grief and confusion. We needed to set up safe places for them. Places where they could take refuge in the arms of caring adults.

In this land of eating bitterness, there were no resources to address trauma of this scale. Most Chinese mental health professionals dealt with disease. They prescribed drugs. A supporter told me about a group of American pediatricians and psychologists who had come together after 9/11 to help communities heal from disaster: the National Center for School Crisis and Bereavement. I contacted them and began to make plans to bring a team to China to train doctors, teachers, caregivers, and volunteers in Sichuan.

I drafted a quick proposal to our ministry partners to allow us to create instant Half the Sky Centers in tents—we'd call them BigTops—in refugee camps or wherever there were large numbers of newly orphaned and displaced children. We'd use our skills to help them heal. We'd stay as long as we were needed.

But, of course, first we must do what we could to get the children out of danger.

Dear Half the Sky Family,

With your help, we have purchased and delivered or are in the process of delivering huge amounts of medicines and medical supplies, tents, cribs, cots, bedding, baby formula, diapers, kids' clothing and shoes, rice, noodles, cooking oil, water, powdered milk, bowls, cups, towels, mosquito repellent, and much, much more. As we finalized plans to ship, then bring in engineers to erect two more giant tents to shelter hundreds of orphaned and displaced children, we got an emergency call from the Aba Civil Affairs Bureau on the Tibetan Plateau.

They are caring for approximately one thousand children, fifty-two of them from the orphanage. There are over a hundred infants. They just received news that seventy more children are on the way. There are no more tents and no more beds for them. Further, they urgently need powdered milk and diapers. And they need foods that don't require cooking, as most of their cooking stoves and supplies have been destroyed. They need so much that they can't even give us an estimate.

IN SOME WAYS, if you ignored the tents and tarps set up on sidewalks and in parks, the city of Chengdu seemed untouched. We had definitely managed to give the Chengdu orphanage a makeover, though. The unsafe Half the Sky activity room, with its cracked walls, was piled high with boxes and sacks of diapers, clothes, food, formula, tents, and medical supplies. Our first BigTop (this one the size of a basketball court, purchased from a Beijing wedding planner and trucked in by our filmmaking friends) stood in the courtyard outside. Aftershocks were frequent and severe; everyone felt safer sleeping outside.

Our trucks ran between the airport, the orphanage, and the places in trouble. When we needed more help, the ministry sent in the army (the PLA). Half the Sky was *zijiren* (one of us)—not so foreign anymore.

A small convoy of red-bannered military trucks filled the orphanage driveway. Forty uniformed soldiers loaded one truck with tents, baby formula, clothing, and blankets. The front grill sported the Half the Sky logo and the characters for "Relief Goods." The army would try to get relief to two thousand children in flood-threatened Leigu, tucked in a valley northwest of the epicenter. Another truck was destined for the children stranded in distant Aba.

ZZ and I climbed behind Mrs. Gan into the ministry minibus. It was already full. The elegant UNICEF China representative—a foreigner like myself—her cameraman, and three Chinese assistants were surrounded by media gear and bulging plastic bags. Everyone wore bright turquoise UNICEF T-shirts. They scooted aside to make a bit of room for us. The UNICEF representative didn't seem particularly thrilled to have us onboard ("What is this Half the Sky?"), but her colleagues welcomed us. I was humbled to be part of the team.

"Do you share our policy on children and institutionalization?" the UNICEF representative asked, moments after we were introduced. I'm embarrassed to say I had no idea what it was. I glanced at the UNICEF team in the backseat. They smiled apologetically.

"Absolutely," I said.

"Good," she said. "Because if you don't, we don't want to work with you."

The minibus headed north toward Dujiangyan, just fifty kilometers south of the epicenter. After careful scrutiny at each stop, guards at the military checkpoints allowed our minibus to pass through into the town.

Dujiangyan, a once-bustling resort town, was in full relief mode. There was quake damage on every street, though not all of it catastrophic. Three-story buildings with faces ripped off, furniture still inside. Shops open for business despite pancaked rooms overhead. Tents crowded onto every possible bit of open space.

Mrs. Gan showed us where the government was erecting Hardworking and Frugal Families Shelter, the first and largest refugee camp. Several acres of farmland had been cleared, and now, prefabricated blue-roofed housing was being erected in neat rows. An instant city, only a bit more than a week after the quake.

We stopped at the local orphanage. The children and *ayi*s were outside, like most everyone else, living in a tent. No one had really slept in days.

Mrs. Gan, ZZ, and I climbed out of the minibus and visited with the children. They were eager to talk; their quake stories spilled out. Meanwhile, two UNICEF workers set about quizzing the workers and filling out questionnaires. The third hauled one of the plastic bags out of the minibus.

The UNICEF representative remained in the minibus, adjusting her makeup and smoothing her hair. Eventually she emerged, smiling and fresh. Diego, the cameraman, filmed her giving toys to the children. Then she posed for stills while her colleagues did the work they came for.

It was the same drill at every stop. Whether makeshift shelter or government refugee camp or hospital ward, each visit was capped with a UNICEF representative photo op.

•   •   •

"WE'VE TALKED TO the Army," Dick said. "The trucks can't get through to Aba."

His call came while the ministry minibus was driving us through more quake-ravaged countryside toward the big refugee shelter in Mianyang.

"They told us that nearly two hundred people have died in the last few days along those mountain roads in mudslides caused by the early rains," he said. "As dire as the situation appears to be, even the Aba director feels the risk is too great."

"So you think there's no way to get to those kids?"

"There's maybe one. Since the ministry was instrumental in launching us on this mission, can you ask if there's any possibility the government could fly at least some of this shipment by helicopter?"

"Okay . . . sure," I said.

I hung up and looked at the back of the head of the Ministry of Civil Affairs of the PRC's sole representative in the vehicle, Mrs. Gan. She was sound asleep and snoring. The UNICEF representative sat stonily beside me. This wasn't the moment for *carpe diem*.

MIANYANG (*XINHUA*)—Chinese Premier Wen Jiabao went to the makeshift tent school established at Jiuzhou Stadium in Mianyang on Friday to visit teachers and students who survived the May 12 earthquake. Wen encouraged them to study harder following the calamity. "Let us not forget the earthquake," he told the students in a tender voice. "Then you will know what life is all about—it is bumpy, as the roads are."

"Trials and tribulations serve only to revitalize the nation," he wrote on the blackboard to encourage them.

"The Mianyang Jiuzhou Stadium is the largest and *most famous* stadium in southwest China," the local Civil Affairs official told us as our minibus neared the sports complex. "It cost 150 million *yuan*! Many people criticized such wasteful spending. Of course, they don't criticize now! No other place is large enough to shelter so many refugees."

We were allowed past another military checkpoint onto stadium grounds. The giant courtyard was ringed by a multicolored sea of tents, tarps, and plastic sheeting. The Red Cross and various government agencies had set up aid tents and kiosks. Cases of bottled water were stacked in small mountains.

Twenty thousand survivors, maybe more, overflowed the grounds. They were camped on quilts or sleeping bags among their few possessions; or standing in line for information or food; or wandering and looking for familiar faces; or scanning for the hundredth time the row of white boards covered with name lists of those in other shelters or hospitalized with injuries; or studying the big notice board and every other vertical space that was covered with missing-person flyers, photos, and posters.

We left the minibus, and while Mrs. Gan went to check in with Civil Affairs officials, ZZ and I wandered over to the notice board. We joined the dozens who were standing stock-still in front of it, staring at the rain-washed notices and fading faces, wanting them to morph into someone they loved but seemed to have lost.

I looked at the faces on the board. Children and grannies and strong young men. All vanished. The same song played over and over again on the loudspeakers, "No matter where you are, I must find you. . . ."

Mrs. Gan returned. She told us that it would not be possible to visit the children inside the arena, the "inner circle."

"But why not?" the UNICEF representative protested. "UNICEF has come expressly to help the children. That is our only purpose for coming all this way. Just today the drive was over three hours."

"I'm sorry," Mrs. Gan said. "The authorities wish only to protect the children. They are concerned about the spread of disease. Since we have come all this way, however, I suggest you visit with the many families here. As you can see, there are thousands of children. I'm certain it will be all right to take their pictures. Our bus will wait here until you return. Take all the time you need."

The UNICEF representative sighed and turned away. She walked into the throng with her crew following.

ZZ and I started to do the same. Mrs. Gan caught us both by the arm.

"Follow me," she said.

A DOZEN MORE checkpoints led us to the "inner circle"—a very big gymnasium housing about a thousand children, volunteers (most in their late teens or early twenties), police, and soldiers.

"No picture taking in here." Mrs. Gan smiled. She'd had it with the photo ops.

Neat rows of red mats striped the wood floors. We walked past a few counseling sessions—three or four earnest psychologists, brought in by the Municipal Committee of Youth League, questioning a single frozen-faced child.

Mrs. Gan introduced us to Mr. Liang, the man in charge. Recently retired from the military, Mr. Liang had a calm and kindly demeanor.

"How do the counselors decide which children to counsel?" I asked.

"We look for the sad faces," Mr. Liang said gently. "Generally, those are the ones who need help."

"That seems the right approach," said ZZ.

"Sometimes, though, if the child looks very sad," he said, "they are counseled by a few different groups."

I wandered through the rows of children and sat down beside a little girl, seven or eight years old. She had a sheet of paper before her, beside a bunch of colored markers. She was looking down at the plain pencil in her hands, chipping the red paint off its outside with her fingernails.

The paper was blank, except for a neatly drawn round sun in one corner. It was black.

"May I sit with you?" I asked.

The girl said nothing. I sat beside her. I touched the black sun.

"Is your drawing finished?"

"Uncle said to draw my home. Draw trees and flowers. Call the picture 'Take Care of Our Planet.'"

"You don't want to?"

"I want to draw earthquake, but I don't know how."

"What is earthquake?"

"Big shaking, big noise, then come aftershocks, then comes epidemic when you die for not washing hands before eating."

We sat for a while and pondered such a fate.

"Do you want some help with your drawing?"

She nodded. Then she climbed into my lap. The tears came before she'd even settled.

"I miss my mama," she whispered, choking on the awful words.

IT WAS RAINING lightly, and mud flowed on the roads. The UNICEF representative decided that her team would not join us for the drive farther north to the small orphanage in Zitong.

When we arrived, dozens of children were huddled in the courtyard, sheltered from the drizzle by a few dazed young *ayi*s holding umbrellas. A large blue government relief tent sat in the center. It was full of babies and toddlers. The walls of the orphanage itself were too cracked to trust.

A sign inside the gate listed the names of new arrivals, some with notations.

Yan 女 [female]—only mother was home

Xianlin and Ligang 男 [male]—brothers, parents unknown

Cheng 女—her father is working in Xinjiang, mother did not survive

Dan 女—her parents are working in Zhejiang

Jun 男—about two years old, parents' whereabouts unknown

Baby Zhou? 男—about one year old, relatives unknown

A toddler with a big bruise on one side of his head hurried up to me and clutched my leg. "Mamamamamama. . . ."

"Oh baby. . . ." I lifted him up. He clung to my neck.

"He does that whenever the gates open," the Zitong director said. "We think it's the only word he knows."

ZZ and Mrs. Gan and I (with the little boy wrapped around me) sat on small chairs and sipped hot water from paper cups. We asked the director how we could help.

"Before the storms of Spring Festival, we didn't know Half the Sky," she said. "Now we know you very well. You helped us then. And this week, you helped us with a whole truckload of clothes, bedding, formula, medicine, and diapers for the new children who arrive each day. It is difficult now to ask you for more."

"That's why they've come," Mrs. Gan said. "They want to help."

"What we need is a van," the Zitong director said.

I flashed back to my very first orphanage visit in Shijiazhuang. *What we really need is an elevator.*

And now this place—Zitong—it wasn't a Half the Sky orphanage. Many of these children weren't even orphans. They had relatives somewhere looking for them. *Talk about mission drift—we can't do it all.* I hugged the little Velcro boy closer.

"Half the Sky doesn't buy vehicles," ZZ said regretfully. "Never. We work only for the children."

"This *is* for the children. We are in the center of nine counties—

all hard hit. We have no way to take the children to hospitals. Emergency vehicles are not available. A van costs only 100,000 *yuan* [12,000 dollars]."

"Can't you make an exception?" said Mrs. Gan. "It may take months to get a vehicle through proper channels."

"Not possible," ZZ said, blinking back inevitable tears. "We have rules. . . ."

Family helps family. The rest doesn't matter.

"Well," I said. "Well, maybe—"

ZZ looked at me, waiting, not breathing.

"Mrs. Gan," I said, "we have a problem getting relief to the children in Aba. The roads are gone. We really need a helicopter."

"A helicopter?" said Mrs. Gan. "You want to trade?"

"We don't need to *buy* a helicopter, just use one of the army's. Just once. Or twice. What do you think?"

Mrs. Gan turned to ZZ. ZZ looked stunned. Tears drizzled down her cheeks.

Mrs. Gan looked back at me. She laughed.

The next day a People's Liberation Army helicopter full of baby formula, diapers, and bedding flew to the Tibetan Plateau. And somewhere in Sichuan, a van bearing the Half the Sky logo still prowls the backroads.

Hongbai Town
Three Weeks Later

An aching sorrow smothered Hongbai. We had made the five-hour journey from Chengdu once before, past broken bridges and collapsed roads, to bring relief goods. We'd been there as the army boys worked to build a cemetery on a hillside with hastily poured concrete tombstones. We'd seen the parents place photographs and stuffed toys and sweet treats beside the small fresh graves. We'd looked away as they built fires and burned paper blessings and tore their shirts with agonized cries.

Now, on this one-month anniversary of the quake, the local volunteers we'd been training in Chengdu asked if we could come back to help mark the day.

I climbed out of the minibus. A tiny grandmother rushed up to show me cell-phone photos of the two children she'd lost. Their parents—her son and his wife—worked in a distant province. She'd been the sole caregiver for the two little girls.

"I couldn't save the children," she said. She thanked me, thanked Half the Sky. I don't know why.

The tent school, decorated with balloons and tinsel, stood in the old schoolyard. Behind it, soldiers and dogs still picked through the much-sifted rubble of the collapsed primary school. Parents sat or stood silently in the courtyard, holding photographs of their lost children. Waiting.

Inside the tent were the children who'd survived, with their volunteer teachers and with desks salvaged from the collapsed school. We talked and played games through the morning. The children relived their disaster experience over and over again. There was a hunger to talk about it now.

There was also a birthday to celebrate—twin girls who should have been turning eleven together, but only one was alive. Still, the group ate cake and sang songs.

"My sister and I loved to sing 'Invisible Wings,'" the birthday girl said. She tried to smile, but it wouldn't come. The volunteers and the children sang together:

I know I've always had a pair of invisible wings
And they take me flying, flying over despair. . . .

"*Sheng wu suo xi,*" ZZ whispered. "Life must go on."

•　　•　　•

AT 2:00 P.M. we went outside. The children and the volunteers and the parents who held photographs gathered in front of the fallen school. The soldiers stopped their work and stepped away. We all looked at the pile of rubble and twisted rebar.

A boy, eight or nine, who'd only listened in the tent, now couldn't bear the silence. His memories came pouring out. He told us that he hadn't been able to bring himself to attend the tent school before today.

"I was afraid to come back here," he said.

He was the last student to be pulled out alive. When the earth shook, he was one of the obedient children sitting with arms crossed at their desks—some naughty boys were still outside, safe on the playground where we now stood.

"My classroom was on the second floor. It fell and I got trapped between concrete and brick. I tried to yell for help, but nobody could hear me. Everybody was screaming and crying. I waited for a long time until it was quiet. I began yelling again. Then they came for me."

"And the other children in your class? The good ones at their desks?"

He bit his lip, shook his head.

At 2:28 P.M., exactly one month after their world changed forever, the children from the tent school placed their hands on their hearts, then bowed three times, saying goodbye to those who had died at the Hongbai Town Primary School.

The boy said, "We will live our lives as best we can."

Although I never knew the ones they lost, I said goodbye too. The loss belonged to us all.

Chapter 20

Count Not What Is Lost, but What Is Left

往事已成云烟　珍惜今日拥有

Dear Mr. Jenny Bowen :

Congratulations! With the theme of "Journey of Harmony" and the slogan of "Light the Passion, Share the Dream," it is a great pride to be selected as a torchbearer of the Beijing 2008 Olympic Torch Relay. The moment when you hold up the flame will definitely be the most brilliant and memorable one in your life.

The Olympics were the last thing on my mind. When the call came reminding me that the torch relay would be starting up again after the three-day official mourning period, I was engrossed in trauma trainings and opening our instantly popular Half the Sky BigTops for kids in refugee camps. The six giant tents each filled with children the moment they were erected, sometimes even before we were able to bring in teachers and furniture and supplies. The need for safe and caring community was great.

Edward, my torch relay handler, said I was now scheduled to run in Chongqing on June 14—just a month after the quake and not far from the affected areas.

"Edward, I would like to ask special permission to run with some children who survived the quake," I said. "To show that they will not be forgotten even during China's big celebration. Under the circumstances, I hope this will be granted."

"It is not possible," Edward said. "Security is too high. Not safe for kids."

"Then I think I can't run," I said.

"You *must* run," he said. "It is a great honor!"

"What's the point?"

"But it is impossible to cater for your request," Edward said. "BOCOG takes security as the top priority. If you do what you say, thirty kids will enter the protected zone of torch relay, which is not allowed. BOCOG has strict rules to ensure smooth, safe relay. How about we can arrange for kids to be along route where you run?"

"I'll think about it."

Edward didn't have the power, and he was all we had. ZZ thought we should make the best of it—get the kids whatever attention we could. The media was eager to cover the big day. Besides the Chinese news outlets, we had been contacted by some Western media—*The Wall Street Journal, New York Times,* Reuters, *Time,* NPR, CNN, ABC, and AP. Most had learned about Half the Sky during the early days of quake relief, when information was hard to come by. They called us almost daily. Some wanted to bring camera crews. Maybe there was a story to be told, even if the children couldn't run.

But then government friends quietly informed us that there was word of protests brewing in this sensitive part of China, so close to Tibet. One told us that there were rumors of some sort of attack or bombing in the works; known activists had been spotted in Chongqing. The date and place of my run were switched, then switched again. And certainly no foreign media would be allowed.

Dear Half the Sky Family,

We got a call today telling us that, for security reasons, our torch leg is now scheduled a day earlier and moved to Wanzhou, a district of Chongqing Municipality that's about four hours outside the city. I will still run for the children, especially those of Sichuan. Somehow, we will manage to bring the children to the site. I hope it doesn't change again!

Yesterday was the one-month anniversary of the earthquake. . . .

That night I left to meet the torch relay in Chongqing. My destination was 360 miles and a world away from the quake zone.

Wanzhou, Chongqing

It was raining in Wanzhou. The bus full of nervous torchbearers made its way past an endless lineup of what looked to be the entire People's Liberation Army. Instead of torches, they carried automatic weapons. We waved at them through rain-spattered windows. They didn't wave back. This was a different PLA than the good-hearted boys picking through rubble in Sichuan.

Up ahead, through the haze, in a new suburban development that appeared to be uninhabited and still under construction, I saw a camera truck and a bunch of athletically clad Public Security Bureau guards. And then, orderly throngs of spectators waiting patiently under umbrellas, waving little Chinese flags. All neatly arranged behind a phalanx of large plainclothesmen.

As our bus approached the scene, a former Olympian, who, judging by the applause aboard, was *famous,* handed out torches to the passengers and told us how to use them. I didn't understand a word. After a month of earthquake, I was exhausted and in what felt like a permanent daze.

The Olympian showed us how to raise our hands in triumph

when we passed the torch. We all practiced. As we finished, the bus stopped.

The first runner was released. The bus moved on but stayed just ahead of the action, stopping, starting, dropping and picking up runners every fifty meters or so. Security guys lit and doused the torches, just in case dummies like me couldn't follow directions. It was hardly what you'd call a strenuous effort on the part of those of us having the most brilliant and memorable moment in our lives. In my case, that was probably just as well.

I did spot the children from Chengdu and Chongqing orphanages. Just barely. Peering out from behind the Public Security Bureau's burly finest, about fifty of them were there, along with Maya, Anya, Dick, ZZ, and our Half the Sky team, all waving little flags and jumping up and down and calling out to me to *Run!*

"*Jiayou*, Jenny! *Jiayou! Jiayou—!*"

For the children, for my big beautiful family, I gave it my all. I waved wildly and raised my torch in triumph as I ran by.

Beijing
August 8, 2008

At the most auspicious moment of what should have been the most auspicious year—8:08 P.M. on 8/08/08—I sat with my family and our friends amid more than ninety thousand human beings in absolute awe. Surrounded by people I loved, I watched the phenomenal display as China told the world she had arrived.

The opening ceremony of the 2008 Olympic Games: 2,008 drummers, 2,008 *taiji* masters, 2,008 parasols painted with children's happy faces. China's proudest, *most famous* night ever.

I found myself swept to another place. Lost in the throbbing of 2,008 *fou* drums. Still raw from the memory of orphans in the rain—*Jiayou, jiayou!*—and the children with their hands over their hearts in Hongbai Town. . . .

And maybe it was the drums and the spectacle . . . and maybe it was the lost children calling to me, all my small teachers—Jingli, Baobao, Baimei, Kailu—the ones I knew and the ones whose names I'd likely never know . . . I now completely understood that *I am part of this*. Not part of China. Nothing to do with borders or blood or beliefs. I am part of a vast shared humanity. I have a role to play. We all do.

Beijing
Spring 2009

"The babies are coming!"

Four nurses, a doctor, thirty nannies, and six foster moms closed in on the elevator doors, impatient for them to open.

Thirteen years before that day, a boy—the young son of a wealthy American financier—was sent to Beijing to live with a Chinese family for a year. His parents had a special fondness for China and wanted to give their son a life experience different than the privileged one he knew. The boy learned the language, completed sixth grade, made some lifelong friends, and then went home. That could have been the end of it.

But China has a way of getting under your skin. The boy loved the people, and he was haunted by the poverty. As an Eagle Scout project when he was sixteen, he started China Care, a charity to benefit Chinese orphans with special needs. He began by raising money from his neighbors, and the enterprise ballooned from there: China Care went on to fund corrective surgeries and medical care for hundreds of children with life-threatening conditions.

When the boy was older and ready to explore new things, China Care's leaders approached Half the Sky. It was during the earthquake days. I was only too aware of the needs we weren't filling. I thought often of that little baby in Harbin whose heart was failing.

So now, in the spring of 2009, we were finally ready to greet the first residents of our new China Care Home, providing pre- and postoperative care for medically fragile orphans.

But the elevator doors didn't open soon enough for the baby girl in Harbin. She didn't survive.

Among our first arrivals, there were three whose complex heart conditions could not be repaired in country. Once again, I stepped into the forbidden waters of international adoption and requested special permission to advocate for the three little girls. We had their medical records reviewed by prominent American pediatric cardiologists. Two of the girls easily found adoptive homes and lifesaving surgeries in the United States.

The third, Fangfang, needed, at the very least, a transplant—a new heart. More likely, new lungs as well. Given her frail condition after three years of struggling to live, it was unlikely she could survive surgery. She was deemed inoperable and terminal.

In the China Care Home, Fangfang was given a mama and siblings. Despite her weakness, and in her own way, she blossomed.

I sat in our playroom with tiny Fangfang on my lap and showed her how to work my camera. She watched carefully with a crooked little smile. I heard her delighted laughter as, despite the congenital malformation of one of her arms, she not only figured the thing out but managed to take some great shots. I looked into the bright eyes of this enormously intelligent and spirited little being. And I simply couldn't believe that her life would soon be over.

Fangfang

Fangfang is a clever girl. She can speak many words and is a quick learner. As we show her photos of some children, she can recognize them and say their names. She can walk steadily and use her little two fingers on the left arm skillfully to pinch things like spoon or ball.

Six months into our search for families for the three little girls, only Fangfang was left. Finally, a couple came forward and told us she was meant to be theirs.

> Fangfang is so lucky that a family is going to adopt her. They sent presents to her and an album with pictures. We are very excited. Her foster mom at the China Care Home burst into tears and said to her, "Fangfang, I'm so happy for you." Fang- fang looks at the album every day and says, "This is my dad, my mom. I also have a sister."

But then, when they truly understood how ill she was, the family withdrew. Soon two other families considered adopting Fangfang, but they also decided not to pursue it. I talked to dozens of prospective parents. I tried to arrange a free heart transplant in the United States. From what I could learn, such a thing does not exist. A healthy child's heart is too rare and precious.

Finally, just before China Care Home celebrated its first birth- day, Fangfang found her family. She would have three big broth- ers and five big sisters, four of them adopted from China. Her new parents said, "We knew from the moment we saw her face that she was our daughter. We were prepared to bring her home and pro- vide her with a family and love her unconditionally for however long God would share her with us on earth."

We all knew they were the ones. Fangfang, of the sweet crooked smile and the iron will to live, became Teresa, the newest resident of Maryland, USA.

She spent three joyous years treasured in the arms of family, but she didn't survive that long-awaited heart transplant. Still, Fangfang's spirit touched the hearts of many; urgent care for criti- cally ill orphans continues today in her name.

•　　•　　•

BY LATE 2009, we had five flourishing programs and operated centers in forty-six cities. Nine of them were Blue Sky Model Centers; we still had twenty-two model centers to go. Half the Sky was legal and had a bona fide partnership with the Chinese government, complete with contract. Our lives were very full.

Despite all that, and after five years in China, the Splendids returned to America. Our daughters, now fourteen and eleven, dearly wanted to be American girls when they entered high school; and, as much as we loved China, the pollution was killing us. Once again, I became an ultra-long-distance commuter: a month in China, a month in the United States. Life was even fuller!

So when both ZZ and Rachel Xing, our operations director, told me that I really should meet the new boss of the welfare department at the Ministry of Civil Affairs, I kept postponing the visit. I figured he was just another bureaucrat and I'd meet him in due course. They persisted. They'd heard him speak at a conference.

"He's different," Rachel said.

I did a little research on the man. He was all over the Internet, most unusual for a government official. And he had done some pretty remarkable things.

"He's nothing like the others," said ZZ. "You should trust us."

Of course, I did. We made an appointment to meet the new director general.

"IT HAS TAKEN you a long time to come see me," said Director General Wang Zhenyao. "All of the other foreign NGO leaders came when I arrived, but *you* were the one I wanted to meet."

Director General Wang had a crew cut and the mild face of an academic, but the man spoke with a passion that rocked the musty walls of the ministry. His underlings gazed at their boss in open-mouthed wonder.

He had been in charge of disaster relief during the earthquake. There were still maps of Sichuan all over his walls. From his desk piled high with reports and charts and loose papers, he grabbed our Half the Sky training manual.

"This," he said, "can change everything."

He told us that, when he made the move from disasters to welfare, like a good academic he did his homework. Every night at home, he sat down to read through piles of research and reports. He glanced at the cover of our book many times. Once or twice he lingered on the photo of a Half the Sky teacher and her young charge, each focused only on the other. The image was so foreign . . . and yet so Chinese. Finally, after many days, he began reading. He read straight through the night.

"When I read this I felt I had failed as a father," he said. "I only knew to push my child to study, but not to think and dream. This way of raising children is missing not just in our welfare institutions. It is missing in Chinese life. Our children grow up not feeling valued; so they have no values. No dreams! As teenagers and young adults, they suffer. Half the Sky has much to teach us. Look at you, coming all the way to China with your big dreams. Why did you come here?"

"I felt I had to."

"Because you believed in yourself—in your dreams," he said. "Most people are not so fortunate. If they have a dream, they immediately think, *Ridiculous! Impossible!* Thank you for bringing *Impossible* to China!

"So we must popularize your way for our children! The way to big dreams. Television, Internet—reach the people. Comic books! How about comic books?"

"Well, we need to start with the welfare institutions." I laughed.

"Sure! How many institutions are you in now? We have to reach them all."

The Yangtze River
Autumn 2010

Five years after the boat ride during which China's Ministry of Civil Affairs informed the world that change would come for orphaned children, Half the Sky chartered an even bigger boat. We invited government officials, two hundred orphanage directors, and our entire board and staff (and Princess Madeleine!) to join us on an almost identical cruise—a national workshop we called Collaboration! Working Together to Make Positive Change for Children. But this time, our ship sailed *up*stream. Against the current.

By now, Director General Wang had reorganized the China Center for Adoption Affairs and made it the China Center for Child Welfare and Adoption—one entity that would be responsible for all child welfare in the country. He moved two trusted colleagues from the welfare department to run the new CCCWA. One of them was our pal Mrs. Gan.

Director General Wang set the stage for Half the Sky's acceptance as China's *most famous* child welfare authority. Working together, we would now begin to reimagine the entire child welfare system.

AFTER TWO DAYS of lively brainstorming sessions, workshops, and, as ZZ calls them, "heated discussions," we were back on the Yangtze's Shennong Stream in the little peapod boats, being pulled upstream by muscular young men wearing clothes.

Dick filmed while I interviewed Director General Wang and Mrs. Gan, both decked out in transparent purple trash-bag raincoats and orange life vests. Like every Chinese citizen I've had the pleasure to know, both relished a good outing. They were in great spirits as they talked about the future.

"Just a few years ago, Chinese people didn't have enough food to eat. Now food is not a problem," Director General Wang said. "Now we must turn to quality of life. Especially for the children. More than orphans—all children in need—this must improve! In the next five years, ten years, China will learn."

"It's an exciting time for China," I said. "Things are changing so fast. We can see the day when all our hopes for the children will come true. Maybe still far away, but we can see it."

"The children shouldn't have to wait. We don't want to wait," said Mrs. Gan.

Director General Wang folded his arms and smiled at me.

"What do you mean, Mrs. Gan?" I asked.

She looked at Director General Wang. "*Ni shuo,*" he said to her. "You talk."

"We want to train the whole country," said Mrs. Gan. "Every child welfare worker in the system. Right now. With Half the Sky."

Now they were both grinning at me. Two high-ranking Chinese government officials in silly outfits in a peapod boat. I squeezed ZZ's hand.

"We know we can count on Half the Sky to help us," Mrs. Gan said.

"You are so sure of that, Director Gan?" asked Director General Wang.

"I knew it in Sichuan, when Jenny bought the van."

SOMEHOW, THE FURTHER we'd drifted from our mission—the more rules we'd broken—the closer we'd come to the heart of it. I think maybe I was following a different set of rules. Immediately after that fateful excursion up the Yangtze River, I returned to Beijing, I thanked Guanyin and the Living Buddha, and I went back to work.

With CCCWA, we developed a comprehensive plan to co-train and mentor every child welfare worker in the country. Besides our Half the Sky training, we'd help the government make its own training more user-friendly. We'd create an online community for caregivers and administrators, an e-learning course for professional certification, and a video resource library illustrating our approach to child nurture, and we'd permanently station our own child development consultants at each of the provincial model centers. Along with the government, the JPMorgan Chase Foundation agreed to underwrite a large share of the costs. And, with Director General Wang's deft and quiet leadership, a plan was made to expand the benefits, over time, to all children at risk, whether institutionalized or not. The government named our joint endeavor the Rainbow Program.

It now seemed that the *most excellent and magnificent* mountain peak I'd been seeking in our Chinese garden was to be found at the end of a rainbow.

THE LAUNCH OF the Rainbow Program was celebrated in China's Great Hall of the People on Children's Day, June 1, 2011.

In typical Chinese fashion, everything came together (and unraveled again) at the very last minute. The e-mails flew:

> *Okay, scratch the live satellite. I've got it! How about we launch a campaign and get videos of children from around the world singing the same song and cut it all together? We'll project it on a giant screen and have a live children's choir singing along.—Jenny*

> *Hi Jenny—Mrs. Gan called today:*
> *1. She stressed again to keep foreign guests low number.*
> *2. No foreign media will be invited to the event.*
> *3. Drinks and snacks—Only water. No snacks.—Rachel*

Hi Jenny—Gan got news from Vice Minister Dou Yupei's secretary. The vice minister will not be available for Great Hall since he will accompany a vice premier for Children's Day visits in other provinces the whole day.—ZZ

ZZ, JPMorgan's senior executives will be at the celebration. They're key sponsors of the Rainbow Program. We've got to have a minister. Also, I just got a call from them. Their Asia CEO can stay at the Great Hall only until 2:00 P.M. He has another agreement signing. Can we move the event up an hour?—Jenny

During lunch?

Right. What was I thinking?

The day before the big party, ZZ called me from the management office at the Great Hall.

"Work on the backdrop is not yet started," she said.

"But the event is tomorrow."

"Great Hall team says they can't include JPMorgan's logo at official government event. Also, they say they are not certain that the children's choir will be allowed. The Great Hall of the People is not a place for children."

"ZZ, JPMorgan is a corporate sponsor. The logo tells the world JPMorgan is helping China's children. I think they'd really like to see their foundation president on the dais at the Great Hall with their logo in the background. We need the logo."

"I'll get Gan to help."

"Thank you. And ZZ, it's Children's Day. The Rainbow Program is all about children. We need children at the Great Hall."

"Understood."

Great Hall of the People, Beijing
Children's Day 2011

"As we are drowned in the vast expanse of verdant green and beautifully blooming flowers on this joyous occasion, we gather at the Great Hall of the People to present our love to the children, in a special way, an extraordinary gift—the collaborative Rainbow Training Program for child welfare workers that will benefit the orphans and disadvantaged children all over China. . . ."

I was sitting on the dais at the Great Hall of the People listening to China's *most famous* television presenter announce Half the Sky's unprecedented national partnership with government to transform the nation's entire child welfare system.

Me. Unsure where the movie ended and real life began.

I unplugged the interpreter from my ear. The presenter's voice softened into rising and falling tones like background music . . . and I found myself drifting . . .

It had been a long journey from the first moment when Meiying, our Maya, was placed in my arms that day in Guangzhou. I could feel her there now—that first moment, at once so foreign and so familiar. And little Xinmei, our Anya, whose physical scars so compounded her loss that she couldn't bear to be touched by one who, at first, could only pretend to love her.

So great was our need, theirs and mine, that somehow we managed to find that love in strangers. Surely, there is a place deep inside all of us that recognizes the need in each other—the very most basic human need, the one that truly distinguishes us from all other creatures—the need to love and be loved.

If we are denied, we cannot thrive.

When I was a very small girl, no more than three or four, my mother would let me take a bath with her every night. She enjoyed soaking in water that was scalding hot. She would lie there in the heat, steam rising, her body turning red.

I sat on the rim of the tub. I would begin with my toes. The hot water was almost unbearable, but if I could hold still, the pain would ease. Then I'd slip my feet in the water, hold still . . . and so it went, until I was crouched beside my mother in the bath and I could feel the soft skin of her legs beside me. We would stay like that until the water cooled and my skin shriveled. It was the closest I ever got to her that I can remember. The closest I came to feeling her love.

When I looked at Anya's little burned feet, instead of anger I felt unbearable, aching, primal sadness for the love she so needed and couldn't have. And how many others I held after that . . . the little girls I couldn't bring home, but whose need I understood in every part of myself. In some way, I knew I had been put on earth to help them find what was missing.

The Chinese, of course, said it best. About seventeen hundred years ago, the philosopher we know as Mencius said, "All the children who are held and loved will know how to love others. . . . Spread these virtues in the world. Nothing more need be done."

SWEET CHILDREN'S VOICES filled the Great Hall of the People. On giant screens, the faces of Chinese children, once in orphanages but now living all over the world, sang along, more or less all together. Then everybody joined in. The lyrics were corny but sweet. It was the China I'd come to love:

Together we strive through twists and turns
Together we pursue the same dreams. . . .

Now, at this moment, in that Great Hall, as wacky and improbable as it was—with the corny song and the wrong minister and the still-wet logo—the movie was far from the one I had imagined. But it was perfect.

I'd found my place and my purpose. Everything in my life, everything I had done, had prepared me for this.

What a gift I had been given!

Epilogue

One hundred thousand children's lives have been touched by Half the Sky. But almost a million still wait.

As the Rainbow Program rolls out, Half the Sky, together with its partners, is reaching hundreds of thousands more by training every child welfare worker across the nation in its approach to providing family-like nurturing care for institutionalized children. China's Ministry of Civil Affairs has further pledged to offer Half the Sky–inspired services to all at-risk children by converting now-isolated orphanages into community service centers, encouraging once-marginalized families to remain together.

In 2012, Half the Sky's sister organization in China, Chunhui Bo'Ai Children's Welfare Foundation, was founded, providing for the first time an opportunity for Chinese citizens to support nurturing programs for children at risk.

A nation fully committed to its children can bring about transformation of an entire child welfare system. We can envision a day in China when all children will grow up knowing love.

No child should have to wait to be loved.

www.halfthesky.org
www.chbaf.org
For China's orphans, a second chance at childhood . . .

Acknowledgments

My thanks must begin with the children—China's orphaned girls—my inspiration and my teachers. Thanks to our Half the Sky Big Family—the many thousands of caring people across the globe who support our work.

I thank our Chinese partners—the government officials and orphanage directors who truly want to make life better for the children in their care—for giving us the gift of their friendship and their trust.

To the women and men of Half the Sky who dedicate their lives so that children who've lost everything can have a second chance. To the nannies, teachers, youth mentors, foster parents, nurses, doctors, and support staff—seventeen hundred strong as I write this—there aren't words enough to describe my gratitude.

With Half the Sky's best-ever board of directors at my back, it almost feels easy. My thanks go to our quiet heroes, Guy Russo, Peter Bennett, Stephen Chipman, Matt Dalio, Tim Huxley, Dana Johnson, Peter Lighte, Joe Longo, Melissa Ma, and Chapman Taylor.

We couldn't begin to achieve what we have without the unstoppable energy, passion, and steadfastness of Half the Sky's amazing leadership team: Emma Chen, Janice Cotton, Mei Jiang, Carol Kemble, Patricia King, Winnie Sun, Roger Tang, Sandy Wang, Ivy Yu, Wen Zhao, and Qian Zhou. My very special thanks and *happy forever wishes* go to Rachel Xing, the gentle powerhouse who leads us into the future.

And ZZ. The magnificent, incomparable ZZ. Well, quite simply, there would be no Half the Sky without her. My *jie jie,* my big sister, my guide, my Chinese voice—she is the heart and soul of Half the Sky.

This book and the opportunity to tell our story would not exist without the collaboration of two big dreamers, Mark Tauber, publisher at HarperOne, and Jeff Skoll, founder of the Skoll Foundation. How lucky I am that they not only live their dreams, but also believe in the dreams of others.

My gratitude goes to all those at HarperOne who helped bring this book to life: Jackie Berkman, Michele Wetherbee, Suzanne Wickham, Laina Adler, Suzanne Quist, Claudia Boutote, Laura Beers, and the entire too-good-to-be-true team; and to Sally Osberg, Sandy Herz, Suzana Grego, and all my longtime friends at Skoll.

To my dear friends and early readers, many thanks for being honest, insightful, and always kind—Karin Evans, Deanne Bevan, Patricia King, and Marion Roach—and to Hendrika Misciagna for her gorgeous map of my adventures.

I owe a very special thank-you to Jeanette Perez, my editor, for putting her own life's journey on hold to work with me, and for her huge heart, her sensitivity, her modesty, and for her stunning ability to get to the heart of the matter.

There is no thank-you great enough for Richard Bowen—my fellow dreamer, my soul mate, and my love. Because he is beside me, I have the good fortune to live in a world where all things are possible. I can't begin to imagine my life if he hadn't come into it.

Credits

Grateful acknowledgment is given to the following photographers for the use of their work in this publication (page numbers refer to the photography insert pages):

p. 1: © Richard Bowen

p. 2: Courtesy of Jenny Bowen

p. 3: © Richard Bowen

p. 4: © Richard Bowen

p. 5: Courtesy of Jenny Bowen

p. 6: Half the Sky Foundation

p. 7: Half the Sky Foundation

p. 8: © Jenny Bowen

p. 9: © Richard Bowen

p. 10: © Richard Bowen

p. 11: © Richard Bowen

p. 12: © Richard Bowen

p. 13 *(top):* Ivy Yu, Half the Sky Foundation

p. 13 *(bottom):* © Richard Bowen

p. 14 *(top):* © Jenny Bowen

p. 14 *(bottom):* © Richard Bowen

p. 15: © Richard Bowen

p. 16: © Jenny Bowen

p. 17: © Jenny Bowen

p. 18 *(top):* Courtesy of Half the Sky Foundation

p. 18 *(bottom):* © Richard Bowen

p. 19: © Richard Bowen

p. 20: Half the Sky Foundation

p. 21: Half the Sky Foundation

p. 22: Half the Sky Foundation

p. 23 *(top):* Half the Sky Foundation

p. 23 *(bottom):* © Richard Bowen

p. 24: © Richard Bowen

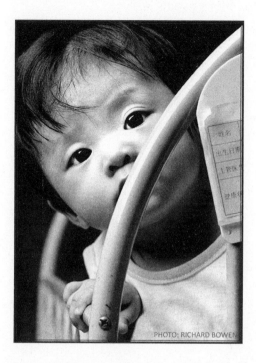

PHOTO: RICHARD BOWEN

We've come a long way, but a million children in
China still wait to know what happy feels like.

To learn more about Half the Sky and the young
lives it transforms, visit us on the web...

www.halfthesky.org

Half the Sky
半边天基金会